The Politics of Culture

The Politics of Culture

The Case for Universalism

Munira Mirza

palgrave
macmillan

First published 2012 by
PALGRAVE MACMILLAN

Palgrave Macmillan in the UK is an imprint of Macmillan Publishers Limited, registered in England, company number 785998, of Houndmills, Basingstoke, Hampshire RG21 6XS.

Palgrave Macmillan in the US is a division of St Martin's Press LLC, 175 Fifth Avenue, New York, NY 10010.

Palgrave Macmillan is the global academic imprint of the above companies and has companies and representatives throughout the world.

Palgrave® and Macmillan® are registered trademarks in the United States, the United Kingdom, Europe and other countries.

ISBN 978–0–230–28453–1

This book is printed on paper suitable for recycling and made from fully managed and sustained forest sources. Logging, pulping and manufacturing processes are expected to conform to the environmental regulations of the country of origin.

A catalogue record for this book is available from the British Library.

A catalog record for this book is available from the Library of Congress.

10   9   8   7   6   5   4   3   2   1
21   20   19   18   17   16   15   14   13   12

Printed and bound in the United States of America

Contents

Illustrations

Preface

A few years ago, whilst conducting some research for my doctoral thesis, I was invited to visit an arts education project in a major London gallery. An arts educationalist was conducting a small group of children from an inner city school around the different galleries in the building. He was an affable and articulate young man who had recently graduated from art school, and he was working part-time in the gallery's education department. Taking such a job is a common step for art graduates who want to work in the cultural sector, because it is flexible enough to fit around studio time and allows them to work in an environment they enjoy.

On this morning, the educationalist took his group of 20 or so eight-year-olds around some of the rooms in the main gallery, before stopping in a room containing works by the twentieth-century British sculptor Eduardo Paolozzi. He asked the children to sit down on the floor and look at the collages on the wall and then, using materials he had brought with him in a bag, to create their own collages. Excitedly, the children rummaged around in the bag, pulled out large sheets of paper, materials, and felt-tip pens. For 15 minutes or so, they worked – some more diligently than others – and then, after a growing number began to get bored and restless, the educationalist called them all back in to sit in a huddle. He asked them to show their work to the group and then told them how good their efforts were. They were asked to look at their work, then at the works on the wall and to compare them.

After some discussion, one boy, clearly struck by a clever thought, confidently put his arm in the air and began to wave it around excitedly. When picked, he asked his pertinent question: 'Why, sir, if our work is so good, is his on the wall and not ours?'

There was silence. The educationalist paused and stared back at the child. A subtle, almost imperceptible, look of terror crossed his face, as he struggled to think of the right thing to say. The pressure was on. All his efforts to engage the children, to make them feel included and creative in this prestigious, daunting space suddenly rested on this moment. For the boy had asked a perfectly reasonable question: what is so special about this guy's work that it should be hanging on the wall, when mine looks so similar to his? In other words, why does his work have *value?*

It is a question that any teacher might recognise. Perhaps 100 years ago the educationalist might have been able to answer simply, 'Because I say so.' But we live in a less deferential era, and institutions and professionals are now expected to explain the choices they make. So, after a few seconds of hesitation, the educationalist regained his confidence and talked about the style, the innovation, and the interesting qualities of Paolozzi's collages. He might even have convinced some of his students that it was worth their effort to look more closely. But it was by no means a done deal. Perhaps he could have talked more about the historical context, the influence of the Second World War and Surrealism, or the way in which collage allowed Paolozzi to juxtapose different images and ideas to provoke a disruptive, psychological reaction in the mind of the viewer. Or he might have explained about the choice of colour and shapes and why they had such an extraordinary sensory effect on the viewer. The educationalist was young, and probably not an expert on Paolozzi. It would be unfair to expect him to possess the skill of communicating what is special about art to the very young – something that can take years of practice.

The point about this incident is that it brings into sharp relief the key issue underpinning a cultural institution – that of cultural value. The point of looking at certain pieces of art, and indeed the very purpose of a school trip to the gallery, is something that children find easy to ask about in their charmingly unselfconscious way. This moment of confrontation, sometimes even framed aggressively ('Why him and not me?'), is at the heart of the cultural institution. Yet, at the same time, it is a question that those institutions and society more generally find increasingly difficult to answer.

Why do we fund the institutions we do? Why does so much money go to opera and national museums and galleries? Why provide resources to small, grass-roots organisations that cannot survive commercially? What makes their work so worthwhile? What do they contribute to our society? Who decides that one young artist has great potential, while another does not? Who is making these choices and are they merely subjective – the reflections of personal taste? Are these judgements biased: racist, sexist, or Eurocentric. Is it all pointless?

The cultural sector is implicitly a place of choice and judgement. Museum and gallery managers, curators, and theatre producers – all these professions presume to show us something we don't already know. When we buy a ticket for an exhibition or play, we place our trust in them. It doesn't always pay off, but evidently most of the time it does because statistics show that many of us are avid consumers and repeat visitors. Nevertheless, those with key roles in the cultural sector remain uneasy. There is acute consciousness of the disconnection between many people and the culture esteemed in our institutions. In particular, there is concern that 'non-traditional' groups (by which ethnic minorities and people from lower socio-economic backgrounds are meant) feel uncomfortable with or indifferent to the culture on display. We are told that unless people see themselves, or people who look like them, reflected in the productions, paintings, or objects on offer, they will not be able to relate to them.

In late 2010, I participated in a public debate at the Whitechapel Gallery in East London about cultural diversity policies, and a young woman in the audience put her hand up and explained that she was torn about how to feel towards culture. On the one hand she listened to her teachers at school talking about wonderful artists, writers, and thinkers throughout history, and she wondered where all the black and Asian figures were. At the same time, she attended various arts events and workshops at galleries and museums where those in charge seemed most keen to talk to her about the importance of her race and identity, and she felt disappointed at this apparent fixation, believing there must be more to her than being black. She wanted to believe that culture should be about more than where one comes from, but at the same time felt sad that she did not see more black people celebrated in the history she learned.

I was very struck by this comment. Here was an articulate young person, clearly interested in culture, but also experiencing disaffection. She was being sent conflicting messages – told that her race, ethnicity, and cultural background are vital elements in defining identity, but at the same time encouraged to engage with outstanding cultural offerings which did not happen to come from people who shared her ethnicity. Like many young people from ethnic minority backgrounds, she had been urged to identify with literature or art that reflected her ethnic identity or experience. Yet great art does not respect such boundaries. It speaks across ethnicity, history, and geography and allows people to transcend their particular experience. That is why cultural value seems to last beyond its own time.

We are currently living in straitened economic times and so it is inevitable that discussion within the cultural sector, particularly in Europe and America, should focus on the challenge of maintaining funding. However, in my view, another, more subtle challenge is emerging. This relates to the nature of cultural value, and how cultural institutions are run and policies developed. At the heart of this debate is an uncertainty about the nature of culture, its value to society, and what it says about being human.

In this book I argue that whilst the cultural sector and cultural policy have evolved in many positive ways over the last two decades, the widespread acceptance and institutionalisation of highly politicised concepts of diversity and inclusion have created contradictions, problems, and unintended consequences in practice. In particular, the emphasis on using culture to engage with (and affirm) people's identity seems to run counter to the universal idea that culture transcends identity and particularism. The word 'universalism' is much maligned and misunderstood in some circles, being associated rather crudely with imperialistic values and hagiographies of dead white men. It is sometimes misunderstood to mean, in a banal way, 'we are all the same' and that the sameness should be white, middle-class, and male. In fact, universalism is not the same thing as uniformity, but instead means something much more profound: we are all shaped and informed by our particular historic, geographical, ethnic, and cultural backgrounds and circumstances, but as human beings we have the capacity to use our imaginations, not merely to understand difference but also to transcend it. This simple quality, which distinguishes human from beast, is the basis of human culture.

To recognise this truth does not mean that one wishes to return to some golden age of cultural policy – such a thing has never really existed. Nor is it about taking sides politically – both left and right contain strong universalist traditions. Developing a historical perspective and an understanding of the ideal of universalism as it existed in the past might help us understand why cultural institutions have developed the way they have, and give us a better insight into their present working. It may also help us navigate through the difficult waters of identity politics. If we want to achieve a truly democratic culture – in both an artistic and a political sense – I suggest this is a good way to start.

To give my own background: I have been involved in discussions about culture and identity for nearly ten years, organising public debates and writing in academic and mainstream publications. After completing my doctorate in 2008, I became the Advisor on Arts and Culture to the Mayor of London. This position has allowed me to see at first hand how ideas in policymaking interact with, and translate into, practice on the ground. My experience over the past three years has taught me many things but has also reinforced the views I developed while conducting my research. One of the privileges of my current role has been the opportunity to discuss these ideas with some of the world's leading cultural professionals, based in London. These conversations have informed many of the arguments in this book.

I would like to thank all the people in Tower Hamlets and Oldham who gave interviews and provided information for the case studies in this book. I am also indebted to Oliver Bennett, Iwona Blazwick, Andrew Calcutt, Dolan Cummings, Alun Francis, Frank Furedi, James Heartfield, Michael Keith, Richard Morris, Chris Pickvance, and Douglas Smith, who read drafts and provided valuable insights. Finally, I am grateful to colleagues at the Greater London Authority from whom I have learned a great deal about policymaking and the challenges of making cultural excellence accessible. This book is dedicated to my parents.

Introduction

On 12 March 1901 the East End Art Gallery in Whitechapel opened its doors for the first time to an excited crowd. The founders, Canon Barnett and his wife, Henrietta, were pioneering Victorian reformers who sought to bring great art to local people. They wanted to create a 'permanent Picture Gallery' to build upon the immense popularity of the temporary art exhibitions they had held in the area for over 20 years and which had attracted thousands of visitors. Their gallery was one of the first public art institutions in the country to be funded by private philanthropy, raising its money through public subscription and donations from wealthy individuals, such as John Passmore Edwards (who also paid for the public library next door).

For the deeply religious Barnetts, art and education were important tools to aid the advancement of working-class people. Observers at the time might have been forgiven for thinking that a fine art gallery was somewhat superfluous to the needs of people living in Whitechapel. Its dingy streets, lined with overcrowded tenement housing, were home to hunger, harsh working conditions, and ill health, and were a hotbed of political activity. But the Barnetts maintained that art could serve a worthy, spiritual function. As Steyn (1990) notes, their aspiration was 'to inculcate in the population a higher subjectivity which could transcend nature by offering experiences, feelings and pleasures that were beyond what were perceived as the mindless routines of the working classes' (44). Canon Barnett frequently referred to Pre-Raphaelite paintings as 'sermons on the wall'. For the next 110 years, the gallery (later renamed the Whitechapel Gallery) would remain free to the public and show some of the most challenging and influential contemporary art in the world, winning both critical success and the affection of local residents.

Front Whitechapel Gallery (reproduced with permission from Gavin Jackson/ Arcaid Images)

Fast forward to 2011. Whitechapel is now part of the London Borough of Tower Hamlets. It is still one of the most deprived areas in Britain. According to the Index of Multiple Deprivation 2004, Tower Hamlets is the most deprived borough in London. It is also one of the most ethnically diverse: most of the Jewish population moved out long ago and there is now a well-established Bangladeshi community. Many of the Georgian terraces that once housed the poor have been converted into stylish apartments, whilst fashionable local restaurants and bars cater for workers from the adjacent financial district of the City of London. Just a few blocks away from the Whitechapel Art Gallery a new arts centre called Rich Mix is open. A renovated garment factory, Rich Mix's vibrantly designed website describes itself as 'a place where the communities of the world who are the citizens of East London and beyond can come together to experience and make world class art and feel that it's a place where they belong'.[1] The project was conceived in the 1990s and funded by a range of statutory bodies including London Borough of Tower Hamlets, Arts Council England, and the Greater London Authority.[2]

Like the Whitechapel Art Gallery, Rich Mix's aim is to provide culture and education for local people. Yet, whereas the Barnetts' institution was devoted to the narrow sphere of 'fine art', Rich Mix's 62,000-square-feet facility has a broader remit and offers 'a mixed arts programme which is representative of our local Tower Hamlets communities, including live music, film, dance, theatre, spoken word, education, and a range of creative activities for people of all ages and all cultures'. Following the contemporary vogue, its definition of culture is protean, referring not only to cultivated art forms such as painting, sculpture, music, and theatre, but also to the daily habits, customs, and traditions of wider society. Nor does it focus on western European culture – Rich Mix is avowedly global and its corporate literature boasts about the ethnic diversity of the borough. The project was developed in the mid-1990s by a group of political activists and arts workers in response to what they claimed was the racism and exclusion of the arts establishment. Cultural diversity lay at the heart of its approach.

Rich Mix states that it aspires to improve the lives of local people, although this ambition is not couched in the Barnetts' language of spirituality and beauty. Instead, this new kind of arts centre is intended to be a flagship for both social and cultural regeneration in East London, and offers training, mentoring, and commercial support to local communities. Whereas the Barnetts saw culture as distinct from the everyday drudgery of life, existing in a separate spiritual realm, Rich Mix links

Front of Rich Mix, Bethnal Green Road, London (reproduced with permission from Rich Mix)

together the everyday world to culture and seeks to generate economic and social value.

These snapshots of the past and present in one London borough demonstrate that much has changed in the meaning, scope, and aims of cultural policy over the course of a century. Whilst the Whitechapel Gallery and Rich Mix are both public cultural institutions, they represent quite different worlds in almost every respect. The Whitechapel Gallery was a bold and unusual experiment developed in an era when it was radical to imagine that the working poor could appreciate culture. Rich Mix, by contrast, has opened at a time when culture is regarded as politically and socially important, and arts centres are a stock feature of most towns and cities.

In the past two decades in advanced industrial societies, the word 'culture' has become more prominent in political discourse. This reflects the increased politicisation of the arts and culture, but also the 'culturalisation' of other policy areas, such as education, economy, urban regeneration, health, and community relations. In the United Kingdom especially, culture has become a part of mainstream political debate. It has been common over the last decade to hear politicians claim that culture today is more important than ever. When the former Arts Minister Estelle Morris MP gave a speech to the Cheltenham Literature Festival in 2003, she stated, 'Art and creativity are more important now than they ever have been' (Morris, 2003). Her successor David Lammy MP addressed the Museums Association in 2005, saying, 'In a fragmented, less deferential, more mobile, more diverse society where globalisation affects us all, the role of museums as places for reflection and understanding ... is more important than ever' (Lammy, 2005). A later holder of the post, Margaret Hodge MP, stated on a BBC Radio 4 programme in 2007 that there is 'growing recognition within the political class of the role of culture in communities, the link of culture to the sense of identity ... I also think there's a growing understanding of the creative industries which come out of culture in the economy.'[3]

It is not only politician who assert the increased importance of culture. The left-leaning British think tank Demos, which has been prolific in producing cultural policy advice, stated, 'We live in an age of globalisation, an age in which culture is more important than ever before ... It is not a case of culture being put at the service of politics, but rather of culture being a determinant part of politics' (Jones, 2007: unpaginated). In June 2006, cultural leaders in Britain launched a manifesto for the arts. One of the signatories, Tony Hall of the Royal Opera House, stated that the arts were 'not some add-on but absolutely vital to the future of the creative economy on which our future will undoubtedly depend' (Jury, 2006). The editor of the *British Medical Journal*, Richard Smith, even suggested only half-jokingly, in 2002, that central funds for healthcare ought to be reduced slightly in return for a substantial increase in arts subsidy, because their spiritual contribution would improve people's health (Smith, 2002).

In Britain this rhetoric has been matched by funding, and over the past two decades there has been a new interest in the potential of culture to regenerate towns and cities. In 1990 Glasgow won the accolade of being the European City of Culture, attracting fresh and positive interest to what had once been thought of as a dirty, crime-ridden, deindustrialising city. Although much of the regeneration funding that would transform the city's buildings and infrastructure was committed before 1990, and marketing campaigns and new cultural programmes had already been implemented, the City of Culture status offered a huge boost to tourism and place marketing. It became firmly established in people's minds that culture had led the transformation of Glasgow, turning it into a visitor destination and a place to do business, even though some would argue that in the end it had relatively little impact on the entrenched social and economic problems of the city (Garcia, 2004).

The experience of Glasgow and the consequent fashion for cultural regeneration in other major cities preceded the creation of the National Lottery in the mid-1990s. This fresh stream of funding was to transform Britain's cultural landscape with a wave of iconic new arts and cultural centres around the United Kingdom, plus the refurbishment of many more. In 1999 the Royal Opera House relaunched following a £178m refit. The following year, the Great Court opened at the British Museum. Yet the most impressive capital projects were those in the most unlikely places. In 2000 Tate Modern opened in Sir Giles Gilbert Scott's disused power station at Bankside in London, widely credited as transforming the deprived wasteland area of Southwark. The Bankside development was followed by the opening of the Baltic Centre for Contemporary Art in Tyneside, the Lowry Centre in Salford, the International Slavery Museum in Liverpool, and many more. Eighteen years after Glasgow's perceived success first put the idea of culture-led regeneration on the agenda, Liverpool hammered the nail in more firmly by becoming European City of Culture in 2008. It is also clear that culture will play a very important part in the 2012 Olympic and Paralympic Games in London. The Cultural Olympiad, the associated cultural programme for the Games, will be the largest of its kind in the history of the modern Games, with over £70m committed from cultural and charitable agencies. Culture is a key part of plans to encourage participation amongst the general public, and is seen as providing a major contribution to the legacy of the Games nationally (Greater London Authority, 2010).

The effect of these projects has been to embed the notion that culture has a powerful economic and social impact. Tony Blair's New Labour government took up this theme enthusiastically when in 1997 it set up the Creative Industries Task Force, and then in the same year the new Prime Minister invited the cultural glitterati to Downing Street, describing 'Cool Britannia' as 'the design workshop of the world', and extolling the nation's fashion designers, artists, musicians, architects, writers, actors, and film-makers (Elliott and Atkinson, 2007: 83). Although some of the artists involved later looked back on this moment with regret,[4] one cannot deny its significance in public life – culture was no longer a sideshow or luxury for an elite, but could play an active part in politics and the future of Britain. The Coalition government of Conservatives and Liberal Democrats which came to power in May 2010 has affirmed its positive support for culture, despite the economic climate and the spending cuts announced in October 2010.[5]

Without doubt the increased focus on cultural activity as a social and economic tool has shaped the way the cultural sector works and behaves. Cultural institutions and professionals are much more preoccupied with understanding and improving their 'usefulness'. They are also more concerned about their audiences – who they are, what they represent, and whether they are large and diverse enough. In *Turning Point*, an Arts Council strategy document for the visual arts, published in 2006, the authors state that the Council will seek to put 'people at the heart' of arts policy, implying that arts policy in the past had not been 'people-centred' enough (ACE, 2006a: 6). The arts have undergone something of a revolution, being encouraged to cater for the many and not just the 'same white middle class audience'.[6] This increased interest in the public consumption of culture has without doubt energised the cultural sector, making it more accessible and a richer experience for many people. The Labour government's policy of making the national museums and galleries free in 1997 has increased the size of the museum-going public (although whether it is more diverse is another matter). The scale of cultural policy has also grown, both nationally and internationally, with a surge in conferences, academic publications, and 'grey literature' (reports and papers produced by government agencies) exploring the politics of cultural policy. All this has occurred at the same time as a demographic shift amongst artists and arts professionals themselves – with more women, ethnic minorities, and people from 'non-traditional' backgrounds seeking to work in the arts and having some influence on the debate. The arts workforce and the kind of art being shown today are slowly starting to reflect the heterogeneity and internationalism of contemporary society.

At the same time, the increasing emphasis on audiences has raised some serious questions about the purpose of cultural and arts organisations and the values they should be governed by. At the forefront of debates about cultural policy today is a set of concepts: 'diversity', 'inclusion', and 'access'. These words have become part of common parlance in the arts and cultural sector since the late 1990s, and have shaped policymaking. They have created a new focus in cultural activity and policymaking and challenged the assumptions in older models of cultural policy. The historian Tristram Hunt, writing in *The Observer* in 2009, explains:

The culture shift began with free entry to museums and has developed down the years to force once standoffish institutions to engage with wider school trips, outreach and working with diverse communities have come to rank as highly as research and fundraising...Of course, there has been some guerrilla resistance by curators concerned more with restoration than education. A leading fine art director, Philippe de Montebello, spoke for many of his peers when he revealed: 'To me, audiences are second...Our primary responsibility is to works of art.' But the combination of social activism and public funding tied to popular engagement meant that such disdain could never be sustained.

Hunt refers to a latent tension between 'guerrilla' curators who adhere to older attitudes about cultural policy and a new generation that seeks to challenge these values. Other commentators suggest that the shift in cultural policy towards access and inclusion has not been wholly positive and has led to a 'dumbing down' of culture. In one of the first critiques of the 'new museology' at the dawn of the century writer Josie Appleton (2001) stated:

A defensive museum profession, riddled with self-loathing and no longer sure of its traditional role, was open to the new Department for Culture, Media and Sport (DCMS) agenda...They seemed to hold the idea that museums – from the objects they chose, to the layout of their buildings and exhibitions – excluded ordinary people...social inclusion has become a key government project. It is not just a lone museum curator using the museum to boost the self-esteem of socially excluded individuals – it is also the government.

Others have also expressed concern about the changing nature of cultural institutions and their purpose (Pick, 1991; Appleton, 2001; Ellis, 2003; Delingpole, 2006; Lebrecht, 2006; Tusa, 2007).

What does this shift tell us about culture today and why should this be of any interest to social scientists? After all, the future of museums, art galleries, theatres, and libraries has traditionally been a 'low politics' issue, of concern to only a minority of academics (Gray, 2002). These institutions receive only a fraction of public spending.[7] Although there is far more rhetoric today about how important culture is, this does not mean it is of greater political significance or that we should be especially interested in how it is changing. Ultimately, cultural policy is unlikely to win or lose an election.

Yet this increased attention to culture from policymakers is important because it reflects wider changes in the way we as a society think about identity, human subjectivity, and social change. The growing sphere of cultural policy (i.e. policies relating to the arts and cultural sector, and also the use of culture in other areas of policymaking) indicates a fresh engagement in the cultural dimension of social problems and a changed understanding of the relationship between culture and society. In this sense, the rise of cultural policy arises as a result of the 'cultural turn', an event which has provoked intense academic discussion since the 1980s, and which means that societies have become increasingly oriented towards cultural issues in political, economic, and social life. Culture is more central to policymaking because it has come to the fore more generally in how people in politics and intellectual circles think about society. Krishan Kumar (1995) argues that the growing attention to culture reflects a paradigmatic shift in thinking and therefore deserves more notice from social scientists:

> Were [questions of culture] simply a matter of culture, in the sense of artistic developments, we might – at least as social theorists – be inclined to leave the whole thing to the cultural critics, if not to late night television programmes and the cultural channels. What continues to make the debates relevant and interesting is that they are part of a much broader debate on the contemporary condition and future direction of industrial societies (112).

The aim of this book is to explore the development of cultural policy in the United Kingdom and the ideas and assumptions that lie behind it.[8] The premise is that culture has risen in political importance, not only in terms of party politics or the machinery of government, but also in the way it has infused wider political discourse. In other words, I try to explain the shift in ideas and values that has taken place in the period between the creation of the Whitechapel Gallery and the creation of the Rich Mix centre. Whilst I note changes within broader cultural or artistic movements, I am primarily interested in the way which state policy and public subsidy for culture works, that is, the public dimension of cultural policy, rather than ideas and trends within cultural practice at large (although there is inevitably some overlap).

Before introducing my argument, I should explain what I mean by the term cultural policy. In the nineteenth century, it would barely have been recognised in public discourse. Government involvement in culture during the Victorian era was mostly limited to providing funding or legislation to support the major national institutions (such as the National Gallery or the British Museum), or administering technical matters such as licensing arrangements and enforcing censorship rules. By the early twentieth century, and particularly in the inter-war and post-war period with the creation of the Arts Council, the British state's involvement in culture expanded to cover more sectors of creative activity: public museums and galleries, and certain types of cultural production, especially visual arts, radio, film, music, literature, and theatre. In the last half of the twentieth century, however, cultural policy grew into an entire area of government, being granted its own government department in the 1990s.

The DCMS came to define culture more widely than before. It now had both a 'material' and 'value' dimension and included a range of new activities and institutions, like the Internet and digital media, the National Lottery, as well as political concerns like community-building, race relations, and well-being. It sought to deliver a variety of social and economic objectives, not only the creation, preservation, and display of conventional cultural products. Although cultural policy throughout the nineteenth and twentieth centuries often had ulterior motives, these were largely implicit rather than explicit. In the late twentieth century, the instrumental use of art was more overt. Cultural policy also extended beyond the subsidised sector into the 'cultural and creative industries', including commercial areas which are, at least in most people's minds, not 'arts-related' as such: tour and travel agents, newsagents, video and DVD rental, TV and radio servicing, jewellers (retail), greetings card shops, furniture retailers, bookmakers (DCMS, 2004b). More specifically, in the past three decades there has been a profusion of 'culture talk' – that is, discourse about cultural policy at different levels of international, national, and local government, and an emphasis on the cultural dimension of social problems, as well as the social impact of culture (Coalter, 2001; Keaney, 2006a).

It could be argued that cultural policy, like other policy areas such as education and health, has expanded as part of 'an international policy boom' in advanced industrialised countries since the 1980s (Hood, 1994, cited in Collyer, 2003: 4). There has been a shift away from bureaucratic governance towards deregulation and privatisation, leading to the idea of the 'enabling state'. Public policy has also moved to colonise the 'life world': the private, intimate concerns of family, community, and leisure (Habermas, 1987). In this wider context, the growth of a more explicit cultural policy is not particularly extraordinary.

Yet the 'culture' of cultural policy has also changed profoundly in meaning. In the late nineteenth century it was relatively easy to speak with confidence about the word 'culture', referring to a canon of literature, fine art, and poetry – what the arch Victorian Matthew Arnold described in *Culture and Anarchy* [1869] as 'the best that has been thought and said in the world' (Arnold, 2006: 5). A century later, the influence of postmodern thought and theories of anthropology have undermined such a neat definition of culture, setting forth the view that culture is relative to particular societies. Culture today is an essentially contested concept (Gray, 2004: 44). The disciplines of sociology and art history have produced a considerable body of literature to challenge the notion of absolute aesthetic value, insisting that 'culture' should refer not only to high art but also to elements of popular culture and that the value of culture exists only in relation to whichever social group is consuming it (for instance, Bourdieu, 1986 and Barthes, 1997). Bennett states that since the 1980s this questioning of the definition of culture has destabilised the rationale of cultural policy. An understanding of culture as something that is commodified and relativistic has ended up changing the remit of cultural policy itself (Bennett, O., 1996).

In both the United Kingdom, but also internationally, the sphere of cultural policy has boomed. This can be seen easily enough in concrete terms: funding, legislation, the number of people employed to work on cultural matters in government departments, non-governmental agencies, supra-national and international bodies such as the United Nations, the European Union and the World Trade Organisation, and the increased number of voluntary and community groups, professional associations, consultants, and academic departments specialising in the field.

Yet the increased significance of cultural policy is evident in more than just the volume of policy being churned out – it is in the changed attitudes and expectations about the legitimate role of government in culture. In the post-war and Cold War era, the very idea of cultural policy – that is, government intervening in cultural life – would have been seen as 'un-British' and typical of the Soviet Union instead. McGuigan (1996) therefore argues for a broader definition of cultural policy – not just about administrative decisions, but the politics of culture in practice.

> [This] emphasizes the relationship of policy to politics as a field of contestation between rival discourses, ideologies and interests rather than confining it to the more technical though hardly unpolitical, connotating of policy and policing. Cultural policy raises questions

of regulation and control but its meaning should not be restricted to an ostensibly apolitical set of practical operations that are merely administered and policed by government officials. (7)

The history of the growth of cultural policy in the United Kingdom but also in other countries, shows how culture is seen as a much more important part of our society and in the way we look at social problems and solutions. It is also a more politically contentious area and there are many debates about the value of culture and whether it should exist for its own sake, or should deliver social or economic benefits, especially if it is funded through the public purse.

In this book I argue that for various reasons policymakers have increasingly come to see culture as socially 'useful'. They have come under pressure to justify expenditure on culture by giving an account of the benefit it brings to society. Many authors have pointed to economic drivers as the reason behind this new reasoning. I agree with them that the impact of the 1970s fiscal crisis and the ensuing drive for economic efficiency altered the rationale of cultural funding. But, economics is not a sufficient explanation for this change. Policymakers have also been driven by political developments – in particular, a new understanding of the individual human subject and an interest in 'identity' and 'diversity'.

In the United Kingdom at least, this discourse of 'cultural diversity' and 'identity' has been framed largely in terms of ethnicity, and to a lesser extent, in terms of disability, sexuality, and gender. This book seeks to analyse what 'diversity' means and how the rise of identity politics in society has influenced the cultural sector.

I want to show how the values and ideas of cultural policy have changed, and how these have shaped the way in which cultural organisations and agencies operate. Whilst many of these changes are positive, there is also reasonable cause for concern and debate. I suggest that these new cultural policy ideas, when put into practice, can reveal some interesting tensions and a gap between rhetoric and reality. I hope that in reading this book, others will find these observations worthwhile and relevant.

There is already considerable academic literature about the change in the scope and character of cultural policy. Yet, as Oliver Bennett (2004) points out, there are two halves of cultural policy study which rarely meet. On the one hand, there is discussion of the technical and managerial nature of cultural subsidy and support. On the other hand, there is the field of cultural studies which tries to deconstruct the very meaning of the category of 'culture' and how it is used by actors and institutions. The ideological component of cultural policy is therefore decoupled, to some extent, from managerial questions of policy development and implementation. Janet Wolff (1999) argues that academic studies of culture can be shallow and insufficiently sociological in their approach – either because they focus primarily on symbolism, interpretation, and 'textual' readings, or else because they are positivistic and focus on empirical data and 'number crunching'. She calls for a more productive encounter between cultural studies and sociology, combining an attention to the critique of categories with an understanding of social and institutional processes, in order to yield a better understanding of cultural policies in practice.

In order to understand deeper changes in cultural policy we need to pay attention to how ideas and values relate dialectically to structural and institutional processes: how each impacts on the other. We also need to appreciate the influence of social and political trends from outside the worlds of cultural practice and cultural policymaking. If we were only to look at the changes in cultural life or the views of actors working in the cultural sector, we would miss the enormous impact of other political factors on social consciousness and cultural policy today.

My argument is that the growth of a more explicit and instrumentalist cultural policy reflects a new understanding of what it is to be human today and the nature of the subject at the heart of policymaking – the imagined individual at whom policies are targeted. This is the result of considerable social and political change in the last two decades and changing attitudes in political life.

One way in which public perceptions have changed is a disenchantment with conventional politics based on class, and the increasing orientation in policymaking towards issues of 'cultural difference', 'identity', and the struggle for 'recognition' (Giddens, 1994; Mulgan, 1994; Kumar, 1995). This trend marks a departure from what might be classed as the old, 'liberal' notion of the political subject. This subject was expected to be able to abstract from his or her immediate personal context in order to develop shared interests with other people in society. This allowed for the possibility of universal interests and values that transcended people's particular social circumstances. Policymaking was based on the notion of the universal citizen and this implied equal treatment for all in the public realm.

However, in the past two decades there has been a shift. The new enthusiasm for 'identity politics' reflects and reinforces scepticism about the universalist approach. For advocates of identity politics people's differences (such as differences in race and ethnicity, gender, or sexuality) are no longer things to be transcended or overcome, but are in fact the basis of their shared experience of social problems and, therefore, their solidarity. To recognise this diversity of identities is to enable self-empowerment. In this context, the field of culture – with its potential to nurture a sense of identity and collective loyalty through emotional and meaningful experience – is a novel way to engage people in a way that conventional politics seems unable to do. At the same time, the failure to recognise cultural difference and identity is seen to lead to people having a lack of self-esteem, confidence, and ability to contribute to society, which leads to a range of social and economic problems. Policymakers are interested in how nurturing individual and community identities might lead to improvements; hence, culture is applied as a tool to achieve social and economic effects through changing individual psychology, personal development and behaviour, nurturing 'community' and 'social capital', and making good, economically productive individuals. In short, cultural policy, with its stress on identity, is seen as a better, more effective way of doing politics than the conventional politics of the past.

How has this change come about? One established school of thought argues that there was a reconfiguration of subjectivity at the end of the twentieth century – as a result we look at ourselves and act differently. Whereas the individual was once presumed to be able to transcend difference, today he or she is supposed to be defined by it. Heartfield (2002) calls it 'subjectivity in denial' (238) – a standpoint that rejects the universal character of the subject as transformative and self-creating, in favour of 'identity', which values the particular, fragmented nature of the subject. The individual is increasingly regarded as vulnerable and in need of emotional support, undermining the idea of the autonomous, robust subject that had once been the basis of political and cultural life (Nolan, 1998; Furedi, 2003), or in need of behavioural re-education (Brown, 2006). By this account the subject at the heart of politics and culture has undergone revision. One manifestation of this (amongst many others, no doubt) is the emergence of cultural policy and the preoccupation with the notions of identity and diversity.

Another factor is a change within thinking about culture itself. In the modern era, the development of cultural policy relied on certain key facts: the existence of cultural authority; the notion of universal cultural value; the criteria of 'excellence' and the possibility of a shared canon, which could (in theory at least) be appreciated by everyone, regardless of creed, colour, or class. This liberal-humanist discourse of culture, as it might be described, was internally related to the concept of subjectivity and the expectation that the individual was able to transcend his everyday 'particular' culture, in order to appreciate a 'universal' culture. However, there have been growing attacks on this notion of universality within the field of official cultural policy. Cultural value is no longer regarded unequivocally as durable and transcendent, but relative to each society or community that produces it. This multicultural argument in cultural policy has gained ground since the late 1990s, bringing a challenge to the universalist approach and placing increased emphasis on culture as an expression of particular identities. Cultural policy discourse at times expresses ambivalence about ideas like cultural authority and expertise, betraying a slight nervousness at the use of such terms. They were, after all, used rather complacently in the past by an elite which could at times be closed-minded about what constituted 'excellent culture'. Today, cultural policy seems to celebrate the idea of consumer choice and difference – each person has their own taste and view of what is excellent. Although the rhetoric of cultural universalism ('excellence') still permeates cultural institutions, it now mixes alongside the rhetoric of 'cultural identity' and 'diversity', which emphasises the partial and inherently socially bound nature of cultural life. This mix of approaches leads to the possibility of confusion and contradiction in the way cultural policy is implemented.

To state my argument in more abstract terms, I identify a major shift at the level of social consciousness (the way we perceive ourselves as subjects and understand the individual's relationship to society), which then leads to twin consequences: a greater interest in culture as a tool in social policymaking, and an increased interest in cultural policy and practice in issues of identity and diversity. My concluding argument, therefore, has a twist – whilst culture has grown in importance, this is not the same 'traditional' culture as from the past, but rather a new *politicised* kind of culture which is a tool for other purposes.

How do these ideas translate into practice? The aims behind cultural policy and its beneficial effects are often taken for granted in most policy literature, but the underlying contradictions are rarely thought through. I suggest that the emphases on diversity and identity run counter to the values of universalism, which had informed politics and culture in the past. How do these conflicting values play out in lived reality?

To answer these questions, I explore two case studies in the United Kingdom.[9] The first is the history of the Rich Mix arts centre in Tower Hamlets, an organisation which was established by a group of political activists in the 1990s around the principle of cultural diversity, and which has evolved over the years into an ambitious (but politically controversial) project with a series of major organisational failures. I chose this institution because it was formed with a self-avowed commitment to promoting diversity and has been cited as a pioneer in urban cultural diversity strategies (e.g. Brownhill and Darke, 2000: 20). The project also received considerable backing from the London Borough of Tower Hamlets, the Greater London Authority, and the Arts Council, reflecting the degree of official support for its aims and objectives when it was set up. I look at how the principle of diversity has been institutionalised in a new setting and the way in which staff, board members, local artists, funders, and residents came to react to it with ambivalence.

The second case study focuses on the cultural policies in the town of Oldham in north-west England. This former cotton mill town received a large amount of media interest following serious riots by local Asian youths in 2001. The riots provoked much reflection within the Council and amongst local people about the tensions between different communities. At the heart of this was a question about the extent to which cultural identity had reinforced such divisions but also whether culture might be used as a tool to overcome these problems. Oldham is seen in local government circles as an important test case in the field of community cohesion, so it is a useful example to explore. It is also the town where I grew up, so I have long been interested in discussions about diversity in the area and the impact of policies.

In both case studies, the use of culture by state and non-state agencies is characterised by a strong economic objective, in particular, the need to counter the impact of deindustrialisation. However, in both cases the turn to culture is also a way of addressing wider social and political issues, such as community engagement, social inclusion, and the relations between the local ethnic communities. Culture is a means to engage people through their identity. By looking at both cases in their historical context and examining how these policies evolve in relation to local circumstances, we can see how ideas about cultural diversity develop under different influences over time. We can also see how philosophical contradictions come to life when policies are put into practice. As Winston Churchill once said, 'However beautiful the strategy, you should occasionally look at the results.'

The research and case studies I explore are based in the United Kingdom, which may seem parochial, but this allows me to explore how national, political, and economic concerns shape policies on the ground. As a result, the arguments of the book are not confined to the United Kingdom and ought to have relevance for countries around the world where there is a well-developed cultural policy infrastructure, such as Europe, North America, Australia, but also increasingly in Africa and Asia. Many of these countries have developed their own diversity policies and participate in intra-national networks and schemes run by organisations like the United Nations Educational, Scientific and Cultural Organisation (UNESCO).[10] Although there are considerable variations in the traditions of cultural policies between countries and the scope of the state to intervene, there are also certain trends which appear consistently – such as the increased interest in culture as a political tool to address citizenship, the desire to nurture the cultural industries for economic growth, a greater emphasis on diversity and access, and an increase in private funding and sponsorship.[11]

I should make clear that I do not try to evaluate the success or failure of cultural policies within their own terms, or even to judge their social or economic impact. There is considerable literature on the evaluation of cultural policies, much of it positive (for instance, Matarasso, 1997) and some more sceptical (for instance, Belfiore, 2002; Merli, 2002; Selwood, 2002). Rather, my intention is to develop an understanding of the broader ideas that frame cultural policies today and to tease out what I believe to be internal contradictions.

Through my empirical research I expose a number of latent tensions. First, whilst the celebration of ethnic difference is welcomed positively by those working in the cultural sector and regarded as an important aspect of being inclusive, there is also concern that the focus on ethnic identity ends up 'pigeonholing' artists and audiences. There is also discomfort from local actors about the extent to which difference can bring communities together or just end up reinforcing divisions between ethnic communities. Second, there is genuine interest in widening cultural programmes and reflecting the diversity of audiences within institutions' work, but at times the rhetoric of diversity is based on challenging the 'exclusiveness' of traditional cultural authority in institutions. This appears to undermine the ability and confidence of organisations. The tension in both these factors is manifest in debates within these institutions but also between institutions and their publics. Most people seem to embrace diversity as a concept, but there is a lot of confusion about what it actually means. This confusion can even turn into hostility when policies are implemented.

How can we explain these tensions? In the arts and cultural sector, many actors tend to blame the authorities, policymakers, and even each other, but there is little discussion about the inherent philosophical contradictions of the policies they are being expected to implement. If we take an abstract view, we can see that there are contradictions in cultural policies today – mainly that the principles of diversity and identity can at times seem at odds with the liberal-humanist discourse of subjectivity and culture. The view of the individual as being defined by his or her cultural identity conflicts with the universalist notion of a subject that can transcend their culture. This clash means that cultural policy often fails to live up to its aspirations and, ironically, can reinforce exclusion as well as inclusion. Although in many cases these tensions do not appear visibly and can be managed successfully, there are also cases when they are not being managed well. Understanding why or how these tensions arise could be invaluable to cultural organisations in the future.

This book is designed to be read from beginning to end, because it builds up an argument throughout. I start by describing in brief terms the historical shift in the way in which culture is perceived and how it has gradually become an object of policymaking. I then draw out some of the conceptual issues and problems with contemporary thinking. I apply this conceptual framework to an analysis of 'real' cultural policies in the United Kingdom. At the end I explore theoretically the nature of the contradictions I have revealed and put forward a case for a universalist approach to cultural policy which attempts to mitigate, if not overcome, these problems.

In Chapter 1, I give a necessarily brief historical account of debates about the meaning of culture and its relation to society in the modern era. Part way along this journey has been a change in the understanding of the relationship between culture and society – from an Enlightenment tradition, which portrayed culture as a realm of transcendental, universal value to be kept free from the influence of social and political forces – to a new expectation amongst the political and intellectual elite that culture should demonstrate its 'usefulness' to society. The rising importance of cultural policy reflects a shift in broader thinking about subjectivity by away from the model of the autonomous, transcendental, individual subject towards 'identity' and a preoccupation with the fragmented and diverse subject.

In Chapter 2 I chart the rise in cultural policy since the mid-1970s within official international and national bodies. This is evident in specific policy frameworks and legislation but also in the way that social problems and issues are increasingly viewed in relation to cultural factors like 'identity' and 'community'. I look in detail at the United

Kingdom where increased rhetoric about culture is matched by the growth of new institutions, legislation, policies, and increased cultural subsidy. Whilst many commentators view this rise of cultural policy-making as a reaction to economic change, I argue that it is also a result of wider political developments and that much of cultural policy is driven by new fashions and intellectual trends in national and local government. Crucially, culture is seen by policymakers not only as an important economic tool, but also as a strategy to develop novel forms of political engagement and a new kind of citizen. At the end of this chapter I examine how the principle of diversity is enacted in the UK context and I explore some of the potential philosophical tensions at the heart of this new model of cultural policy.

In Chapters 3 and 4, I explore two case studies which exemplify the broader narrative I have described in the previous chapters, of a move towards a new model of cultural policy that seeks to use culture to deliver both economic and social/therapeutic benefits. I then explore some of the ambiguities and problems that seem to occur and relate these back to my theoretical framework.

In Chapter 5, I analyse the findings from my case studies and theorise the contradictions at a more abstract level. I show that the legitimacy and authority of cultural policy is inherently compromised by the appeal to diversity and that this leads to conflicts when policies are put in practice. The end results are the destabilisation of cultural authority, the reification of difference between groups, and the requirement for external authorities to manage tensions and disagreements which arise. Despite good intentions to bring groups together into a unified framework, the use of identity-oriented cultural policy reinforces their division. Paradoxically, the philosophy of diversity fails to live up to its aspiration. By contrast, I argue that a universalist orientation is better equipped to deal with the nature of difference and artistic creativity.

1
From Confidence to Uncertainty – Cultural Value and What It Means to Be Human

Cultural autonomy in the modern era

There is evidence of human culture and creativity in almost every part of the world since the beginning of humanity. From the ancient cave paintings of Lascaux in the south of France, dated to c.15,000 BC, to the colossal pyramids of the Nile Valley of over 4000 years ago, or the fifteenth-century Renaissance church paintings of Florence, human beings have left their cultural mark on the earth for future generations to study and admire.

Yet, whilst the existence of culture may be a universal phenomenon, the understanding of what culture is and its role in human society has been quite different throughout history. Over the centuries, philosophers and artists have developed their own definitions, bringing forth their own values about what it is to be human. From the eighteenth century in Europe, the meaning of culture was especially a matter of intense political, as well as intellectual, debate.

The word 'culture' derives from the Latin *colere*, meaning 'to cultivate'. In *The Idea of Culture* (2000), the cultural theorist, Terry Eagleton, states that our modern conception of culture is intertwined with the birth of modernity in the eighteenth century. Prior to this moment, the word 'culture' referred to the 'thoroughly material process' of cultivation of soil, agriculture, and crops. Only as humanity developed did the word acquire a spiritual, transcendental dimension (Eagleton, 2000: 1).[1] During the European Enlightenment in the eighteenth century, the leaps in artistic and scientific knowledge and the emergence of a public sphere of debate and discussion made it possible to forge a new understanding of culture as a profoundly *human* quality. The concept of culture was born at the point when humankind began to abstract itself to an

20

unprecedented degree and reflect self-consciously on the society around it. Culture indicated humanity's ability to think rationally about the world and to act purposefully on it, rather than being shaped passively by circumstance.

The Enlightenment marked a point in history when human beings began to ask questions about the world in which they lived and also the nature of authority and God. The sense of liberation this brought and the enthusiasm for new ideas drew attention to the seemingly infinite capacity of human beings to think in innovative ways and to challenge the shackles of superstition, myth, and ignorance. In this new world, culture was something that humans – not nature or God – created and therefore was something to be cherished. It is not hard to see why the thinkers of the Enlightenment were so joyous about the power of culture, for it marked the superiority of humanity and their own sense of freedom from control by the natural world, religious or political authority, and God. This major break in philosophical and scientific thought produced volumes of philosophy, heated debates in salons in elite eighteenth-century society, and the bold creation of new works of art, poetry, and music, which licensed human beings to *self-consciously* think for themselves for the first time – lacking the inhibition to think only as the church or government would like them to. Not without reason did the ancient Greek myth of Prometheus (the champion of humanity who stole fire from the gods to give it to mortals) become popular amongst artists and poets in the eighteenth and nineteenth centuries.

Of course, there had always been cultural activities – music, art, literature, theatre, and sculpture – in pre-Enlightenment times. However, the belief in an autonomous aesthetic realm, which had a value *for its own sake*, came into proper existence later: first amongst certain artists during the late Renaissance period in Europe, and then more widely in the consciousness of the intellectual and social elite in the eighteenth century. Up till that point, church patrons or merchants and lords tended to hire their artists, musicians, and sculptors as skilled labourers to decorate their homes and provide pleasure or instruction. The value of the work was essentially judged to be in the eye of the beholder, and ultimately depended on the taste of the patron. Music was regarded either as a religious prop or part of ordinary folk culture, and therefore seen as tied to social circumstance and occasion without any greater aspiration for aesthetic value (Hewett, 2003). Even in great artistic centres of early Renaissance Italy, it was widely accepted that art must ultimately serve the desires of patrons – for it could not survive without their support.

It was slowly with the establishment of formal art schools and art history writing in Europe from the sixteenth century (for instance, Giorgio Vasari's influential text *Lives of the Artists*) that art as a sphere began to acquire its own independence and respect. In the eighteenth century, this growing awareness came to a point with a fundamental break between artistic and cultural practice and the institutions of social life. The church and royalty continued to fund their favourite painters, but the artist also emerged dramatically as a being with his own impulses, beholden to new obligations to society. This Romantic approach viewed the artist as someone who existed within a particular social and cultural milieu yet could also exist in a world apart from it. The artist had a consciousness of himself as an autonomous being whose responsibility was to the Truth, transcending the quotidian demands and fickle fashions of society. In his inner, private life, he was free to explore the nature of the human condition without the polite social constraints or political demands of the external world. His responsibility was to universal Truth, to which all humanity is subject.

For this reason, the writer and music critic Ivan Hewett (2003) explains that classical music is a 'child of the Enlightenment', in that 'it can never answer to an aesthetic or cultural particularism; it aspires to be the voice of anybody with a modicum of training and experience in its language' (23). The influence of Kantian aesthetics throughout the late eighteenth and nineteenth centuries established a view of cultural value as innately natural to humanity, and therefore ahistorical. Humanity's appreciation of beauty lies constant beneath the surface differences of plural cultures.

This idea of durable cultural value was connected to the idea of man as universal, or essentially unified. As Friedrich Schiller stated in his *Letters on the Aesthetic Education of Man* (1795):

> Every human being, one may say, carries within him, potentially and prescriptively, an ideal man, the archetype of a human being, and it is his life's task to be, through all his changing manifestations, in harmony with the unchanging unity of this ideal.
>
> (Schiller, 1967: 178, cited in Eagleton, 2000: 8)

At the heart of this almost heroic (what some might call naïve) conception of culture was a belief in the universality of human beings, and the possibility that through culture all individuals can achieve a truer understanding of the world. It was a view of the human subject which would dominate modern society – a being acting on the world, not only being acted upon, and with an infinitely complex consciousness. The very word 'culture' embodies a 'momentous historical transition', encoding within a vast set of philosophical issues: 'freedom and determinism, agency and endurance, change and identity, the given and created' (Eagelton, 2000: 2).

This explanation of the birth of culture closely follows that laid out by the British post-war cultural theorist Raymond Williams. In his introduction to *Culture and Society*, published in 1958, Williams describes culture as a faculty which challenges the unseen and often uncontrollable forces of the world, particularly the market. Culture is:

> ... first, the recognition of the practical separation of certain moral and intellectual activities from the driven impetus of a new kind of society; second, the emphasis of these activities as a court of human appeal, to be set over the processes of practical social judgement and yet to offer itself as a mitigating and rallying alternative.
>
> (Williams, 1963: 17)

In modernity, man developed new intellectual and aesthetic tools with which to contemplate his world, being freed to a considerable extent from existing social institutions. This process of gradual self-consciousness, Williams suggests, develops in tandem with the emergence of 'aesthetics' and a notion of artistic truth and value that was distinct from other kinds of human activity (Williams, 1963: 15).[2]

At the same time, however, we must acknowledge the existence of an opposing tradition during the same period, in which culture came to be seen as bound to particular societies and inherently differentiated. This understanding of culture found its earliest and fullest expression in the German Romantic philosophy of Johann Gottfried von Herder and Johann Fichte in the eighteenth century, which proclaimed the centrality of culture to the national identity or 'soul of the people' (*Volksgeist*), through its language and folk culture. Culture was part of a collective, historical memory of a nation and could not be understood properly outside that framework. Their conception of culture as inherently differentiated was a deliberate rejection of the Enlightenment ideal of universal man, which transcended difference. As Herder stated, 'Let us follow our own path ... let men speak well or ill of our nation, our literature, our language: they are ours, they are ourselves and let that be enough' (cited in Malik, 1996: 78).

There is, therefore, in intellectual thought, an understanding of the twin movement within culture; it reflects our particular circumstances, time and background, yet also wrests us away into a universal, timeless place in which we are part of a common humanity. Culture is part of society but also something which lives beyond it, and which can view it and criticise it from a distance. Williams, in his 1958 essay 'Culture is Ordinary', expressed culture's reciprocal relationship to society as both 'ordinary' and part of common consciousness, but also something autonomous and 'special':

> We use the word culture in these two senses: to mean a whole way of life – the common meanings; to mean the arts and learning – the special processes of discovery and creative effort. Some writers reserve the word for one or other of these senses; I insist on both, and on the significance of their conjunction... Culture is ordinary, in every society and in every mind.
>
> (Williams, 2000: 17)

In the fine arts during the eighteenth and nineteenth centuries, this twin movement was reflected in ongoing debates about the idea of a national aesthetic versus a civic humanist and universal aesthetic.[3] The two models of culture which were being debated can be summarised using the German distinction between *Kultur* and *Zivilisation*: the former is associated with the notion, developed by German sociologist Ferdinand Tonnies, of *Gemeinschaft*, and is local, experiential, and unique, transmitted through socialisation and an unconscious absorption of knowledge. The latter is associated with Tonnies' notion of *Gesellschaft*, which is global, cognitive and universal. It can be passed on through learning and education. For instance, to demonstrate the difference between the two, it was frequently said about the Jews in the interwar Germanic world that 'they could acquire our civilization, but never our culture' (Hylland Eriksen (2001: unpaginated)).

In the mid-nineteenth century, Marx presented the transcendent quality of culture (or if we accept the German term *Zivilisation*) as internally related to the social being of man and the individual's dialectical relationship to society. For Marx, man is special in the animal world not merely by dint of his consciousness or emotional depth, but because of his unique ability to abstract himself and see beyond his individual being towards a shared interest with others. He is a social creature who can imagine the interests of others and join together with them. This capacity allows him to not only appreciate other persons and cultures as an outsider, but come to believe them to be part of his being too.

This social nature of humanity which fascinated Marx had been brought into sharp relief during the nineteenth century, as social relations changed rapidly: entire populations were experiencing the transition from rural to urban life, and there was the emergence of private and public spheres and the development of the state. People were brought together into a much more complex and interdependent relationship than ever before, as strangers came together to work in cities and exchange commodities. Human labour conjoined to create new inventions, commodities, urban environments, and ideas. The growth of society and human progress generated new forms of identity which extended far beyond the scale of small peasant communities, and grew into large cities, nations, and empires. One's culture and identity could not be static or tied down to where one was brought up or how one lived, but to a more profound, more abstract sphere – new connections around nationhood, class, and ideology became prominent.

Thus, in the *Grundrisse* (1858) Marx reflects on the way in which human consciousness transcends the limits of daily, personal interactions. In a short commentary about artistic beauty, he notes how whilst art is undoubtedly made in a particular historical time and place, human beings' appreciation of art seems to transcend history. For him,

> the difficulty lies not in understanding that the Greek arts and epic are bound up with certain forms of social development. The difficulty is that they still afford us artistic pleasure and that in a certain respect they count as a norm and unattainable model. A man cannot become a child again, or he becomes childish. But does he not find joy in the child's naïveté and must he himself not strive to reproduce its truth at a higher stage?
>
> (Marx, 1978: 246)

In reading these words it is perhaps ironic to think that a large amount of contemporary Marxist art criticism focuses on reading texts politically and decoding their social meaning, because here Marx seems to be perplexed by something quite different. Although culture and consciousness are tied to a historical moment ('bound up with certain forms of social development') and therefore inherently differentiated and relative at one level, why is it that we can still enjoy this art centuries later when the society in which it was created is so different from ours? The answer, he concludes, is that humans have the capacity to transcend their particularity; hence, we can appreciate the value of art *qua* art. Artistic value has a degree of durability and provides continued fascination for humans, long after the historical period of their creation has passed.

Or, as the Romantic poet, John Keats, put it more poetically in 'Ode on a Grecian Urn', written in 1819:

> When old age shall this generation waste,
> Thou shalt remain, in midst of other woe
> Than ours, a friend to man, to whom thou sayst,
> 'Beauty is truth, truth beauty,' – that is all
> Ye know on earth, and all ye need to know.

(lines 46–50)

In other words, when time withers human beings, works of artistic beauty remain true and remind us of some deeper meaning. Though they capture a moment of time and feeling, they become immortalised through art and are forever beautiful.

It was this notion of transcendence – being able to see outside one's particular social context – that lay behind the recurrent view of culture as a form of critique during this period; culture is a way of looking critically at society from a distance. It is 'other-worldly', a universal existence beyond the everyday experience of society.

In Britain, the most influential thinker in this respect was the Victorian writer and poet Matthew Arnold, whose conception of culture's importance left an indelible influence on the liberal-humanist model of cultural policy in the United Kingdom in much of the twentieth century (Bennett, O., 2005). Arnold regarded culture as a kind of objective critique that could reveal our 'best self', as opposed to the impulses and thoughts produced by an atomised and subjective market place (Arnold, 2006: 149). Culture was the inheritor of a religious sensibility that enabled humans to turn 'a stream of fresh and free thought upon our stock notions and habits, which we now follow staunchly but mechanically . . . ' (5). Culture therefore allows us to think for ourselves, challenge orthodoxy, and be true.

Views like Arnold's dominated intellectual debates about cultural policy and the importance of culture long into the twentieth century. Writing in 1948 T.S. Eliot (1962) developed the notion that culture had a critical, reflective value and was closely related to religious life. He distinguished carefully between different levels of culture in society, each with their own value and special contribution: the lowest being 'a way of life', whilst the highest was the most consciously developed and specialised, which required maintenance by an educated elite. For Eliot, a vocal advocate of such 'high' art institutions as the BBC's Third

Programme (today, Radio Three), it was the responsibility of the state to maintain cultural perfection above the lowest levels of mass culture.

Arnold and Eliot conceptualised 'high' culture as separate from society, distinguishing it from 'low' culture and entertainment, which was determined by social forces like the market and everyday politics or propaganda. They insisted on the authority of an expert elite that could maintain this distinction, seeing ordinary people as a polluting influence. This view of culture reflected ambivalence towards the masses, sometimes openly expressing itself in contempt. For conservative writers like Eliot, the cultivation of a higher, civilised culture was tied to the class structure, and required the domination of a stable and enduring elite. Only such a group would have the qualities and commitment required to maintain the standards of culture and act as guardians for the preservation of civilised values and art (Carey, 1992).

Meanwhile, there were many artists and writers of the first half of the twentieth century that also claimed to be speaking to a higher truth but kicked against the cultural traditions that were passed on to them. Dadaists, Surrealists, Imagist poets, and Absurdists all developed their art in defiance of what went before – taking succour from the sense of a new modernity that would break up the traditional outlook. This *avant garde* was just as sure that it stood apart from the crowds, but also gave life to the idea that tradition was a deadweight on the imagination and truth.

There were also more radical proponents of cultural autonomy, specifically on the political left, who regarded the masses as the beneficiaries of culture, not merely the barbarians at the gate. In his 1967 essay 'Culture Industry Reconsidered', the Marxist writer Theodor Adorno expressed concern about consumerism and the state control of culture as a tool of oppression which dehumanises the population and presumes their lack of critical faculties: 'The culture industry misuses its concern for the masses in order to duplicate, reinforce and strengthen their mentality, which it presumes is given and unchangeable.' He then argued that culture did not 'simply accommodate itself alone to human beings; but it always simultaneously raised a protest against the petrified relations under which they lived, thereby honouring them' (Adorno, 2001: 99–100). Cultural autonomy could be a tool of conservatism, but also of radicalism. For thinkers like Adorno, culture could lift people from their state of nature, endow them with a truer consciousness and way of seeing which empowers them to take a more active role in society. Adorno's critique reflects the way in which the left was just as concerned as those on the right about the need to distance autonomous 'high culture' from the 'cultural industry', which was shaped by the vagaries of the market and treated people like mere consumers, pandering to their immediate likes and dislikes. Time and time again, writers have insisted that culture should be allowed its autonomous space, to develop freely from market or state interference.

The German-born philosopher Hannah Arendt, who refused most of her life to fit into any political category, shared with these writers a concern for the need to maintain culture's 'superior' character. In 1961, writing poignantly in the shadow of totalitarian regimes in Europe, Arendt attacked the way the Nazi state used culture for 'ulterior motives' such as 'self-education', 'self-perfection', and 'entertainment'. She insisted that culture required its own valuation according to aesthetic criteria, regardless of the tastes of individual men or governments. Culture was not useful like other things, but valuable precisely for this reason.

> 'From the viewpoint of sheer durability,' she wrote, 'artworks are clearly superior to all other things; since they stay longer in the world than anything else, they are the worldliest of all things. Moreover, they are the only things without any function in the life process of society; strictly speaking, they are fabricated not for men, but for the world which is meant to out-last the life span of mortals, the coming and going of the generations. Not only are they not consumed like consumer goods and not used up like use objects; they are deliberately removed from the processes of consumption and usage and isolated against the sphere of human necessities'.
>
> (Arendt, 2006: 206)

For Arendt, culture was a necessary source of critical distance from the state and the market; it was also a key aspect of human feeling and judgement. A logical and rational philosopher who took pleasure in poetry and art, Arendt valued the human quality of culture as something that existed beyond politics. She saw no contradiction in her condemnation of German society, whilst retaining a profound love of German culture and literature. When asked about her return visits to Germany after the Second World War, she dismissed concerns of fellow German-born Jews who felt she remained too attached to her native culture, saying, 'It wasn't the German language that went crazy.'

In this necessarily truncated historical account, I have tried to show how a particular idea of culture in the modern era has been bound together with key concepts – the *transcendence* of human beings and artistic value, the need for culture to be a form of *critique*, the *authority* of experts. In this spirit, culture is regarded as something that exists beyond particular societies and belongs to the subject of, what might be called for want of a better phrase, 'humanity in general'. I have also shown that culture is, at its very heart, a reflection of human experience – they both come from a place, but are also capable of moving beyond it.

The idea of the autonomy of culture – freedom from society – is evident in the early development of arts policy in the United Kingdom in the early twentieth century. By seeming paradox it was a desire to keep the cultural sphere protected from the pressures of society and the market that led politicians and thinkers to develop state intervention in the cultural sphere. Public subsidy enabled culture to exist as a 'public good', free from any reliance on the market, wealthy patrons or changing public taste. In 1940, the government created the Council for the Encouragement of Music and the Arts (CEMA) which championed the idea of 'The Best for the Most'. It pioneered arts initiatives to cheer up an embattled country and encourage a sense of national pride and camaraderie.

Following the war, the influential economist John Maynard Keynes was a forceful advocate for the arts and drove forth the creation of Britain's first Arts Council in 1946. The respected economist had just told Churchill's outgoing Cabinet that Britain was facing 'a financial Dunkirk', without foreign reserves, industry, shipping, raw materials, and carrying a debt to America that would take 70 years to pay off. There was even to be bread rationing. And yet despite this, Keynes asked the Prime Minister for half a million pounds to set up an Arts Council. He managed to secure £235,000, a considerable sum in those days, especially given the circumstances (Lebrecht, 2010).

According to Maynard Keynes, the founding principle of the Arts Council was artistic autonomy. 'The artist,' he wrote, 'walks where the breath of the spirit blows him. He cannot be told his direction: he does not know it himself... he teaches us to love and enjoy what we often begin by rejecting, enlarging our sensibilities and purifying our instincts' (cited in Garnham, 2001: 456). This pure-minded dedication to art was tempered with not a little reservation about the influence of commercial American culture. Only a few lines later he exclaims, 'Death to Hollywood!', echoing Adorno's concerns about industrialised culture as well as British anxiety about the brash power of America in old Europe. In the early days of British arts policy, state funding was therefore directed to preserving creativity, culture, and knowledge which could not survive by the market or popular taste.

The Arts Council was also to work at 'arm's-length' from government when choosing which cultural practitioners and organisations to support. This was an innovative (although arguably a frequently compromised) type of organisational existence. The Arts Council's policies would go on in the twentieth century to play a crucial role in providing the conditions for artistic autonomy by giving grants, supporting artistic development and practice, encouraging touring, and running educational programmes to increase cultural knowledge and interest in the population. Today, the Arts Council is divided into four national bodies but it continues to espouse the old ideals, albeit with a new slogan, 'Great Art for All'. Its budget has increased from £235,000 in 1946 (£9.4m in 2010 values) to £450m in the 2010 financial settlement. Its formation also influenced the creation of an entire movement of semi-independent arts bodies in other countries, including the National Endowment of the Arts in the USA and the Australian Arts Council (Upchurch, 2004).

Without doubt reality did not always match up with the ideal of autonomy. The history of state subsidy shows how culture has been used frequently for other, non-artistic ends: the preservation of national identity and heritage; the refinement of public 'taste' and consumption; the need to boost morale during the world wars and post-war period and to promote the egalitarian ethos of the welfare state by bringing great art to the people (Minihan, 1977; Williams, 1979; Pearson, 1982; Hewison, 1995). Instrumentalism has been a feature of much cultural policy and although cultural policy adopted the rhetoric of the Romantic viewpoint – in which culture exists partly outside society, as suggested by Arnold, Adorno, Arendt, and others – it was also subject to bureaucracy, arguments for 'the public good', censorship, and political propaganda (Belfiore and Bennett, 2006; Levine, 2007).[4] The instrumentalist use of culture by the state is nothing new.

Yet importantly, the notion of the arm's-length principle and *art pour l'art* remained the ostensible justification for arts subsidy in the post-war period and most of the twentieth century. The rationale for cultural policy adhered, at least in its presentation, to the Enlightenment view of culture as something that should be allowed to exist freely of social pressure and need. It indicated a belief in the need to defend culture's autonomy. The criteria by which it was judged would not be the arbitrary tastes of individuals, private institutions, or politicians, but of experts who had transparent authority and could ensure standards of excellence.

This ideal was linked to a belief in democratic egalitarianism. Roy Shaw (1987), the General Secretary of the Arts Council in the late 1970s, who rose to prominence through the Workers Educational Association, was a strong believer in the aspiration to democratise great culture, encouraged by his own experience as a working-class man, and personal passion for the arts. He wrote, 'the task of education, broadcasting organisations and arts organisations...is to make excellence accessible. This is to make the eminently democratic assumption that people deserve the best and need it' (81). The role of the state was to preserve and disseminate those forms of culture worthy of support and incapable of surviving in the commercial climate. This naturally involved judgments about artistic merit and public worth, a process that was not deemed particularly controversial for most of the history of cultural policy. Up until the 1970s at least, there was a fairly durable 'order of discourse' that posited culture as universal – belonging inside society, yet at the same time, existing outside it.[5]

Growth of discussions about cultural policy since the 1970s

In the 1970s and 1980s a growing chorus within the cultural sector and academia challenged the comfortable consensus of the post-war period. They argued against the idea that culture can and should exist autonomously from the state and society, scrutinised the notion of the Romantic artist or the autonomous museum or gallery, and regarded artistic value as 'an arbitrary aesthetic system', contingent upon the tastes of specific groups who wield social influence. Pierre Bourdieu's work on the sociology of taste, most notably his *Distinction: A Social Critique of Taste* (1986), along with other left-wing critiques of the cultural sector, pushed the idea that cultural value is not transcendent, but grounded in social conditions of power and class. This 'exposure' of the essential contingency and relativism of cultural value became an important influence in academia, first through the growth of the discipline of anthropology in the 1950s, and then later in cultural studies in the 1960s.

These arguments culminated in what has become known as the 'cultural policy debate' of the early 1990s (Rothfield, 1999). The debate amongst predominantly left-wing figures in cultural studies centred on the political ambitions of the discipline and the role of academics as shapers of policy. On one side were those who believed that the importance of cultural studies lay in its capacity for autonomous critique: impartial analysis of cultural products and representations in order to generate a greater understanding of the dynamics of capitalist society. This position had dominated early cultural studies in Britain and America, with proponents such as Raymond Williams, who sought to radicalise Matthew Arnold's idealist 'criticism of life' (Jameson, 1993; McGuigan, 1996: 13).

On the other side were those who argued that it was naïve to believe that cultural studies could operate in a transcendent space, immune to political and social influence. All cultural study and analysis, they argued, was itself implicated in the very fabric of state power. For instance, the university (in which cultural studies academics are based) is never free of practical considerations, regulations, or agendas. As a result, culture – down to its very practice, display, and dissemination – has always been 'useful' to those in power. Probably, the single most forceful exponent of this position is Tony Bennett, trained in the British school of cultural studies and working throughout his career in universities in the United Kingdom and Australia.[6] In 1992, in his article 'Putting Policy into Cultural Studies', he argued that the notion of culture as critique was problematic because it had always been used for the exercise of power in modernity, borrowing the term 'governmentality' from the postmodern theorist Michel Foucault to describe how it wields influence over citizens (Bennett, T., 1992). Bennett challenged an account of culture moving from being 'pure' and autonomous towards being a subject of policy. Instead, culture is always compromised and partial. Even academics who spend their lives deconstructing texts and art works are themselves situated in the ivory towers of a university, with its own particular demands, expectations, and rules of compliance.

Bennett first described culture as a 'technology of the self' in his 1995 historical account of the emergence of the modern public museum, *The Birth of the Museum* (itself a nod towards Michel Foucault's *The Birth of the Clinic*). Following Foucault, Bennett argued that the state's relationship to the citizenry went through a qualitative transformation in the early nineteenth century. The state shifted from a juridical-discursive mode, with explicit expressions of absolutist monarchical power and coercion, towards a new mode of 'governmentality', through which the citizenry is fashioned to be self-disciplining and the state is able to 'work at a distance ... achieving its objectives by inscribing within the self-activating and self-regulating capacities of individuals' (20). The shift marked a move away from an explicitly oppressive and coercive state that imposed rules of behaviour onto people towards a relationship of mutual interdependence, in which citizens were encouraged to think and act in a certain way and appear to do this voluntarily. The lack of explicit coercion was extremely effective and efficient, making citizens more compliant, easier to manage, and more willing to develop the appropriate personality, values, and attitudes.

Within this historical account, Bennett suggests that museums were part of a battery of new cultural technologies such as parks, leisure facilities, theatres, and halls that were aimed at reforming individual citizens through ideas about good behaviour, self-fashioning, and self-education. The public museum, with its emphasis on a universal regard for the object and a shared story, reinforced a particularly liberal model of subjectivity. Yet the narrative of a free, disinterested cultural sphere, Bennett argues, is itself a fiction. The 'passionless reformers' of the new public museums were just as concerned with fashioning citizenship as promoting cultural value. For instance, the architecture and organisation of public museums were oriented towards teaching people how to behave in public and emulate the middle classes; the visitor was moulded through the assertion of new norms of accepted conduct (no eating, no drinking, dress codes, and so on) (1995: 24). Although museums were ostensibly about engaging people with 'the best that has been thought and said', they were also tools of citizenship creation and behaviour management.

Most provocatively, Bennett has argued that the claim to cultural universalism is itself spurious, brought into existence for the purpose of fashioning a new kind of citizen for the modern state. Universalism presupposes an autonomous, rational subject who is capable of self-discipline, improvement, and making a contribution to the social order. It is an affirmation of the bourgeois ideal of citizenship, and a way of inducting people into this new subjectivity. Instead of insisting on seeing culture as impartial and independent, Bennett insists it is better to understand it as a tool of government.

Instead of attacking the prescriptive use of cultural policy and trying to wrestle culture away from power – to make it 'pure' again – Bennett argues that society should emulate this approach to achieve the desired moral objectives of our own age. We cannot create an autonomous cultural sphere, so why not use it to promote the morality and values of the contemporary era? The Victorians spoke the language of universal citizenship and autonomy, but we can turn this on its head and emphasise new values; in particular, the language of diversity and inclusion:

> Are museums not still concerned to beam their improving messages of cultural tolerance and diversity as deeply into civil society as they can reach in order to carry the message to those who the museum can only hope to address as citizens, publics and audiences? And do we not, through a battery of access policies, wish – indeed require – that they do so?

> (1998: 213)

In Bennett's account, power does not emanate solely from the top, but from a multiplicity of sites, including government but also non-governmental organisations, civil society, and even just individuals in their day-to-day lives. Cultural policy can allow for a more 'prosaic politics' that involves 'tinkering with the routines and practices through which [cultural institutions] operate' (1998: 195). For museums specifically, they can discard old universalist logic and create space to discuss diverse narratives and values (Bennett, T., 2001b: 37). The role of the curator should be reoriented away from expertise and claims of knowledge towards being a facilitator whose function is to help groups outside the museum influence its content and express themselves. This is not about establishing a singular truth claim or narrative, or universal standards of 'the best', but to expose the inherent instabilities of truth claims and narratives, and give different individuals and ethnic or social groups the opportunity to present their own perspectives on cultural value. Government needs to include those who are not represented in the hegemonic national picture – ethnic minorities, the working class, women, and other marginalised groups.

This approach may be highly appealing to the socially conscious. But it also knocks culture off its perch and with it the unified, transcendental human subject. Without objectivity or claims to truth, the subject itself is compromised. The writer James Heartfield (2002) notes the way in which challenges to universal truth are essentially also a challenge to the liberal-humanist subject: 'If the singular objective ground is called into question, then so too is the singular and unified subject' (20). It is the capacity to transcend and develop objective knowledge that allows the subject to act upon the world and change it. Without such capacity for transcendence, subjectivity is not possible. Individuals remain trapped in their partial, different identities, and can only ever understand their own private truths.

Bennett's theorisation of cultural policy and subjectivity leaves in doubt such notions of transcendence, critique, and authority, which had been the basis of legitimacy of cultural institutions in the modern era. The task for a twenty-first-century cultural institution is not to naïvely assume its work is 'true' or at least 'truer', but to recognise its own fallibility and even embrace it actively. Museums and galleries are to be more self-conscious, to see culture in terms of the distribution of power and to use their collections and interpretations to impart moral values and attitudes, in the end making themselves more relevant to contemporary society. Cultural institutions are expected to become facilitators of identity and narrative construction, rather than as guardians of objective knowledge and expertise. Indeed, the notion of knowledge and expertise is itself called into question.

All this calls into question the legitimacy of cultural policy in the past – a rallying cry which has been taken up with enthusiasm by many in working in and writing about cultural policy over the two decades. With reference to museums, Stanbridge (2002) argues that cultural policy should challenge traditional hierarchies ('universalising modes of thought') (127). Lloyd and Thomas (1998) and Lewis and Miller (2003) assert that traditional cultural policy in the past was about creating a 'compliant citizen' and is in need of reform to produce a more democratic citizenry. Clifford (1997) has argued that the role of the museum is no longer to simply display objects unequivocally but to facilitate different voices and opinions in 'conversation'. Hooper-Greenhill (1992), a prominent 'new museologist' in the UK, has argued that 'history must abandon its absolutes, and instead of attempting to find generalisations and unities, should look for differences, for change, for rupture' (10).

Stuart Hall, perhaps the United Kingdom's foremost theorist of cultural diversity and a major figure in the field of cultural studies, has argued for the need to challenge the implied universalism of the museum display and to develop an explicit subjectivism that shows how unreliable, temporary, and relative interpretations of cultural objects can be. Hall has also been a very active member of the cultural sector, leading on the development of key black cultural institutions in Britain. He was a member of the influential Runnymede Commission on *The Future of Multi-Ethnic Britain* and until 2008 was chair of The Institute of International Visual Arts (Iniva) and Autograph ABP (The Association of Black Photographers), based in London. Much of his work has revolved around the notions of identity, culture, and difference, and he has argued for cultural institutions to better reflect these ideas. The museum, he writes, 'has to be aware that it is a narrative, a selection, whose purpose is not just to disturb the viewer but to itself be disturbed by what it cannot be... Its purpose is to destabilise its own stabilities' (Hall, S., 2001: 22). Hall's work on championing cultural diversity in the UK cultural sector – primarily by promoting ethnic-led organisations and practice – reflects this logic.

The championing of diversity and access (i.e. the imperative to include new visitors and audiences) is often posed against notions of excellence, universal truth, and standards. In the field of museums today, a range of cultural professionals are fighting a campaign against the old values which have supposedly excluded people. One museum professional, Jocelyn Dodd, wrote in 2002, 'Art and design museums work well for those who speak the right language, for people who understand the right codes... However, many people find no connections, no relevance. They see serried rows of precious objects unfathomably presented, with texts that presuppose considerable knowledge and provides a very hands-off, alienating experience' (Dodd, 2002: 1).

Beyond museums, these arguments have become commonplace in the fields of visual and performing arts. Justin Lewis, a prominent cultural policy academic and practitioner in the United Kingdom, has argued that there is a conflict between 'an aesthetic based upon "the artist's point of view" and the needs and interests of people as potential cultural consumers'. Arts centres in Britain are wrongly concerned 'with the culture of the arts centre rather than the culture of the area it operates in' (Lewis, 1990: 35). Cultural professionals should pursue a broader range of objectives than mere aesthetic excellence and be used to address issues of economy, individual personal development, tourism and industry, and community.

A new understanding of subjectivity

At a profound level, the new discourse about the value of culture has been shaped by wider debates about what it means to be human and what the human subject is. In political theory and wider academia, there is a view that old 'liberal' or 'humanist' models of subjectivity are out of date with contemporary social experience. The Enlightenment notion of the individual subject and his or her ability to act autonomously and exercise freedom of choice and agency is now under scrutiny. This is because major institutional and material developments have ruffled the fabric of society and had a profound impact on how human subjectivity is understood: the rise of the transnational corporation, the expansion of the international economy, the proliferation of global forms of communications, major changes in the production and consumption of goods and services, global population movements, the techno-industrialisation of war, the emergence of identity politics and the dominance of mass media, and communications technology in daily life. There is a new discourse which emphasises the vulnerability, atomisation, and fragmentation of individuals in modern industrialised societies. Modernism, with all its accompanying ideals and values, has lost its confidence and 'all that is modern melts into postmodern' (Elliott, 2006: 134–5).

The result of this is a new interest in culture and issues of selfhood and self-fashioning. For some thinkers, the old model of subjectivity was based too narrowly on the taken-for-granted experiences of white, privileged males, and did not take into account the particular experiences and disadvantages of minority or victimised groups, such as females, ethnic minorities, gays, or disabled people. The 'rational subject' model only applies to those people in society who have power. The remainder of people are not in control of themselves or their lives (Hall and Paul du Gay, 1996: 4; Keith, 2005: 114).

Many intellectuals have welcomed this change, seeing it as belated recognition that human beings are not always the history-making agents they have been portrayed to be. Rather, humans are vulnerable and determined by social, cultural, even genetic, factors. To treat them as autonomous agents is to underestimate their weakness and partiality. A more balanced account would be fairer and more realistic. However, we need to recognise what such a shift means for human society and the culture of our age. If we cannot believe ourselves to be autonomous, robust individuals, able to transcend our background, much else falls away too. Heartfield (2002) has coined the phrase 'subjectivity in denial' to depict a society that is inescapably bound to the notion of the subject (as the central unit of all legal, political, economic, and social contracts) yet feels ambivalence towards it. He argues that the increasing orientation towards 'identity' reveals a reaction against what he regards as the positive attributes of the Enlightenment subject:

> ...identity is markedly different from subjectivity. Whereas the Subject presents itself as pure, abstract and universal, identity is specific and local... Those very features that were portrayed as flaws, or even impurities by Enlightenment thinkers are instead held up as a badge of pride. The particular stance that was rejected before for its partiality is now recognized for its special insight. And that insight is precisely the limit point of the presumed generality of the dominant identity. (89)

In other words, the criticism of the Enlightenment subject is that it had always presumed that certain abstract principles were applicable to all human beings, regardless of their specific cultural or social experiences as subjects. This approach presumed the commensurability of all people, despite ethnic or cultural differences, and belief in the general progression of lifestyles and ethics in a similar direction. All of public and political life therefore derives from a universal or 'colour-blind' orientation, which treats all citizens the same; with the same rights and legal status as each other.

By contrast, advocates of 'identity politics' argue that there is no such thing as abstract truth that transcends particular differences. The notion of 'truth' is always imposed from a position of privilege and power and any truth perspective is just as partial and biased as any other. Going a step further, such arguments insist that it is actually human differences that give people their identity and basis of self-worth, rather than their grasp of a universal truth. Being a woman, black, disabled, or gay gives a partial but special perspective on reality, which should be recognised as equally valid as any other.

Yet this emphasis on identity means that one is wholly tied to one's background and experiences and unable to transcend them. It is an essentialist view: something which posits that people are determined according to a particular identity and cannot change or transform themselves (for critiques of essentialism, see Kuper, 1999 and Bayart, 2005). Kenan Malik, one of the first critics in Britain to write theoretically about multiculturalism, has argued that it is not unrelated to older forms of racial discourse, in that it rejects the universal nature of humankind. He writes about the consequences of such a shift:

> Multiculturalists have turned their back on universalist conceptions not because such conceptions are racist but because they have given up on the possibility of economic and social change. We live in an age in which there is considerable disillusionment with politics as an agency of change, and in which possibilities of social transformation seem to have receded. What is important about human beings, many have come to believe, is not their political capacity but their cultural attachments. Such pessimism has led to multiculturalists to conflate the idea of humans as culture-bearing creatures with the idea that humans have to bear a particular culture.
>
> (Malik, 2002a, unpaginated)

For Malik, this understanding of culture is used to entrap humans in the status quo despite the radical rhetoric of identity politics. Of course, no human can live outside of culture. But nor do they have to live inside any particular one. 'To view humans as culture-bearing,' he writes, 'is to view them as social beings, and hence as transformative beings. It suggests that humans have the capacity for change, for progress, and for the creation of universal moral and political forms through reason and dialogue.'

The rise of identity politics is more than an emphasis on cultural difference, or ethnicity; it is a reformulation of how humans behave and feel about their lives. The new fixation with identity reflects the wider ambivalence about individual agency. The subject increasingly appears unable to control his or her life choices, circumstances, or reactions to situations. They are 'vulnerable' and in need of support from external agencies. This has prompted some sociologists to bemoan the growth of a therapeutic culture in modern society and the massive growth in state-supported counselling and 'therapeutic' interventions which are designed to strengthen the individual subject whilst at the same time undermining their autonomy and independence. The taken-for-granted relations that had existed between people have weakened and people are forced to rely on themselves to make sense of their individuated life-journeys and experiences (see Nolan, 1998 and Furedi, 2003).

Not only have therapeutic interventions like stress counselling expanded in places like the workplace, but people's experiences are also mediated through a new 'cultural script' which emphasises their feelings of vulnerability and insecurity. There has been a growth of agencies, professionals, government, and corporate policy or funding themed around therapeutic concerns. Between 1989 and 1999 the number of members of the British Association for Counselling rose from 4500 to 16,000. In 300 UK newspapers for the year 1990 Furedi did not find a single mention of the word 'self-esteem'. A decade later, there were 3328 references. A similar rise is evident for the words 'trauma', 'stress', 'syndrome' and 'counselling' (Furedi, 2003: 3–10).

This new trend towards a therapeutic state appears to parallel the rise of identity politics and the politics of recognition; both indicate a search for meaning and stability at a time when traditional institutions find it harder to confer a sense of identity or authority. In this sense, we are not just witnessing a 'turn to culture in general, but towards one with an intense therapeutic sensibility' (Furedi, 2003: 163).

This preoccupation with the self became a feature of left-wing political discourse throughout the 1990s in Britain, Europe, and America, treating individual vulnerability and weakness as an important and inevitable new aspect of politics in a post-industrial world. Left-wing writer Geoff Mulgan in his 1994 book *Politics in an Antipolitical Age* argued that the 'industrial logic' of socialism is no longer sufficient to meet advances in flexible forms of production, working patterns, lifestyle, and attitude. The problem, for Mulgan, is how to re-engage the electorate and find a new kind of politics that appeals to their needs, because 'symbolic inequalities are as significant as material ones' (138). This concern for the individual psychology of the citizen and the 'reflexive self' was a cornerstone of 'Third Way' writing in the 1990s, which would go on to shape the New Labour project (Giddens, 1991, 1994).

Political theories of recognition also became influential in the social sciences in Europe and North America during the 1980s and 1990s (Fukuyama, 1992; Taylor, C. 1994; Fraser, 1995; Kymlicka, 1995; Honneth, 2001; and for application to local government in England and Wales, see Perrons and Skyers, 2003). This approach argues that individuals in contemporary society require not only material welfare provision, but also the positive affirmation of their identity and that governments must address 'the everyday dimension or moral feelings of injustice' (Honneth, 2003: 114, cited in Thompson, 2006: 108). Government should seek to empower the individual by changing structures, but also help individuals reach their 'authentic' self by realising their own distinct cultural lifestyle and choices. The key to restoring a sense of agency is to nurture one's sense of identity through therapeutic or other means.

The consequence of this approach is that politics should not only aspire to conditions of universalism, where everyone is treated the same regardless of their cultural or private identities, but also to a politics of difference, in which cultural identities are given freedom and also validation in some form. Culture, just as for other spheres like education and housing, requires intervention, because it relates the individual's psychology and relationship to society.

Many of these arguments have found their way into academic and mainstream discussions about the role of culture in society and the relevance of cultural policy. There have been calls for the respect for 'cultural rights' in addition to the portfolio of liberal rights, which will embed diversity and identity as core features of citizenship (Rogers and Tillie, 2001; Stevenson, 2001; Turner, 2001). Some have also argued the need to use culture to manage the changing nature of national and local identities in a globalised world. In a United Nations document about cultural rights in 1995, Diana Ayton-Shenker writes about the importance of cultural identity in helping people to cope with economic recession, environmental changes, increasing disparities in wealth around the world, mass migration, the displacement of people, and an alarming increase in violence. She argues that such changes have made people more vulnerable and likely to resort to isolationist cultural identities – hence, the need for cultural rights to ensure that minorities do not become marginalised:

There is an understandable urge to return to old conventions, traditional cultures, fundamental values, and the familiar, seemingly secure, sense of one's identity. Without a secure sense of identity amidst the turmoil of transition, people may resort to isolationism, ethnocentricism and intolerance.... This climate of change and acute vulnerability raises new challenges to our ongoing pursuit of universal human rights.

(Ayton-Shenker, 1995)

The result of this shift in political theory and academia is a new understanding of the value of culture in terms of identity creation, citizen engagement, and social justice. This thinking has come to permeate the cultural sector itself.

2
The Development of Cultural Policy in the United Kingdom

Since the 1970s the debate about the perceived usefulness of culture led to an expansion of cultural policy structures and language at local, national, and international level. Whilst the idea of universal, autonomous culture did not disappear, it came under increasing scrutiny.

In the 1970s the United Nations Educational, Scientific and Cultural Organisation (UNESCO) began to put culture onto the international political agenda, reflecting increasing concerns about citizenship and the impact of post-colonial migration and displaced minorities within Europe.[1] It announced the 'World Decade for Cultural Development' in 1989, followed by the establishment of the World Commission on Culture and Development in 1991. Its definition of culture was strategically broad enough to encompass artistic but also political concerns. In its major report, *Our Creative Diversity* in 1996, the authors acknowledged the growing clamour about the cultural dimensions of development, 'as people realised that economic criteria alone could not provide a programme for human dignity and well-being' (World Commission on Culture and Development, 1996: 8). Importantly, the UNESCO definition, whilst paying lip service to the notion of culture as autonomous and universal placed greater emphasis on it as 'a way of life'.[2]

Following suit, cultural policy statements from national and international bodies during this time were broad in their definition of culture. For example, Australia's cultural policy strategy, *Creative Nation: Commonwealth Cultural Policy* (1994), deploys an anthropological meaning of culture: 'the work of Australians themselves through what they do in their everyday lives, as communities and as individuals (whether it be as workers in industry, farmers, parents or citizens') (DOCA, 1994: 9, Bennett, T. 1998: 89).[3] Similarly, the South African government's

Creative Nation document also states that 'arts and cultural policy deals with custom and tradition, belief, religion, language, identity, popular history, crafts, as well as all the art forms including music, theatre, dance, creative writing, the fine arts, the plastic arts, photography, film' (ANC, 1996: 1, cited in Bennett, T., 1998: 89–90).

At the national level in many countries cultural policy became increasingly visible from the late 1980s onwards. Whereas before it had been done largely as a 'labour of love' (Pankratz and Morris, 1990: xiii), cultural policy studies began to grow in stature, generating a considerable volume of academic journals and books, prestigious annual conferences, and the creation of numerous university departments worldwide. Since the late 1990s, major think tanks in the United States, Europe, Britain, and Australia have also produced pamphlets and research about culture.[4] There has also been some demand by those within cultural policy studies to have a more prescriptive influence on government policy (Lewis, 1990; Rothfield, 1999; Lewis and Miller, 2003). These academics have written for state and supra-state authorities, crossing the divide between academia and policymaking.

UK context

I have outlined a shift in the ideas shaping cultural policy in academia in various countries. More specifically, we can also see how this has been translated into practice in the United Kingdom with the move from a 'policy-light' approach to a 'policy-heavy' approach since the 1980s.

As suggested earlier, Britain's post-war governments tended to keep a distance from culture, adhering to the 'arm's-length principle'. Government officials would 'write the cheque' but were, in large part, either disinterested in culture or else sufficiently satisfied with the judgements of the arts elite to allow them to distribute funding in their own, unregulated way. Even during the 1960s when the position of Arts Minister was created for the Labour MP, Jennie Lee, the government allowed the Arts Council to manage their limited funds with relative freedom from government guidance or diktat. The arts writer, Norman Lebrecht (2010) writes about how arts administrators in the Arts Council were at liberty to use their own discretion with artists, choosing to supplement their funds as and when required:

> John Denison, the Council's director of music from 1948 to 1965, would get a call at times from David Webster, the Covent Garden manager, asking him to drop by after dinner for a chat. On a

fine night, the pair would take a stroll down Weymouth Street and Webster would confess that the box-office was a bit low: 'I don't know if we can pay the wages next week,' he'd mutter. Next morning, Denison would send him an Arts Council cheque for £1,000 as an advance on the next year's grant. 'That's how it was done,' he told me. 'No forms to fill, no fuss.' *Autres temps, autres moeurs.* Public administration has moved on. Today, a senior official biking round an unvetted advance would have the fraud squad on his doorstep before the banks opened.

From the 1980s onwards, the arts were no longer afforded this kind of light-touch treatment, and government's involvement in the arts and culture began to grow. Politicians took a rather keener interest in what was being funded and why (Hewison, 1995; Blandina-Quinn, 1998; Gray, 2000; Selwood, 2001).

To a large extent this increased interest from government was driven by economic pressure – in particular, the fiscal crisis of the welfare state in the 1970s and 1980s and the ensuing emphasis on economic management and efficiency. In 1987, the Arts Council's reduced grant meant that it was forced to halve the number of organisations it funded and it became subject to new accounting procedures. It was also instructed to encourage the sector to seek funds from corporate sponsors, rather than the public purse, and improve the efficiency of organisations. The 'New Public Management' approach in government, which sought to increase efficiency and standards in the public sector, applied managerial methods to a range of policy areas and introduced models of market-based competition in order to drive up standards (Hood, 1991, 1995).

For the cultural sector, this meant an increase of targets and performance measures (largely unrelated to aesthetic values) and usually tied to funding. Whereas in the 1970s decisions over Arts Council subsidies were decided by a panel of art experts – what Hutchison has scathingly called 'little more than the rich looking after its own pleasures' (1982: 68) – in the 1980s new criteria and assessment came into being. This took place alongside more formalisation and bureaucratisation; increased centralisation through the creation of government departments and quasi non-government organisations (quangos); and the growth of statutory and non-statutory guidelines and policy frameworks. The arts became subject to more intense scrutiny in this period and were increasingly judged in terms of consumer-choice and the criteria of economists or 'marketers' (Blandina Quinn, 1998; Selwood, 2001; Caust, 2003). Gray has argued that over this period the values of art and the art elite have been replaced by the values of bureaucrats. He calls this process of change 'commodification' (2000).

New quangos such as the Association for Business Sponsorship of the Arts (now Arts and Business) were set up to help cultural organisations build up another income stream. The major national galleries and museums also set up their own dedicated fundraising and sponsorship departments, cultivating long-term relationships with corporate supporters. Although some arts administrators (for instance, Roy Shaw, the General Secretary of the Arts Council in the 1970s) expressed concern about encouraging more business sponsorship and making the arts more reliant on commerce, the trend was unstoppable. Business sponsorship of the arts rose from £600,000 in 1976 to £20m in 1986, peaking to around £171.5m in 2006/7.[5]

Government and policymakers also emphasised the economic impact of the arts from the mid-1980s onwards, producing more research in this area (Myerscough, 1988). The arts sector, faced with funding cuts, felt the increasing demand to prove their social and economic worth. As if to reinforce the relationship between art and business, the commercial arts sector in the 1980s economic boom appeared more 'business-like' and was oriented towards profit-making practices and speculative investment. This culminated in the 1990s with the dramatic success of the Young British Artists under the patronage of advertising guru Charles Saatchi (Ford and Davies, 1998; Stallabrass, 2006).

In response to these trends, the Conservative government decided to create a new department in 1992 – the Department of National Heritage (DNH). This changed its name in 1997 to the Department for Culture, Media and Sport (DCMS) under the New Labour administration. The new title had a more modern tone, placing further emphasis on contemporary culture as well as heritage. The Department also took a greater interest in the 'creative industries'; art and culture were not merely assets that one looked after for future generations, but were creators of wealth and social cohesion.

After arriving in government in 1997 Labour boosted funding for the arts, but was no less enthusiastic about the managerial approach. It went even further by introducing new three-year Public Service Agreements (PSA) with funded cultural organisations as part of its Comprehensive Spending Review (CSR).[6] DCMS was awarded an additional £290m from the Treasury over the next three years and created new intermediary bodies to manage relations with its 'clients' (grant recipients) (Creigh-Tyte and Stiven, 2001: 184; Selwood, 2001: 2). In 1998 DCMS also established the Quality, Efficiency and Standards Team (QUEST) to scrutinise the effectiveness of the system, although the watchdog was dismantled only four years later, without much fanfare – its functions absorbed within the DCMS.

Alongside this drive towards efficiency – championed by both main political parties – was a new expectation that culture should deliver social and economic objectives. Under the Conservatives, and later under Labour, the Arts Council and DCMS extolled the social and economic benefits of culture: urban regeneration; improving health outcomes; increasing educational attainment; and integrating ethnic, cultural, and religious minorities (see DCMS, 1998a; DCMS, 1998b; ACE, 2004, 2006b). Museums and galleries were even described in one DCMS document as 'centres for social change' (DCMS, 2000). A new crop of arts centres, museums, and galleries were planted around the country, intended to kick-start urban renaissance in previously blighted inner cities and provincial towns.

They were good times – in financial terms at least. The total expenditure on the arts by DCMS rose dramatically between the early 1990s and late 2000s, largely due to lottery funding. It grew from £196.4m in 1997–8 to £435.8m in 2008–9 (although in real terms, the 1997–8 Arts Council budget (including lottery funding of £369m) was £602 m, while the 2006–7 figure was £590m (including lottery funding of £150m)).[7] In 2010, the government announced cuts to cultural expenditure, although it stated its desire to limit the impact on 'frontline organisations' (i.e. those actually producing or showing culture), by awarding them only a 15 per cent cut and asking funding and regulatory bodies to find the remainder of the savings from their own budgets.

An equally interesting change is the growth of support from other government departments. Rather than being treated as a separate area with its own values, cultural policy has gradually become 'attached' to other policy areas such as regeneration, social inclusion, and education (Gray, 2000). In 1998–9, the arts and cultural sector received an estimated £230m in funding from other central government departments – evidence of the perceived relevance of cultural issues to other social problems (Selwood, 2001: 39).

By the 2000s, under New Labour there were even more criteria for assessment, such as participation rates and audience attendance figures (Gray, 2000; Brighton, 2007). With this growth came increasing disquiet from cultural professionals. The notion of art or culture 'for its own sake' was not dead, but it now had to sit alongside an explicit and domineering kind of instrumentalism.[8] Numerous writers and cultural figures – often using the national media – complained about this instrumentalism, which they argued undermined the importance of cultural value (Pick, 1991; Brighton 1999; Appleton, 2001; Ellis, 2003; Delingpole, 2006; Lebrecht, 2006; Tusa, 2007). What was driving this new approach to culture and cultural policy? Why did government suddenly become so interested in an area in which it had expressed little interest before?

Some have argued that the new political attention to culture reflects its increased importance to the economies of advanced industrial nations following a decline in the Fordist model of politics and economic production (Zukin, 1997: 8; Driver and Martell, 1999: 247). As cities throughout Europe, America, and Australia experienced a decline in their industries and a growth in unemployment, urban change, and social crisis, they sought to find alternative ways to generate their economies. In this context, culture was perceived to be useful, as a new area of consumption and industrial growth creating jobs, and tackling a wide range of social problems like crime, ill health, and juvenile delinquency (Gray, 2000; Caust, 2003; Miles, 2005).[9] This idea became particularly prominent at local government level, perhaps most famously expressed as the 'Bilbao effect'. Bilbao is an industrial town in the Basque region, Spain, which received a new lease of life when in 1997 the Solomon R. Guggenheim Foundation opened an architecturally stunning new art museum in the downtown area, designed by Frank Gehry. The subsequent boost in marketing and tourism apparently transformed the town's fortunes, now attracting approximately one million visitors a year. Perhaps unsurprisingly, it led leaders in municipal halls around the rest of the world wondering if they might be able to achieve a similar effect. By the early 2000s, over 50 local authorities in the United Kingdom had developed or were developing cultural quarters or districts, usually large-scale redevelopments of disused industrial areas into retail, leisure, or educational zones, centred around a single capital project like a major art gallery or museum (O'Connor, 2001), and over 150 were thought to be in the process of development worldwide (Comedia, 2004). Some high-profile examples in the UK included the redevelopment of the docks in Liverpool in the 1980s, creating luxury apartments, retail and art spaces; the development of the 'Northern Quarter' cluster in Manchester in the 1990s to boost retail and creative industries and studio spaces; the reconstruction of the riverside area in Gateshead in the 2000s surrounding the lottery-funded capital project, the Baltic art gallery; and most famously of all, the landscape redevelopment of Tate Modern at Bankside in 2000 – a converted power station on the south of the Thames river. As Keith (2005) states, 'the cultural industries have, over the last decade, belatedly achieved a collective identity in the imagination of government officials and city planners in Britain and elsewhere' (115). This same degree of local government interest in culture has been noted in the US context (Zukin, 1997; Florida, 2002; Schuster, 2002) and also parts of Europe (Skot-Hansen, 2002).

The language of cultural policy in the 1980s and 1990s had a strong economic character. Charles Landry and Franco Bianchini, amongst the most influential urban policy-thinkers in this field, stated: 'Future competition between nations, cities and enterprise looks set to be based less on natural resources, location or past reputation and more on the ability to develop attractive images and symbols and project these effectively.' (Landry et al., 1995, 12, cited in Cochrane, 2007: 104). Economics dominated discussions amongst academics, government agencies, and cultural organisations. In 1997 the Labour government established the Creative Industries Taskforce, which aimed to maximise creative activity as an economic asset. In 2001 Lord Evans, a publishing industry heavyweight and Chair of what was then known as Resource (Council of Museums, Archives and Libraries), used the phrase 'the economy of the imagination' in his New Statesman Arts Lecture to describe how culture was now a central plank in the country's economic strategy. This reflected a new interest in how creativity and culture might be used as new indicators of economic growth. In 2003, US academic Richard Florida published the 'Boho Britain' index with the think tank Demos, identifying the top 40 creative cities which would experience economic growth, putting Manchester at the top (Demos, 2003).

However, it would be misleading to see the shift towards culture solely in economic or 'neo-liberal' terms, or to accept without some scepticism the supposed increased economic importance of culture. Whilst it is true that the cultural and creative sectors, particularly in the United Kingdom, have shown remarkable growth in the last three decades (in 2006 DCMS stated that the economic contribution of the creative industries was £57.3b gross value added (GVA) or 6.4 per cent), some have argued that the stated importance of culture and the official economic figures have been exaggerated (Elliott and Atkinson, 2007: 88–9). They argue that the political enthusiasm towards culture has been more about rhetoric and pragmatism than any profound transformation in the real economy.

Policymaking is rarely a simple case of creating a solution to fix a problem and policymakers are themselves shaped by the attitudes, beliefs, and even misconceptions prevalent in wider society. Social scientists need to ask not only what is the 'rationale', in the positivistic sense, but how that rationale is constructed and imagined in the first place (Berger and Luckmann, 1966; Lukes, 2005). This involves looking at a range of factors that motivate people and how these shape their consciousness and behaviour in response to experiences. There may be a fashion today for 'evidence-based' policy, but history shows that policy is quite often legitimised through values, myths, hopes, maxims, and even clichés, not simply 'what works'. Indeed, with regard to cultural policy, some have argued that the state's involvement has been characterised more by incoherence than coherence and that evidence of success is rarely the decisive factor (Pick, 1991; Taylor, A. J., 1994).[10]

So, whilst it is a commonplace idea, in policymaking circles at least, that the 'creative economy' will address Britain's economic situation and the many problems associated with deindustrialisation, one ought to be cautious. Even the term 'creative economy' is fraught with so many difficulties that it is rendered almost meaningless, and probably best viewed as a piece of political rhetoric. The DCMS definition of creative industries covers 13 commercial industry sectors (excluding publicly funded areas of cultural provision such as libraries, museums, and galleries), but the term is also used to cover less obvious areas in tourism (including gambling and tour agencies), or the production of relevant capital and consumer goods (e.g. cinema projectors, broadcast transmission equipment) (see DCMS *Evidence Toolkit*, undated). The creative and cultural industries also contain a considerable diversity in practice, size of organisation, and even ethical values. As Keith (2005) cautions, 'When Rupert Murdoch's News International multinational corporation and a squatting artist are lumped together as part of the cultural industries, it might be time to think about whether there is a degree of chaotic conceptualisation behind the term itself.' (114). It is also obvious to note that not everyone who works in a creative industry will be doing a 'creative' job – indeed, they may be doing administration, support, and technical roles which are also found in other industries.

Such problems cast into doubt the boosterism about the creative industries and the economic value of culture. The Greater London Authority was a great champion of the creative industries in the early 2000s, regarding them as a valuable way to regenerate deprived areas in the city and funding the establishment of 'creative hubs' around the city to support development of creative businesses. The Greater London Authority commissioned research to show how fast the sector was growing in London and deserved serious policy attention. However, it adjusted its view and adopted a slightly more sober tone in 2007, when it noted that whilst the creative industries sector rose in the capital between 1995 and 2001, at a faster rate than other commercial sectors, it also declined more sharply between 2001 and 2004 (Freeman, 2007: 28). Around the rest of the country, this initial excitement about creative industries growth has not been matched by reality. Manchester, Sheffield, and Liverpool are proud of the success of their cultural quarters, but the creative industries sector remains dominated by London with 58 per cent of all jobs based there (Freeman, 2007: 39). More generally, there is scepticism from economists about the supposed size and impact of culture and the creative industries on national income. They have cautioned, for instance, against believing too readily so-called 'economic impact studies' of culture that over-claim on multiplier effects and confuse the size of sector with net financial gain to the economy (Madden, 2001: 168).

None of this is to suggest that the cultural and creative industries did not grow in the 1980s and 1990s or did not have an important economic (and for that matter, social) impact, for they certainly did. Rather, these facts show that the enthusiasm for the creative industries and its potential to transform the United Kingdom in this period (particularly in cities and towns) seems out of proportion with the reality. It is more accurate to see the embrace of cultural policy as primarily a *political* response, to mediate a set of far-reaching changes in society – namely, the processes of deindustrialisation occurring at the national level since the early 1980s and the reframing of national economic challenges such as unemployment, deteriorating public services, and inner city tensions as 'urban problems' which require local government intervention (Pahl, 2001; Cochrane, 2007: 2, 85–103). Local authorities in the United Kingdom, charged with the task of fixing broken areas, looked to develop large-scale regeneration programmes and secure housing and infrastructure investment from substantial pots of available national and European Union regeneration funding. As part of their strategies, councils began to look to culture and flagship cultural developments as a way to rebrand their areas, increase their attractiveness to investors and tourists, and cultivate a more creative workforce that could compete with those in other cities in Europe (Quilley, 2000: 608; Mommaas, 2004; Cochrane, 2007). High-profile international examples such as Bilbao, but also within the United Kingdom, persuaded many officials in local government of the potential of culture to transform a city. Whether such political strategies actually worked, especially for local residents, is still open to debate. Bianchini and Parkinson (1993) admit that 'the direct impact of 1980s cultural policies on the generation of employment and wealth was relatively modest' (2). In discussing the arts specifically, Lewis (1990) argues, 'it is slightly disingenuous (perhaps deliberately so) to argue that local government arts funding is informed by a considered economic rationale' (89) (see also Kawashima, 1997; Cohen, 1998; Miles, 2005).

The mixed outcomes of culture-led regeneration are apparent in one of the best-known examples of this approach – the city of Glasgow. In the mid-1980s, Glasgow had experienced a major decline in manufacturing and was slowly beginning to establish a new cultural presence. Its flagship gallery, the Burrell Collection, opened in 1983 and the refurbished Glasgow Concert Hall and McLellan Galleries boosted the city's reputation as a centre of art. Glasgow won the European 'City of Culture' title in 1989, and instituted the 'Glasgow's Smiles Better' publicity campaign which was seen to be a resounding success and has since been cited in a number of advocacy reports (e.g. Comedia, 2002). However, Gomez (1998) argues that despite these ostensible successes there was no substantial growth in employment in the city; indeed, employment in Glasgow actually fell between 1981 and 1991; the city lost 39,773 jobs in manufacturing and gained only 2843 service sector jobs. Jobs in tourism and leisure fell by 13 per cent compared to a national rise of 14 per cent (115). The major rise in employment was in the banking and finance sectors, which rose by 17 per cent in the same period. The image and physicality of Glasgow was considerably improved '[b]ut this seems to refer only to a very constrained and poor idea of urban regeneration' (118). Meanwhile, Garcia (2004) argues that Glasgow's cultural projects were not integrated into a coherent urban strategy, meaning that the short-term economic achievements were not sustainable in the long-term. Mooney (2004) also argues that the regeneration campaign had very little impact on the city's poorer residents and that culture-led urban regeneration strategies were doomed to failure because they are primarily concerned with symbolism and representation. Some of Glasgow's wards – Shettleston, Springburn, and Maryhill – remained the most deprived in the country. This criticism is part of a wider critical tradition which suspiciously regards cultural politics as 'political displacement' (Eagleton, 2000; Jensen, 2002; Merli, 2002).

However, the fact that culture-led regeneration projects did lead to a changed perception of cities, and became orthodox in places as far afield as Bilbao, Barcelona, Berlin, Vienna, New York, and Los Angeles reinforced the idea in municipal government at least that such a strategy is desirable, even inevitable, to maintain global competitiveness. Also, it must be remembered that whilst cultural solutions often failed to address many deep-rooted problems in cities, they did, in the United Kingdom at least, allow authorities to access public sector funds for large-scale capital projects or infrastructural improvements, and they generated 'symbolic' effects, if not concrete or measurable economic and social impacts (Edelman, 1967). In the competition for investment, a handful of cities, such as Manchester, won significant prizes. Its charismatic leadership made an opportunistic grab for central and EU funding, producing spectacular projects that were the envy of neighbouring northern towns (Quilley, 2000).

Some writers have bemoaned the fact that economics has hijacked cultural policy and pursued a neo-liberal agenda in places like Glasgow and Leeds, where cultural regeneration projects have been characterised by the drive for new jobs and attracting inward investment (Chatterton and Unsworth, 2004; Garcia, 2004: 324). However, the support for arts and culture was always articulated in more than just economic language. As suggested earlier, culture began to reflect a new subjectivity. It began to take on a more therapeutic character, oriented towards supporting personal development and individual growth, raising 'self-confidence in individuals', and acting as the 'cornerstones of urban renewal' (Arts Council of Great Britain, 1989, cited in Selwood, 2002: 30). State institutions were developing policies that used culture in building communities, addressing health and mental well-being, improving educational outcomes, engaging with young people, and ameliorating crime and reducing recidivism rates. A report by Comedia (2004) pointed out a shift in advocacy in 1993 from economic arguments towards more socially oriented justifications. It listed 50 social aims including: 'Increase people's confidence and sense of self-worth'; 'Extend involvement in social activity'; 'Give people influence over how they are seen by others'; and 'Provide a forum to explore personal rights and responsibilities' (11).

One of the causes for this change in attitude was the considerable influence of what is often called the 'community arts movement' in the United Kingdom in the 1970s and 1980s, which led to a radical questioning of the function of art in society. The history of community arts goes back to the early twentieth century, when artists and arts organisations sought to engage the majority of ordinary people in arts and cultural activities through touring, and modest public participation initiatives such as the Art Laboratory centres, Pavilions in the Park, and the 'Scratch' Orchestra (in which people were invited to play in a musical ensemble and improvise the music). The aim was to broaden access to art and help artists reach a wider audience. However, in later years, especially from the 1960s onwards, the philosophy of community arts began to evolve and became more oriented towards the political and social value of artistic creativity, seeking to use the arts and creative activity as a form of 'empowerment' for people.

In art colleges across the country a new generation of art education-alists, influenced by the Modernist ideas of pioneering art institutions like the Bauhaus in Weimar, Germany in the 1920s and 1930s, began to rethink creative practice and develop radical 'student-centred meth-ods' that privileged the psychological process of unrestrained, creative thought above strict adherence to categories, standards, and skills within traditional artistic media. Their aspiration was to promote a new, 'democratised' view of creativity as inherently human and universal – everybody was an artist. Arts educationalists were also heavily influ-enced by psychological theories in the 1960s and 1970s which linked creativity with individual self-fulfilment and argued that society was increasingly concerned with 'post-material' values (Laing, 1967; Maslow, 1971). The changes to arts education also influenced a younger gener-ation of artists. In 1960 the *Joint Report of the National Advisory Council of Art Education and the National Council of Diplomas in Art and Design*, chaired by Sir William Coldstream, advocated a move away from tra-ditional 'craft' or 'skills-based' education towards a more 'attitudinal' understanding of the arts. By the early 1980s, this approach had become mainstream in secondary schools and arts colleges.[11] Art colleges also began to adopt a different view of the creative process, seeing each indi-vidual's experience of making art as inherently different and accepting that skill and perception were relative (Pearson, 1982: 6; De Duve, 1994).

In the 1970s community artists, buoyed up by these wider changes in artistic practice, became a highly vocal force. In 1978, community arts worker Su Braden published *Arts and People* and estimated there were around 5000 projects carried out by members of the Association of Community Artists, with a particularly large presence in the cities of Birmingham, Liverpool, Manchester, and London. She called for artists to use culture as a weapon for class politics, citing the scale of creative activity at grass-roots levels as evidence of the challenge against con-ventional thinking and the values upheld by the Arts Establishment (Braden, 1978: xvi).

The community arts movement believed creativity was universal and that traditional aesthetic standards were just a way of reinforcing the low status of ordinary people. The aim of 'cultural democracy' was not to teach art or artistic standards to ordinary people (what might be called the 'democratisation of culture'), but to use art to empower working-class people psychologically and enhance their identity and self-confidence. Art was a way of recognising their unique experiences, rather than belittling them or asking them to meet the standards laid out by the arts elite. Explicit in this approach was the rejection of traditional criteria for cultural policy and subsidy – aesthetic excellence and tradition – which were seen as bourgeois values for the middle classes (Braden, 1978; Kelly, 2003).

In this sense, the term 'community arts' did not refer to a particular aesthetic style or process, but rather to a set of political assumptions about the arts: placing greater emphasis on active participation in creative activity, rather than the appreciation of existing art works; less emphasis on academic standards and skill-sets, and more on the 'creative process' of using one's own imagination; challenging traditional methods of critical judgement as 'elitist'; valuing art as a therapeutic practice that increases self-confidence; harnessing art projects and creativity as a way to build social networks and activism; and stressing the diversity of art tastes, standards, and practices, in opposition to the hegemonic paternalism of government, academia, or commercial art galleries. This new philosophy of art was also reflected in the campaigns by black and ethnic minority artists around the same time who felt marginalised by the arts establishment and sought recognition for their creative output outside mainstream institutions (Owusu, 1986).

At the time it was a powerful, radical challenge to the establishment. Many artists found the ideas appealing as they strained against the tight-knit circles and conventions of what was, by most accounts, a deeply hierarchical arts world. However, the intellectual challenge of the community arts movement was much more than simply calling on the arts elite to open itself up to new ideas and art forms. Some detected a more significant attack on the notion of excellence and the ideal that all could aspire to it. Writing years later, in his book, *The Arts and the People* in 1987, Roy Shaw criticised what he regarded as a romanticised view of working-class life and a patronising approach to ordinary people: 'I was reminded of the Tory peeress who in the 1930s went round telling housewives in depressed areas how to make soup out of cods' heads. She was generally well received, until one housewife asked challengingly: *"Who gets the rest of the cod?"* ' (93).

Shaw argued at the time that education was vital to enable people to enjoy the arts, and whilst at the Arts Council persuaded its major clients, including the Royal Opera House, to set up education departments. At the time he championed the importance of 'bourgeois art' and angrily rejected the idea that it was not for working people, or that they should be discouraged from enjoying it because it rendered them passive:

Those who contrast the alleged passivity of looking at a work of art and the creativeness of doing your own thing clearly have little idea about what is involved in the appreciation of a work of art... To encourage people to write their own poetry instead of reading Eliot or Philip Larkin, is to encourage blinkered narcissism and consequent cultural impoverishment. (135)

Yet despite such vocal criticism, the community arts movement grew in influence and shaped a large part of the new generation of arts practitioners and administrators. Community art was also intertwined with developments on the political left and the emergence of cultural or identity-led politics, against the backdrop of more conventional class politics. In this sense, there was often a tension within the political left between those who espoused the new philosophy of community art and those who preferred older ideals of the *avant garde* and high Modernism. Both saw themselves as radical inheritors of a tradition: folk music on the one hand, Stockhausen on the other.

The leaning towards identity politics was manifest in the emergence of new social movements and the 'New Left' in the 1970s and 1980s, which expanded the terrain of politics from the realm of production (class-based politics) to the realm of representation (community- or identity-based politics). The new social movements in European cities in the 1970s were not defined along class lines, but rather according to specific issues in the local community (like local environmental problems and local public services) or cultural or lifestyle identities (such as gender, ethnic, cultural, and sexual identities), or broader, single-issue concerns (feminism and women's rights, peace movements, nuclear disarmament, or animal rights, for example). Although it is difficult to generalise about these groupings, it is widely acknowledged that there was 'a clear cultural dimension' to them (Bianchini and Parkinson, 1993: 9; also Thompson, 2006: 2) and that they began to emerge as appealing alternatives to conventional modes of engagement through mass political parties (Kumar, 1995: 122; for advocacy of this approach, see Laclau and Mouffe, 2001).

Hoggett (1997) points out that during the 1980s and 1990s, 'community' itself became a ubiquitous term in local government discourse, marking a shift away from older models of engagement through the political party process. Community engagement appeared to be an alternative way to address the declining membership of political parties and decreasing engagement of the electorate in conventional political life and the party structure (Quilley, 2000). Certainly, interest in conventional party politics dropped dramatically from the 1980s onwards (Hay, 1996; Pierson, C., 1998).

The New Left celebrated groupings arising from shared identity, culture, and history, and marked a shift away from the traditional left-wing preoccupation with class. The radicals embraced culture as 'an enlarged sphere for the operation of politics and constituencies for change' (Hall and Jacques, 1989: 17). The Centre for Contemporary Cultural Studies at the University of Birmingham was formed in 1964, and the writings of Raymond Williams, Richard Hoggart, and Stuart Hall called for greater attention to culture as a factor in political life, both as a source of oppression and a means of liberation. The link between intellectual developments and cultural policy was sometimes quite direct. Not only did these writers influence a generation of cultural political activists, they were themselves deeply involved in arts and cultural policymaking: Williams and Hoggart served as members of the Arts Council, Hall has been a notable figure within black artists networks in Britain since the 1970s (Owusu, 1999: 4), and Bennett (as discussed earlier) has emerged as a key figure in Australian and international cultural policy since the 1980s. Although it should be noted however, that both Williams and Hoggart were highly sceptical about the relativism of community arts and warned that it would erode the democratisation of 'high culture' in the name of consumerism (Sinclair, 1995).

Malik (1996, 2002a) links the privileging of culture and community in radical political discourse during this period with the emergence of identity politics amongst ethnic minority communities in the United Kingdom. He charts the way in which anti-racist groups changed their focus, starting initially with campaigns about material and political issues such as immigration, employment laws, and policing, but moving eventually towards more 'cultural' issues relating to identity, cultural views, and lifestyle choices. In the Muslim community, for instance, there was a shift towards preserving and protecting cultural choices in the community such as religious dress and the provision of halal meat in schools – issues concerning one particular community, rather than a more general political struggle. There was also interest at local government level in bestowing cultural 'recognition' and respect, by providing funding and support for distinct community events and cultural activities. This reflected a view amongst some political activists that older modes of engagement based on class identity marginalised the problem of racism which excluded ethnic groups. Malik (1996) argues that local government policies of 'community engagement' provided specific resources to ethnic communities which reinforced their feeling that they had separate, particular needs which differentiated them from others. These multicultural policies, in emphasising difference in treatment (as well as through 'educating' local populations about diversity), he suggests, created a sense of division and alienation (189–90). Eade (1989) outlines a similar growth of multicultural community engagement in East London during the 1980s, whereby Muslim groups were encouraged by local official policies to relate to each other and to the Council as a distinct cultural group with specific needs. This transition towards a more identity-oriented approach was by no means universally accepted. As I explain later, there was some disagreement amongst ethnic minority arts activists and community leaders about whether they should seek inclusion into a sometimes unwelcoming mainstream, or whether they should try to secure separate support and funding structures instead.

Despite misgivings, the growing influence of community and identity politics meant that culture itself became regarded as a key political tool amongst activists. Left-wing local authorities in the 1980s sought to use culture as an alternative form of communication and mobilisation in response to the flagging base of their core political support. Where traditional political strategies were failing to engage the public, at least the appeal to culture, community, and identity seemed to attract some interest. The Labour leadership of Glasgow City Council reversed its traditional 'anti-culture' stance by supporting local museums and galleries, in order to enhance the city's political identity, distinct from the Conservative central government, to encourage a strong sense of distinctive cultural identity (Bianchini and Parkinson, 1993: 11; Hare, 2000: 220).

At the same time, 'community-engagement' was emphasised by local authorities as a counter to the alienating effects of private-property-led regeneration initiatives created in the 1980s by the Conservative government, including the Urban Development Grants, Enterprise Zones, City Action Teams and Task Force, the Action for Cities programme, and the Urban Development Corporations. Such schemes were criticised for only tackling prime, marketable sites with flagship projects and assuming a trickle-down effect on the worst areas. As a result they were perceived to alienate local residents (Fremeaux, 2002; Imrie and Raco, 2003). Zukin (1997) has compared such rebranded cities to Disneyworld, seeing them as sanitised, inauthentic simulacra of the original place (see also Harvey, 1989; Garcia, 2004; Mooney, 2004). Ironically, those very regeneration schemes which had utilised culture to attract private investors were also the ones that community-based cultural initiatives were supposed to ameliorate. Culture was both the cause of the problem and its solution. In both cases, culture was being asked to resolve the crisis left by the collapse of old industrialisation, and various cultural and community initiatives were seen as a way to help forge a new relationship between the state and the local communities.

Conscious of these problems, local authorities since the 1980s began to talk about the need to 'engage' with local people and represent their culture in an authentic way. They may have used economic arguments on one level, but softer, more socially conscious arguments on another. Culture was a way to support a more localised, bottom-up approach to regeneration that supported diverse identities and needs. In his 1990 book on British arts centres and policy, Justin Lewis argued against an exclusively economic agenda in arts policy, stating that the arts are crucial to 'self-development... personal fulfillment' (Lewis, 1990: 36). Similar arguments have been made for the link between the impact of arts involvement on physical and mental health and wider issues of community (Madden and Bloom, 2004; Staricoff, 2005). Commenting on the notion of arts-led regeneration, one artist, David Mach, and Peter Jenkinson, Director of New Art Gallery Walsall, stated, 'The true regeneration is the regeneration of local people's hearts and minds' (cited in Briers, 2001: 37).

It is important to recognise that there has always been a gap between official cultural policies and the reality of most people's everyday consumption of culture, which has been, more often than not, centred on commercial and popular forms, rather than local authority-led activity. But the drivers for policy have been preoccupied with wider objectives than just cultural consumption alone.

Urban planning started to take local ethnic identities into account; for example, the promotion of 'Banglatown' in London's East End, or the 'Balti Triangle' in Birmingham, home to one of the highest concentration of Indian restaurants in Britain (Cochrane, 2007: 119). The concept of 'diversity' became recurrent in local government discourse, marking a concern to recognise local community identities. It was used to denote an approach to culture which is inclusive, relative, and achieves a range of effects, including community cohesion, increased social capital, enhanced city competitiveness, creative industries development, and personal well-being. Taken together with the wider economic, social, and political rationales, the term 'culture' was endowed with novel meanings that distinguished it from the liberal-humanist definition that had underpinned older models of cultural policy.

The great moment of transition came with the Greater London Council (GLC), under the Labour leadership of Ken Livingstone. Between 1972 and 1986 this was the most pioneering and radical institution of government, and adopted a new type of cultural policy as an explicit challenge to older models. The GLC played a pivotal role in bringing together diverse strands of cultural policy thinking at that time – combining its marketised and community-focused aspects (Brighton, 1999; Garnham, 2001; Hylton, 2007). The GLC's cultural policy arose from the confluence of different factors: the surge in the radical left of the Labour party, the increased volume of community-led arts in London, the nascent 'creative industries' which were growing in the metropolis, and a generation of young, active leaders in the anti-racism movement. Although the arts had no mention in the 1981 GLC Labour Party Manifesto, cultural historian Robert Hewison (1995) notes that by 1986 the arts were regarded as the leading edge of a radical social and economic agenda (238).

The GLC focused on the Southbank site, the home of the Royal Festival Hall and National Theatre, investing in a new pier, and keeping the Festival Hall open in the evenings. The strategy boosted attendance at the concerts amongst first-time attendees. The investment in culture was about projecting a more caring, compassionate image, and it combined with a major advertising and awareness-raising campaign. The GLC's budget for open-air entertainment – an effective strategy to grab public attention – quintupled from £480,000 in 1980 to £2.5m in 1985. However the GLC also pursued more overtly political campaigns through the arts, using them as a way to transmit messages and ideas in a way conventional politics could not seem to do.

Cultural policy was also a strategy of empowerment for the political constituencies that the GLC sought to engage. The GLC's cultural manifesto, *Saturday Night or Sunday Morning? From Arts to Industry – New Forms of Cultural Policy,* written by Geoff Mulgan and Ken Worpole (Mulgan was later to become a key adviser to New Labour), shows the heavy influence of the community arts philosophy, stressing that official support for high culture enforced the psychological subjugation of the working class and that the left should support the 'people's own forms of expression and experience' (Mulgan and Warpole, 1986: 29). It also argued that culture was not only political, but superseded conventional politics by engaging with people's emotional worlds: 'People cannot simply be defined by their work, or as it is often expressed, "their objective position in the social relationships of production"' (1986: 12). Art became a direct political tool through the initiation of festivals, commemorative years, sponsorship of community arts projects, and direct funding for cultural activities amongst minority groups (Hylton, 2007). It fulfilled a straightforward propaganda role – promoting anti-racism, pro-gay rights, feminism – but was also concerned with establishing new political and cultural constituencies through funding. The black arts budget – to promote art made by and for the ethnic minority populations of London – grew from £400,000 in 1982–3 to £2m in 1985–6 (Hylton, 2007: 47). Araeen (2010) notes critically that the accommodation of black artists through separate funding structures during this period did not lead to increased recognition but would be followed by their continuing exclusion from the mainstream over the following decades.

At the same time, the GLC was also in favour of promoting a more consumerist ethos in terms of arts funding. Mulgan and Worpole argued that 'the real popular pleasures have been provided and defined within the marketplace, not the elitist museums, galleries and theatres funded by the state' (Mulgan and Warpole, 1986: 10). The GLC pioneered the earliest creative industries strategies, funding community radio stations, community magazines and newspapers, and providing studio spaces and support for artists and new media practitioners. These were cultural forms that had not been supported by public subsidy up till that point because they were regarded as being satisfactorily supported by the market or having little cultural value. The re-orientation of public subsidy to these forms showed a desire to emulate a market system, rather than to respond to the weaknesses and gaps in consumption that such a system might produce. The GLC Economic Policy Group advocated a shift away from grant in aid towards providing loans and equity, plus advice on business management, new technology, and other consultancy services. The left-wing taste for community arts converged with right-wing support for a more marketised arts system, with both approaches focused on the individual consumer as the ultimate arbiter of taste.

The GLC was abolished in 1986 by the Conservative government, and many of the arts organisations it supported suffered severe financial cuts as a result. However, its legacy was far-reaching, in that it tested a model that linked together the economic case for the arts and culture with the case for social justice and community engagement. Both the left and the right had begun to recognise the value of culture for their divergent reasons (Abercrombie, 1982). By rejecting the old model of 'cultural authority' as the arbiter of taste and subsidy, the GLC combined the marketisation of the arts with cultural democracy. The GLC approach avoided the paternalism of old cultural policy and promised a new, consumerised approach to culture, in which people's choices could be celebrated for being relative and diverse. Cultural policy had entered into a new phase. Importantly, the GLC also supported a whole range of new, cutting-edge cultural forms such as photography, film, outdoor events, and design, which received a significant boost in interest. Whether this greater interest validated the political thinking behind such support, and whether it significantly altered cultural consumption in comparison to other commercial providers of culture (such as Hollywood or the emergence of satellite television), is a different matter – what is undeniable is the impact these ideas had on cultural policy more generally. It also pointed to the way in which the old conventional model of arts subsidy had failed to keep up with its time and why the new left-leaning engagement with culture appealed to a cross-section of society.

Another, more subtle shift denoted by the GLC's approach was a detachment on the political left from what was predominantly a class-based analysis of social problems, to one which focused on culture, identity, and self-development. In his analysis of 'commodification', Gray argues that the relationship between the citizen and the state was transformed: 'it was only individuals, and not state organisations, that were in a position to decide what it was that they actually wanted and needed' (Gray, 2000: 106). Whilst Gray is writing primarily about economic consumerism, the point can be applied more broadly to the ideas of cultural democracy. There was now a new belief in the power of the individual consumer to choose culture, above the authority of the expert, or the state-subsidised cultural institution. In this sense, there was increasing scepticism from parts of the left and the right towards 'one-size-fits-all' policies and the idea of 'universal citizenship' which had been characteristic of the welfare state. The wider consequences of such an approach were a reformulation of social problems as local pathologies (Cockburn, 1977; Cochrane, 2007: 3). These needed to be solved through urban entrepreneurialism, competitive place marketing, and engaging with local communities and identities.

A new cultural script

The impact of the GLC, the community arts movement, and the new enthusiasm for urban entrepreneurialism spurred a new orthodoxy in cultural policy. Arts administrators and activists coming out of universities, think tanks, and local authorities championed the success of cultural regeneration strategies. They argued that other local authorities should emulate British cities such as Glasgow as well as international cities such as Sydney, Barcelona, and New York. Partly because of its reputation as 'radical' thinking and partly because of the lack of viable alternatives, local authorities and state agencies enthusiastically embraced the 'added value' of cultural policy and planning. The most important consultancy pioneering and advocating cultural policy approaches was Comedia, a Gloucestershire-based organisation established in 1978 that published some of the most influential pamphlets and research papers of this area in the 1980s and 1990s.[12] It worked with numerous local authorities and agencies to propagate the power of culture in urban development. New ideas about culture flourished in this environment, facilitated by support from the state. A new generation of arts and cultural policymakers were being trained and gaining experience on regeneration projects which had a specifically cultural dimension, and eventually were themselves contributing to the enthusiasm for such ideas within local government.

The arts sector and artists were also experiencing considerable change in the 1980s, as the demographic of publicly funded and also commercial organisations started to shift: more young people, women, and ethnic minorities began to work in this sphere and influence the cultural agenda. Visual arts curators, in an increasingly globalised art market, explored new types of work that challenged the perception that art was dominated by white European men. There was also increased interest in the global dimension of the Modernist movement and recognition of the lacunae in knowledge about important non-western and female artists in art history. Contemporary art galleries held ground-breaking exhibitions showcasing international artists, and works by women artists (e.g. *Women's Images of Men*, at the Institute of Contemporary Arts in 1980) and British Asian and Afro-Caribbean communities (*The Other Story – Afro-Asian Artists in Post-War Britain*, at the Hayward Gallery in 1989). Although black and Asian artists had enjoyed a brief moment of recognition in the 1950s and 1960s, a new generation of young, second-generation artists were starting to emerge in the 1980s and make an impact; for example Keith Piper, Donald Rodney, Sonya Boyce, and Eddie Chambers, who formed part of what would be known as the 'Black Arts Movement'. In addition, certain ethnic minority artists in Britain were attracting critical acclaim and interest from the commercial art world; for instance, Indian-born artist Anish Kapoor, who was hailed as part of the movement of New British Sculpture, along with white peers such as Antony Gormley and Tony Cragg.

At a national level, the Arts Council began to take up the cause of diversity more seriously. Up till the 1970s the organisation had been relatively insulated from the criticisms of community arts and black arts groups. It set up its first Community Arts Committee in April 1975 with seed funding, and also commissioned and funded Naseem Khan's landmark report on ethnic minority arts practice, *The Arts Britain Ignores,* although its immediate impact was limited (Khan, 1976; Owusu, 1986: 47; Hylton, 2007). The Community Arts Committee's budget for the first year was £176,000 which was allocated to 57 projects. This rose to £350,000 in the second year for 75 projects (which still represented less than 1 per cent of the Arts Council's total budget in 1975–6, although this was a significant achievement considering the degree of hostility from some Arts Council panel members to community arts practice).

In the 1980s more significant changes occurred. A number of authors have described the 1980s and 1990s as a period of disorientation for the Arts Council (Pick, 1991). A. J. Taylor (1994) describes its policy during this period as being in a state of paralysis (136). The Arts Council was attacked by the left for being culturally elitist, and by the right for not being 'value-for-money'. These criticisms were particularly forceful in the context of wider disillusionment from artists who felt that the Arts Council was out of touch with contemporary practice and had become largely unaccountable. Its dependency on government for funding and policy guidance, and its genuine failure to connect to a new generation of artists made the Arts Council increasingly unable to stand up to critics and assert a confident institutional identity. Like many other post-war institutions of the state, the Arts Council began to experience something of a crisis and a fundamental questioning of its core values (Hewison, 1995: 3).

As an institutional response, the Arts Council (Arts Council of Great Britain, 1984) formulated its first strategy document, *The Glory of the Garden* in 1984, in an attempt to develop a more transparent and coherent strategy. This embraced the economic and social agenda for the arts. The concession to the demands of government and bureaucracy would mark a shift towards a more instrumentalist view of the arts and orientation towards the consumer. The report highlighted the social benefits of subsidy and its diversification of support for community/ethnic/regeneration arts activity (Sinclair, 1995). During the mid-1980s, the Arts Council commissioned research and advocacy papers about art practice from 'non-traditional' areas, such as community arts and ethnic arts (see, for instance, *An Urban Renaissance,* Arts Council of Great Britain, 1989).

In particular, the Arts Council began to develop its focus on cultural diversity and the role of the arts in shaping identity. This chimed with the wider growth of multicultural arguments, being developed at local and national level, for instance, the *Swann Report* in 1985, which advocated multicultural education as a way to assist the integration of ethnic minorities in the United Kingdom. The arts and culture were increasingly seen as important in this new approach to cultural diversity. Internal correspondence of the Arts Council during this period reveals the way in which the body was becoming concerned to rid itself of any past prejudices against marginalised groups. In 1987, one member of staff confided to his colleague in a private memo that subsidised art might be about raising black consciousness but it is 'largely realised within a contemporary, Eurocentric tradition' (Arts Council of Great Britain archive material, undated). Staff members were required to attend cultural awareness training courses in which they learnt that racism was primarily an emotional problem that could only be tackled with emotional tools. In an internal briefing document written in 1988, an officer in the Arts Access Unit justified the consideration of ethnic minority art in the United Kingdom because the arts 'predetermine the mental state of each individual; how we perceive each other; form attitudes and opinions; relate our heritage to those of others; how we attribute respect and social status' (Arts Council of Great Britain, undated).

The changes in the 1980s led to the growing acceptance of 'diversity', 'access', and 'inclusion' as defining principles of arts subsidy, along with more traditional notions of aesthetic excellence (Owusu 1986; Hylton, 2007). A new discourse about the importance of applying culture and creativity to a range of social problems was becoming established. Whilst this was widely welcomed and adopted in the arts sector, there were those who, as stated earlier, expressed serious reservations about the creation of a specifically 'ethnic' strand of arts policy and support, for fear that it would reinforce the exclusion of black artists from the mainstream rather than raising their profile (Araeen, 2010).

New Labour's cultural revolution

Whilst many of the political and economic shifts taking place in the past three decades have contributed to the rise of cultural policy, it was the advent of New Labour and the notion of 'Creative Britain' that intensified the developments in cultural policy of preceding years and provided a 'policy window' in which these ideas became firmly institutionalised (for descriptions of 'policy windows', see Hannigan, 1995: 88).

The attention given to cultural policy was one of the Labour government's most novel features in the late 1990s. In his insightful study of New Labour discourse, Fairclough (2000) shows that the early years of the administration were dominated by the rhetoric of 'modernisation' in an attempt, he suggests, to distance itself from past socialism as well as previous forms of government more generally. Cultural policy was used to dramatic effect to demonstrate the 'revolutionary' credentials of New Labour against the staid traditionalism of its predecessors.

Perhaps the single most important policy enacted by the Labour government was the introduction of free admission to national museums and galleries, which has demonstrably increased the number of visitors, although not necessarily the proportion of visitors from priority groups.

However, Labour's cultural policy went further than removing pricing barriers to existing cultural activity. Culture was to become more socially and economically oriented, and made 'relevant' to the needs of society. In the name of modernisation, Labour's recruitment of business leader Gerry Robinson in 1998 as the Chairman of the Arts Council led to the removal of arts experts from the specialist panels, and an influx of managers and experts with little formal expertise in the arts. In a now widely cited annual lecture for the Arts Council of England in 1998, Robinson made it clear that his strategy was to make the arts more attentive to political and social needs, and implicitly to prove how modern and forward-thinking New Labour was:

> Too often in the past, the arts have taken a patronising attitude to audiences. Too often artists and performers have continued to ply their trade to the same white middle class audience. In the back of their minds lurks the vague hope that one day enlightenment might descend semi-miraculously upon the rest; that the masses might get wise to their brilliance.
>
> (Robinson, 2000: 18)

This 'revolution' required that culture be made more useful to society, implicitly attacking older justifications for cultural value and authority. First, there was a call to make culture more economically valuable by developing the creative industries and the establishment of the Creative Industries Taskforce in 1997. The Department for Trade and Industry (DTI) also became interested in the potential of the creative industries as an exemplary model for the wider economy. The Secretary of State for Trade and Industry, Peter Mandelson MP, commissioned Charles Leadbeater to write *Our Competitive Future: Building the Knowledge-driven Economy* in 1998, which developed into the influential book *Living on thin air: The New Economy*, and presented the creative sector as an exemplar for the wider economy (Leadbeater, 2000).

At the same time, however, New Labour's embrace of culture was not merely economically driven, but inspired by political developments since the 1980s, as described earlier. Culture was integral to the new discourse of 'social inclusion'. This was marked by the moment when the Social Exclusion Unit set up Policy Action Team 10 (PAT 10) in 1998, to explore how to use arts, sports, and cultural activity to address social exclusion (DCMS 1999; Social Exclusion Unit, 2001; for analysis, see Buckingham and Jones, 2001).

The term 'social inclusion' has circulated in European academic circles since the 1970s, but New Labour made it one of its defining ideas (Fairclough, 2000; Britton and Casebourne, 2002). It was related to communitarian ideas emerging from radical politics in the 1970s and which came to New Labour's political philosophy through the writings of 'communitarian' theorists such as Amitai Etzioni in his seminal work *The Spirit of Community* (1995). The social inclusion discourse presents a departure from more traditional poverty-reduction strategies associated with the left, towards individuated strategies of self-reliance and self-improvement. This promises to transcend the perceived limitations of the welfare state by shifting emphasis away from class-based, structural factors and towards the maximisation of individual skills and earning capacity of individuals. Under New Labour, this revealed itself in a concern to nurture the entrepreneurial nature and 'creativity' of the individual citizen. For instance, Pierson (1998) notes how the Borrie Commission on Social Justice in 1993 – under the helm of New Labour's favourite political think tank, the Institute of Public Policy Research – sought to reconcile economic opportunity with social justice through a particular focus on education and individual self-development (188).

More specifically, the discourse of social inclusion proposes a modified role for government by redefining poverty as a subjective, as well as objective, phenomenon. Social inclusion is supposed to deal with both the conventional range of problems associated with material poverty (such as poor housing, malnutrition, or weak employment prospects) but also the subjective and psychological experience which such problems entail (e.g. diminished self-confidence, inability to integrate into wider society, isolation, lack of meaning). As Prime Minister Tony Blair stated in his speech to launch the Social Exclusion Unit, social exclusion 'is about prospects and networks and life-chances. It's a very modern problem, and one that is harmful to the individual, more damaging to self-esteem, more corrosive for society as a whole, more likely to be passed down from generation to generation, than material poverty' (Blair, 1997, unpaginated).

In the field of urban regeneration, culture has become seen as a way to improve the political engagement of local residents, where conventional politics has failed to do so. Non-government actors have widely welcomed this approach and called for greater inclusion of racial and gender dimensions, that is, 'diversity' (Brownhill and Darke, 2000).

In the context of this reform, arts and cultural policy was seen as another tool to engage with people's needs and, in particular, to address the psychological aspects of social exclusion. In 1999, at a lecture to the Royal Society of Arts, Chris Smith MP, then Secretary of State for Culture stated, 'Involvement in art can give someone, however marginalized they may be from society, a sense of self-worth, self-confidence, something to live for and to feel good about' (Smith, 2000: 15). His successor, Tessa Jowell (2004), ostensibly eschewed instrumentalist arguments for the arts, arguing that for too long policymakers had tried to justify the arts on the basis of economic value, the creation of jobs, cutting crime, or improving education. However, she went on to assert only a few paragraphs later that culture should serve a different function – to address the 'poverty of aspiration', that is, addressing the subjective, psychological barriers that limit the individual's potential. Such claims about the psychological value of the arts and culture are a staple in cultural policy documents under Labour, for instance, in the *All Our Futures*, a report compiled by The National Advisory Council on Creative and Cultural Education in 1999. This document, compiled by a taskforce of leaders in the arts and education sectors, called for the inclusion of creativity in the education system, and argued that this would help Britain respond more effectively to a new creative economy, plus the changing nature of identity in a multicultural society.

The concept of social inclusion also reshaped the way in which cultural institutions were expected to operate. The onus was placed upon cultural organisations to actively market and attract new visitors, placing emphasis on 'access', 'relevance', and 'inclusion'. The 1998 DCMS policy document *A New Cultural Framework* made funding dependent on improved visitor numbers, especially from disadvantaged groups. The outcome was that spending within cultural organisations between 1993 and 1999 became increasingly tied to access and educational programmes (Selwood, 2001: xli).

Since the late 1990s, the subsidised arts and cultural sector, encouraged by funding frameworks and performance targets, also increased its focus on cultural diversity as a key objective in its work. This aligned with Labour's official support for multicultural policies and was encouraged by various lobby groups, for instance, the *Parekh Report* which came out of the Commission on the Future of Multi-Ethnic Britain, chaired by political theorist, Bikhu Parekh and published by the race relations campaigning organisation, the Runnymede Trust (Commission on the

Future of Multi-Ethnic Britain, 2000). This taskforce was composed of leading figures in the media, culture, politics, education, and social policy, and advocated a stronger commitment to multiculturalism and diversity in British public life, making a number of recommendations for the arts sector. The report argued that the arts and cultural sectors did not realise the extent to which institutional racism was a problem and they needed to tackle inherent bias in staffing, representation, and programming.

The Arts Council published its *Cultural Diversity Action Plan* in May 1998, along with numerous other reports on diversity and access in the arts (ACE, 1998, 2001, 2002a, 2002b; Jermyn et al., 2000). In 1998, it established a number of schemes, including a £20m New Audiences Programme, a Fellowship Programme to place black, Asian, and Chinese Managers in key arts organisations, and a Black Regional Initiative in Theatre (ACE, 2002b). Its flagship scheme for diversity in the arts, 'decibel', started in 2003, with a £5m launch fund and £1.3m per year until 2008. It was followed by Inspire in 2005 – a scheme to place ethnic minority curators in key galleries, which would evolve to become an MA course pathway and bursary scheme at the prestigious Royal College of Arts, only open to ethnic minority students. The Arts Council made diversity one of its five core aims and set a target of making 10 per cent of all its Grants for The Arts funding (non-regular funding to arts organisations and artists) to black and minority ethnic groups. In 2002, the Arts Council held a conference entitled 'Connecting flights: New cultures of the diaspora'. The organisers even dedicated the event to the cultural theorist, Stuart Hall, who has been influential in his critical approval of identity politics (and was also a signatory on the *Parekh Report*).

Hence, the Labour government's adoption of cultural policy accorded with its 'Third Way' approach to social development, embracing both the promise of culture as economic wealth (creative industries, new public management efficiency) and also social justice (diversity, community, social capital, and social inclusion). Today, recognising diversity is presumed to boost people's sense of identity and 'well-being', build cohesive communities, and contribute to individuals' employability and productiveness. It is also a strategy for developing creative and cultural industries, and reinvigorating national and local economies. In both senses, the consumerist ethos – judging the value of culture on how much of it is consumed, as opposed to the quality of what is consumed – has become prevalent.

It is difficult – perhaps too early – to judge the wider impact of these changes on Britain's cultural life, consumption patterns, and attitudes towards culture more generally. Have the audiences for cultural activities

changed? Do we have a more democratic cultural life? It is hard to measure. Despite attempts to make culture more accessible, it is still largely
consumed by 'traditional groups': that is white, affluent, and educated
people. The policy of free entry to the national museums and galleries
and various outreach and access programmes have not dramatically
shifted the profile of visitors (Holden, 2006: 37–9). However, the public
does value culture and seems to believe in public subsidy – even if audiences for museums, theatres, and galleries are still very small compared
to those for commercial mass culture like television, film, and popular
music. Politicians are also much more supportive of subsidy for culture
(or at least those who are not, are much quieter). This support, however,
has come to be framed in terms of usefulness and impact, rather than
as a public good in itself. There are some signs that the Coalition government elected in May 2010 is more willing to adopt an 'art for art's
sake' approach which relies less on instrumentalist arguments, but how
this affects policies and funding on the ground will be hard to judge for
some time yet.

Tensions in cultural policy today

The changes outlined in this chapter have led, almost certainly, to policymakers (and arguably cultural professionals) having less confidence
in their position. They are less willing to appeal for public support on
the basis of their authority and expertise, instead arguing for their case
according to 'evidence'. This evidence may be related to both the size
and types of audiences being reached and quantifiable economic and
social impacts of the cultural activity. This is not to say that notions
of aesthetic value or universal standards (i.e. 'excellence') have disap-
peared altogether within official cultural policy discourse – they appear
frequently in policy literature and ministerial speeches (Bennett, O.,
2007). Nor is it to deny the importance of engaging a mass audience
for culture. However, there is far more ambivalence about referring to
concepts like excellence and quality, as if these are somehow elitist and
not 'useful' in themselves.

Cultural organisations have become articulate at demonstrating their
economic and social value in terms that policymakers will understand,
publishing and commissioning a range of reports and economic impact
studies.[13] The DCMS initiated the £1.8m Culture and Sport Evidence
(CASE) Programme in 2008 – a three-year study about the strategic evidence for values and impacts generated by culture and sports.
Meanwhile, the Arts Council ran a major public consultation between
2006 and 2008 about 'public value' and the arts (Keaney, 2006a). These

exercises have become particularly pertinent since 2010, as cuts of 15 per cent to museums and galleries and Arts Council 'frontline organisations' mean there is extra pressure for cultural organisations to make the case for what they do.

However, there are signs that cultural organisations themselves are increasingly aware of how difficult it is to make economic claims for what they do. Since the early 2000s, there has been a growing chorus of criticism about the quality of evidence for culture's social and economic impacts, and the inherent bias of much grey literature churned out by agencies and cultural organisations seeking to prove their worth (Selwood, 2002: 15). Certainly, there have been some rather exaggerated claims made for cultural interventions. In some cases, positive benefits of the arts are exaggerated by actors, and negative impacts underplayed.[14] There are those who argue that the use of culture to address social and economic problems is nothing more than mere 'displacement' activity which distracts from policies that could be used to improve schools, healthcare, employment, and other spheres (Jensen, 2002; Merli, 2002). This is part of a wider criticism of culturally oriented politics which only focus on the fields of representation and consumption, as opposed to the very forms of social organisation that give rise to such problems (Hughes, 1993; Gitlin, 1994; Calcutt, 2005).

Therefore, cultural organisations have started to revise their approach and reconsider the importance of their 'cultural value'. In a more recent report commissioned by the National Museums Directors Conference (NMDC) in 2010, Selwood acknowledged that in the difficult economic climate, in which funding was expected to shrink, there was a need to provoke thinking about museums' *cultural* impact and to demonstrate it to funders. The report studied 85 projects from 22 NMDC members around the country and documented a range of cultural impacts, including promoting an interest in history, generating empathy for and understanding of minority groups, encouraging community engagement, addressing marginalisation, challenging perceptions, and creating associations and identities (Selwood, 2010: 4).

In 2008 Sir Brian McMaster produced the report, 'Supporting excellence in the arts: from measurement to judgement', which was commissioned by DCMS. It argued for the concept of 'excellence' to be restored to the centre of arts policy and funding, rather than instrumental aims which discouraged risk-taking, innovation, and creativity. The report was warmly received and has been regarded as a turning point in policymaking, at least in DCMS and the Arts Council. The Arts Council has since moved to using peer assessment in its funding decisions as an attempt to reinforce the principle of cultural expertise.

But the ground has shifted in the last two decades, and it is clear that the demands of the new cultural policy have changed the way organisations operate and the balance of their priorities. The Art Fund's survey of 300 museums and galleries (representing a sixth of the total in the UK) in May 2006 showed that respondents had suffered funding cuts for certain core activities (namely acquisitions of artefacts) whilst funds for numerous other areas (education, outreach, and marketing) had grown. *The Goodison Review* (2004) of arts organisations expressed serious concern that cultural institutions had far less funds for new acquisitions than before. For five major museums in the United Kingdom (British Museum, Victoria and Albert Museum, National Gallery, National Portrait Gallery, and Tate) funds for acquisitions had declined by 90 per cent over the previous decade (Art Fund, 2006). No doubt, the increased funding from government programmes like Renaissance in the Regions for museums have not been tied to policy demands for more audience engagement and inclusion. There has also been a reduction of time and resources devoted to scholarship and research of objects in museums and galleries. In an interview in 2005 in *The Times*, Julian Treuherz, the Director of the Lady Lever Art Gallery in Port Sunlight, said, 'A lot of museums pay lip-service to it but their staff are too busy on access-type projects to do any serious research' (Delingpole, 2006).

Is this a top-down, target-driven culture that the arts sector is desperate to resist? The Minister for Culture, Ed Vaizey MP, who assumed the role in May 2010, has stated that he will free the arts from the bureaucracy of government policy and diktats about inclusion and diversity. In an interview to *The Guardian* newspaper in 2009, he said, 'We should be saying, "You're fantastic at what you do. We want you to carry on doing it and doing it brilliantly." I don't want to set them a target and say, "You need to diversify audiences".'[15]

It is true that much of the innovation in cultural policy has been driven by government, but it would be wrong to see this only as a one-way imposition on the arts. Indeed, many the cultural sector have embraced targets as a way of 'keeping them on their toes', and have shared in the spread of these ideas through their own networks and publications. Although the state has driven the new instrumentalist agenda, arts institutions have joined together with the government in reshaping state support according to a new political vision.

David Fleming, the Director of National Museums Liverpool, and named in 2002 by *The Independent* newspaper as one of the ten leading people in UK museums, embraced this new ideal of the museum in his speech at the opening of the International Slavery Museum in Liverpool in August 2007:

> ...Make no mistake, this is a museum with a mission. We wish to help counter the disease of racism, and at the heart of the museum is a rage which will not be quieted while racists walk the streets of our cities, and while many people in Africa, the Caribbean, and elsewhere, continue to subsist in a state of chronic poverty. This is not a museum that could be described as a 'neutral space' – it is a place of commitment, controversy, honesty and campaigning.
>
> (Cited in Selwood, 2010: 39)

Fleming's remarks typify a belief in the cultural sector in the power of culture to change human attitudes and behaviours, and tackle social problems like racism and prejudice. The International Slavery Museum opened in 2007, the same year as the Bicentenary of the Abolition of the Slave Trade in Britain, which was marked with commemorative events, exhibitions, and programmes across the country. This programme encouraged many institutions to work in a new way by engaging with local communities and using their voices to draw meaning on the histories being considered (Cubitt, 2009: 259–75; Selwood, 2010: 15). As Tony Bennett and others have argued, culture is used as a tool to fashion a new type of citizen and social values. Unlike their Victorian predecessors, museum professionals today appear to be somewhat more explicit about this aim, and less concerned about proclaiming the disinterested nature of their work.

A greater engagement with minority (or marginalised) groups was advocated around the same time by The Mayor's Commission on African and Asian Heritage, established by Mayor Ken Livingstone in 2003 and composed of 20 professionals in the cultural and heritage sector. Two decades after the GLC first experimented with black arts and cultural provision, this group and the high-profile nature of the membership showed how such ideas had since become institutionalised. This group produced a major report in 2005 entitled *Delivering Shared Heritage* which outlined a number of recommendations to the cultural sector, including greater investment in black and Asian heritage organisations, more equitable partnerships between major institutions and community heritage organisations, increased ethnic representation in the cultural workforce, and greater engagement with ethnic minorities in the interpretation of collections.

The push to engage local communities and ordinary people has led to some museums working with refugee communities, and seeking to promote a more sympathetic view of their experiences. Meanwhile, other museums have tried to engage the public by asking people to shape their programmes by contributing personal or family stories, objects and recollections, often through online activity. Selwood (2010) gives a number of examples of this type of work. Tyne and Wear Archives and Museums initiated a programme called 'Culture Shock', to collect 1000 digital stories from people across the North East of England, inspired by museums and galleries collections. A similar interactive project 'Make History' was developed by the National September 11 Memorial and Museum, in which 1000 users contributed more than 3000 photos, videos, and personal stories. Many museums choose this approach as a way of sending a signal to visitors that their perspective is of equal significance to the curators – a way of reinforcing the importance of identity in making cultural judgements. For example, Tyne and Wear museums justified 'Making History', a project where members of the public were asked to donate objects, on the basis that 'This project shows that everyday objects today are valued and their owners are valued too. [It conveys] the feeling for members of the community that the museum collection belongs to them, that they are a valued part of the whole and have helped to tell their own area's story' (Appleton, 2001).

Even the architecture of new museums and galleries since the late 1990s shows a difference in the tone of cultural institutions. In the eighteenth and nineteenth centuries, cultural institutions were built with an explicitly monumental quality, in a neo-classical style often featuring columns of Corinthian marble, sweeping staircases, and large atriums (see, for example, the British Museum, Tate Britain, National Gallery, National Gallery of Scotland). This fashion for the quasi-religious space in which visitors were expected to walk in silence helped to inculcate in the visitor a sense of awe and deferential behaviour that reflected elite expectations of how a citizen ought to act.

In the last two decades this style has been self-consciously rejected with a new type of cultural building – no less impressive, with deliberately colourful, playful, and contemporary interiors. For example, The Public in West Bromwich, designed by the architect Will Alsop and opened in 2008 (after much controversy about cost overruns and delays), is a large oblong building clad in dark grey and silver metal, with irregular-shaped magenta windows. The Sage Gateshead which opened in the North East of England in 2004, designed by Foster and Partners, features a large concourse, covered by a curvilinear stainless steel roof which is often likened to a major railway station, or, less charitably, a silver slug.

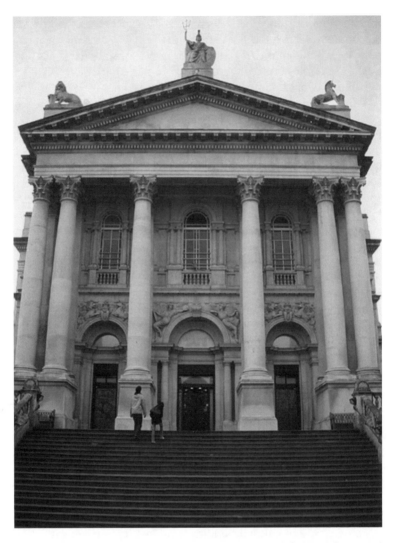

Front of Tate Britain, London (reproduced with permission from stuckism.com)

Probably the most striking and well-known example of the contemporary art gallery is Tate Modern. Built in a power station, which closed in 1982, it is designed in a way which deliberately retains the architectural features of the original building, including the 35m-high and 152m-long Turbine Hall. The symbolism of an art gallery being housed inside an old power station speaks volumes about the new

Front of the National Galleries of Scotland, Edinburgh, Scotland (reproduced with permission from Wikimedia/Kilnburn)

Front of British Museum, London (reproduced with permission from Fotolia/Kadal)

fascination with culture as an 'industry', creating new economic and social energy. Its escalators, rather than staircases, reminiscent of a large shopping mall, remind visitors that culture is something that is consumed, not merely revered. Major commissions in large spaces like the Turbine Hall at Tate Modern have been likened to funfair rides, such as Carsten Holler's *Test Site* slides which he described as 'a playground for body and brain'.

What is the response of cultural organisations to these changes? Overall, they have been largely positive about their twenty-first-century makeover, seeing it as a vital way to engage new audiences, fulfil new social functions, and become more relevant to society. They value their role as agents of social change as much as (if indeed not more than) repositories of cultural knowledge and expertise. In some cases, cultural institutions have argued that the efforts to bring new audiences into their buildings and also to find new ways of interpreting history or cultural objects have contributed to their cultural mission.

Government – particularly at the local level – has also responded positively by investing more heavily in culture, justifying such support on the basis that it will deliver a range of social and economic objectives. The partnerships they develop with cultural organisations mean a grouping together of many different aims, some of which might seem to be in conflict, or at least in competition. For instance, the creation of a cultural space in a town centre may be justified by a number of arguments, both economic and social, in terms of attracting night-time visitors to an area, boosting trade for local restaurants and bars, creating a public space for diverse groups to meet and feel part of a community, to help tackle social exclusion and offer training facilities, to improve the 'brand' and identity in an area, to widen access to art, and the therapeutic tools it might offer.

So there is little doubt that the cultural sector – both the institutions that provide 'frontline' services, and the policymakers and politicians that fund them – has experienced a dramatic change in attitude and approach. Whilst there are some who complain about a 'top-down' imposition by government, I have tried to show that the shift in thinking has a much deeper foundation, and arises partly from the cultural sector itself.

Yet, despite the widespread consensus on the need for diversity and a redressing of what 'cultural value' is, there is disquiet in certain quarters about the policies that have developed.

There are those critics who feel that the emphasis on what people want and what is popular inevitably leads to the 'dumbing down' and infantilisation of audiences and visitors. The dismantling of cultural

Exterior of Sage Gateshead, Gateshead (reproduced with permission from Nigel Young/Foster & Partners)

Exterior of The Public, West Bromwich (reproduced with permission from West Bromwich, Sandwell Arts (The Public))

Test Site 2006, The Unilever Series: Carsten Holler at Tate Modern (reproduced with permission from Fotolia/Jeremy Baile)

authority and expertise in favour of the 'ordinary person's' opinion devalues cultural institutions and encourages a lack of confidence. This criticism has emerged from writers on both the political right and the left, who pick up on the uncomfortable tension between cultural and political objectives.

Since 2003, John Holden has written extensively about 'cultural value' in the UK context, and has argued that cultural organisations have understated the importance of quality and excellence in their work. He argues that there are three different types of cultural value: intrinsic value (the emotional, subjective reaction to art), instrumental value (how art can help deliver social and economic outcomes), and institutional value (the way an organisation behaves and engages with its public). There are also three different stakeholder groups in the cultural sector who are each preoccupied with these different values: the professionals (intrinsic), the politicians (instrumental), and the public (intrinsic and institutional).

This mismatch of values between groups creates a 'dysfunctional' relationship – professionals in cultural organisations spend too much time and energy chasing statistics, trying to produce evidence and meet bureaucratic targets to convince their paymasters they are achieving all kinds of social and economic outcomes, frequently resorting to overblown claims. Meanwhile, the very real needs of their organisation – related to intrinsic cultural value – lie neglected. Holden calls on professionals to focus less on serving the needs of politicians by proving their instrumental value, and instead engage better with the public through their joint interest in intrinsic and institutional value. Unfortunately, the language of 'art for art's sake' and intrinsic value is also tainted with associations with hierarchy, elitism, and paternalism. What can be done? The solution, he suggests, is a commitment on the part of professionals to be transparent and open about what type of cultural value they are using, and not to mystify or impose their choice on the public. Such an approach would allow cultural organisations to build legitimacy and a broader public support for culture, even where politicians are more sceptical (Holden, 2004, 2006).

Holden expresses well the very real tension between different values and is right to recognise the importance of quality and excellence as the basis for state support, not just instrumental objectives. After all, without an interest in the intrinsic quality of art, why would cultural organisations exist? His advice to bring together these different forms of value is a useful and pragmatic way to re-focus the minds of institutions on what should matter most. He is also correct to call for cultural professionals to be transparent about their choices and engage positively with the public about them. Often, the public values cultural expertise and most surveys show steady support of public funding for the arts. The public is not merely a passive consumer of 'elite choices' but is often actively engaged in debates about art and (especially with the advent of the Internet) more able to contribute to cultural creation.

However, there will also be times when there is a conflict or difference between 'public' and 'elite' choices, especially in cultural institutions. The Turner Prize winner is not always the public favourite (conversely, designer fashion may be influenced by street design, but it is tightly controlled by an industrial elite). Our patterns of cultural consumption still mainly fall on class lines – the working class still do not do 'high culture' as much as the middle and upper classes. Does this mean that high culture is the problem? Or could it be that many working people lack the education or even the time to engage with high culture. Holden argues that 'cultural snobs' and 'gatekeepers' are deliberately preventing people from accessing culture by making them unwelcome in buildings, which may be partially true, but not enough to explain the marked class divide in cultural consumption. He adds that the phrase 'art for art's sake' should be abandoned because of its connotations of elitism, and argues that the legitimacy of cultural organisations should rest on public support. Governments should not fund culture chosen by a few and appreciated by others, but instead validate a wider range of choices and support conditions that allow everyone to make culture. This would send out a more democratic message.

Rupert Christiansen (2008), opera critic for the *Daily Telegraph*, echoed this sentiment, when he wrote in reaction to the McMaster report:

> Who exactly arbitrates this quality, and on what basis? ... it's a pity that McMaster didn't have the courage to point out that most art is culturally highly specific and aesthetically focused, and that what matters more than dragging people into to [sic] art galleries and opera houses is inspiring and encouraging them to create their own art, be it am-dram or bhangra.

Yet the question remains – to what extent does the expert have the last word, and does the popular verdict come second? And what would good public engagement look like? On the one hand, organisations can offer tours and talks by their programmers and curators, to show the public how they make their decisions. This would make their cultural choices transparent and engaging, but still does not ultimately hand them over to the viewing public. At the other end are those organisations that willingly embrace being 'taken over' by a non-expert audience (for instance, the Roundhouse in North London has a day when it is 'taken over' by young people who run the building and programme, or museums that allow the public to curate their collections).

Whilst it would be an exciting experiment and quite illuminating to let young people choose their favourite objects from the British Museum for one day, what would happen if this was done permanently? To what extent should such engagement be an occasional event, or should it be a more integrated approach? One would not allow young people to 'take over' a hospital, so how is a cultural institution different? Importantly, what message do such activities send out and what does it say about our relationship to culture? Is it honest to say that the non-expert opinion is of equal worth in the cultural institution as the expert?

Ang (2005) argues that despite the desire to develop multicultural practice in the art gallery or museum as a social mission, the institutions' adherence to the principle of 'art for art's sake' remains a fundamental barrier to achieving plural perspectives and more accessible exhibitions. 'The idea of cultural diversity cannot be taken too far', Ang asserts, 'because to do so would destabilise the very purpose of the art museum as a site for universal appreciation of knowledge' (316). We might then ask, could the desire to use the gallery or museum as a space for social change or inclusion run against the more 'traditional' intention of the gallery or museum to be a place of cultural appreciation? As I have argued, the abandonment of the notion of excellence (no matter how difficult to define) would effectively undermine the basis of state support for the arts.

Of course, culture is not solely what is created by a narrow professional elite, and is constantly refreshed and energised by a diverse range of influences in the commercial and amateur world. Is it not a good thing that the Arts Council now takes seriously classical music from non-western traditions? Is it not worthwhile to fund centres for folk dance and music, recognising that these organic cultural traditions have artistic quality too? In the past, elites had too limited a view of what is great art. But is this still true today? For instance, most music critics and music educators would agree that jazz is as complex, characterful, and rich a form as classical music. At the same time, they would not value all music equally or expect the state to subsidise the latest winners of television music competitions like the immensely popular and enjoyable British-invented format, 'X Factor'. Is it anti-democratic to say that the state should fund and support some types of art over others, because it is not popular but has value anyway? Would such a choice be exclusory? Likewise, museum professionals would today recognise the value of engaging non-professional experts and interest groups, or even non-expert visitors in dialogue about how their collections should be curated and displayed. But how far can this go and who makes the final judgement?

Writing in 1987, Roy Shaw expressed concern that the word 'quality' was being dismissed as an elitist category. He argued that 'the task of education, broadcasting organisations, and arts organisations... is to make excellence accessible. This is to make the eminently democratic assumption that people deserve the best and need it. It is also to incur the charge of claiming to know better than the public itself what the public should have.' Against Holden, Shaw argues that an elite is not only necessary for culture, it is an important feature of democracy. He also argues that the cultural sector has a responsibility to 'offer people opportunities to develop and improve their tastes' (81). In other words, the cultural sector has a responsibility to shape others (1987: 81). To some ears, this will sound too hierarchical and patronising. There is certainly a risk that if cultural organisations are too closed minded and arrogant about their own superiority they will alienate people – but can a balance be struck?

In the context of ethnicity, there are those who fear that the stress on cultural diversity and identity politics undermines the fundamental premise of art and artistic creation. They argue that the emphasis on difference can reify cultural identity, and assume an artist or audience's background is the determinant of their cultural taste. Lurking beneath the argument for cultural relativism and difference, therefore, is a far more contentious argument for cultural essentialism (Kuper, 1999; Bayart, 2005; Appiah, 2006; Brown, 2006). If cultural organisations try hard to make things 'relevant' to particular groups and second-guess what they will like or identify with, they may risk reinforcing stereotypes. This view also militates against cultural change and 'mixing'.

In the arts this is particularly problematic, as most artists and arts organisations make a claim for the 'universal' power of art. Some critics despair that the stress on diversity presents an essentialised, and effectively racialised, view of artists and arts audiences (Araeen, 2004, 2010; Mirza, 2004, 2010; Dyer, 2007). In his comprehensive survey of diversity policies in the UK arts sector, Hylton (2007) explains that such initiatives have tended to deploy conflicting strategies – offering separate funding streams to black artists whilst at the same time espousing the need for equal opportunity (13).

Araeen (2010) offers possibly the most trenchant critique of cultural diversity policies, from the perspective of an ethnic minority practitioner. A Pakistani-born artist, Araeen's academic journal *Third Text* has been critical of Arts Council policies of targeted ethnic programmes and funding since the 1970s.[16]

Araeen's argument is two-fold: first, that art history today ignores the contribution of post-war African, Asian, and Carribean artists who enjoyed success between the 1950s and 1970s, such as Aubrey Williams and Ernest Mancoba. Second, that cultural diversity policies, as they have been conceived, separate off contemporary black artists into a category and of exotic difference. Here they are patronised with offers of support presumed to be unable to aspire to serious art practice within the Modernist tradition. In both cases, black artists have been carved out of the picture and denied recognition of their imagination and intellect to transcend their cultural upbringing. They are treated as exotic and as producers of anthropological culture that is a 'way of life', rather than art. Araeen argues that black artists should instead be assessed for their aesthetic quality, standards, and contribution to understanding of the world; that is, as artists.

This benevolent racism displays similar features to the kind practiced in the 1960s and 1970s. However, it also represents something new:

> At the turn of the twenty-first century, the struggle that non-Western contemporary artists face on the global stage is not Western resistance to difference, as might have been the case in decades past; their most formidable obstacle is Western obsession with an insistence on difference.
>
> (Oguibe, 2004: xiv–xv, cited in Wainwright, 2010: 98).

Furthermore, this 'new' racialised arts sector has grown with the assent of ethnic minority communities, and they now have a stake in it. To cut policies today and expect a number of subsidised black artists to comfortably find a new home in the mainstream would be challenging. From their perspective, it would be like trying to jump from one train to another whilst both are moving – inevitably some of them may miss the jump and fall down in the middle. The institutional structures that have grown up around this model of diversity cannot be easily swept away without damaging those who depend on it.

Many ethnic artists have deliberately avoided being labelled according to their ethnicity, by situating their work in a wider context and seeking mainstream acclaim. For instance, Turner Prize winner, Chris

Ofili draws on his Nigerian heritage in his art, but is also recognised as one of the Young British Artists of the 1990s and has gone on to work as a commercially successful artist. Likewise, Indian-born Anish Kapoor is regarded foremost as a British artist, emerging from the 1980s New British Sculpture movement, and has resisted the label of Indian artist quite explicitly.[17]

At the same time, we need to ask whether 'diversity' is a sufficient answer for addressing inequalities and lack of access to the arts sector – an industry that relies on low-paid labour and unpaid work experience and in which those with privileged backgrounds and networks are more able to succeed. Do diversity policies which only focus on ethnic minorities actually exclude certain groups, such as white people from disadvantaged backgrounds?

Outside the realm of cultural organisations, a number of authors have pointed to the harmful political consequences of diversity policies. They argue that the emphasis on cultural identity and 'background' is not particularly well suited to delivering the aims of community, or a common political discourse which can transcend ethnic or lifestyle differences. Although authors like Keith (2005) are optimistic about how cultural quarters can curate the 'ambivalence' of fixity and fluidity, others have argued that multiculturalism and its stress on difference inevitably brings notions of universalism, politics, and solidarity into crisis (Gitlin, 1994; Malik, 1996; Savaric, 2001; Brown, 2006). If cultural policy is being used to fill the gaps left by the decline of conventional politics – as so many local authorities seem to wish – is it able to do so? Can the stress on difference realistically provide a way of including more people and making them feel more engaged, or does it lead to a further sense of division? At the same time, is it realistic or even desirable for cultural organisations to ignore particular identities and traditions – what is the role of state funding and where does it become constructive or counterproductive?

Taking these criticisms and questions into account, my empirical research in the following chapters explores how this 'new cultural policy' is enacted in reality, and some of the contradictions and tensions that surface. The diversity of objectives now driving cultural funding opens up the possibility of conflicts about priorities. We might then ask to what extent do different values and expectations affect cultural activity in practice? In the lived experience of cultural diversity policy, we can begin to see some of its inherent problems.

3
Rich Mix Centre – A Case Study of a New Arts Centre in East London

In this chapter I will examine how the contradictions of culture I have outlined become manifest in a real example – the Rich Mix arts centre in East London.[1]

The East End of London, sometimes simply known as 'the East End', has historically been seen as the poor part of the capital – long associated with overcrowding, poverty, criminality, political radicalism, and disease. In the nineteenth century, the area became a major centre of shipbuilding, light industry, railways, and docks, leading to the massive growth of the poor working population. For centuries the area was also home to large immigrant communities – the French Huguenot silk weavers in the seventeenth and eighteenth centuries, and a significant number of Irish labourers and Jewish, Russian, and German refugees at the end of the nineteenth century. In the twentieth century, and especially following the two world wars, the area saw considerable social, economic, and political change as old industries fell into decline, and there was cumulative underinvestment from local and national governments in transport and housing.

Today, the East End largely corresponds to the London Borough of Tower Hamlets, east of the financial district and north of the River Thames. It is home to a large 'knowledge economy' as well as a thriving creative and night-time scene, and the area still has one of the highest proportions of ethnic minorities in London. Since the 1980s, the local council under Labour Party leadership developed a cultural and community policy in response to social and economic changes in the area and became regarded as a pioneer of culture-led regeneration. Like many other local authorities in Britain during this period, Tower Hamlets Council looked to the principle of diversity as a way to address regeneration and community development in the area. However, as I will show, the results of this approach have been somewhat mixed. In particular, I will look at one of the council's flagship projects, the Rich Mix arts centre, which was developed in the late 1990s and which has become the subject of considerable controversy and debate.

Background

Like many parts of Britain in the 1970s and 1980s, Tower Hamlets underwent the process of deindustrialisation, and experienced a range of associated social and economic problems. The decline of the docks and the closure of local factories and garment warehouses meant that unemployment rates were among the highest in the country and there were serious problems of overcrowding, poverty, and educational under-achievement. Social tensions grew in this period, between the local white population and the Bangladeshi immigrants who had settled in the area from the 1960s onwards. The presence of extreme right organisations like the National Front and the British National Party exacerbated racial violence and friction, and many anti-racist groups and networks formed during this period.

In the late 1980s and 1990s, however, the area began to change rapidly. Its proximity to the financial centre of the City of London meant that it benefited from its rise as a global financial hub, with booming residential and commercial property prices, as well as the influx of new 'knowledge' workers (London Borough of Tower Hamlets, 2005: 37). Tower Hamlets also gained a strong reputation as a creative nucleus when artists moved into the area, attracted by cheap accommodation and studio space. This Bohemian trend soon led to the influx of more commercially oriented creative industries: designers, advertising agencies, fashion and textile workshops, and web-based companies. The area was able to exploit its 'cultural capital' in a number of ways, turning into what the council has described as 'London's creative engine-room' (London Borough of Tower Hamlets, 2003: 31). The area also acquired a positive reputation for ethnic diversity, becoming a desirable place to visit, eat, and shop. The 'Banglatown' area around the Brick Lane area grew into a busy centre of restaurants, bars, street festivals, and community group activity and the council actively engaged Bangladeshi community groups in its political strategy (Eade, 1989). Today, more than 48 per cent of the population belongs to an ethnic minority – 33.4 per cent are of Bangladeshi origin. Tower Hamlets Council also sought to develop a 'brand' for the area to increase its marketing appeal to tourists and businesses. It invented names like 'Eastside' to brand the area and give it a distinctive feel: local, yet exotic. It sought public funding to develop major capital or community-led projects which often had a cultural regeneration dimension, making successful applications to various government regeneration pots, such as the Neighbourhood Renewal Fund and the Single Regeneration Budget, regional sources of money, such as the Thames Gateway Partnership (set up in the 1990s to regenerate the east corridor of the city), and various grant programmes under the European Union, including the European Regional Development Fund and European Structural Funds.

Yet, whilst Tower Hamlets prospered to some extent in the 1990s, the boost to the local economy at the time was not equally distributed and many residents continue today to suffer from high rates of unemployment, poor health, and educational attainment, as well as poor housing and public service provision. The 'knowledge economy' which had supposedly transformed Tower Hamlets was concentrated overwhelmingly in banking and finance – making up 40 per cent of all jobs – and these were mainly occupied by highly skilled people from outside the borough. The growth of the local cultural sector was portrayed as a potential source of employment, particularly for the young ethnic minority population (even in more recent policy literature, diversity and youth are presumed to be natural aptitudes for working in the cultural industries, without explanation). Yet figures for the cultural industries in Tower Hamlets show it remained a small sector in the mid-2000s and formed only a fraction of total creative employment in London (5.5 per cent of the total) compared to Camden (10.2 per cent) and Westminster (17.3 per cent). Today, the majority of cultural industries in the capital are still based in West London (Freeman, 2007: 31). Furthermore, some have noted that whatever growth there has been in the creative and cultural sectors, it has had limited impact on the area's poorer residents, especially the ethnic groups that furnish the area's reputation for cultural diversity (Cohen, 1998). In 2003–4, 15 per cent of all creative jobs in London were held by ethnic minorities, compared to 23 per cent of all workforce jobs (Freeman, 2007: 44). Indeed, Oakley (2006) has pointed out that the creative industries in general, with their patterns of informal hiring and career progression ('it's not what you know but who you know'), can indirectly exclude those from disadvantaged backgrounds.

So despite the considerable changes in the late 1990s, Tower Hamlets remained a relatively poor borough in London with serious underlying economic and social problems. According to the 2001 census, nine of the borough's wards were in the top 10 per cent of the most deprived in the country. The fast-paced cultural and social change in the borough also, at times, came up against anxiety and resistance from some of the local population, who saw the investment by property developers and commercial interests as exploitative and potentially damaging to the social fabric of the area. The re-branding and nostalgic 're-imagining' of the East End even provoked some resentment from local communities who felt their own culture and identity was being marginalised (Eade and Mele, 1998). For example, in the late 1990s, the council's plans to redevelop the site of the historic Victorian-era Spitalfields Market with new office blocks met with strong opposition from campaign groups who amassed 20,000 signatures on a petition in protest.

Mindful of these criticisms and concerned not to alienate local residents, the council began to subtly change the tone of its regeneration strategies in the late 1990s and early 2000s and place an increased emphasis on 'bottom-up' and equitable development. For instance, it committed in its employment strategy in the early 2000s to concentrate on nurturing those industry sectors which could quickly employ a significant number of unemployed people with a relatively low skills base, including tourism, hospitality, and retail (London Borough of Tower Hamlets, 2005: 70). In addition, the council developed a Community Plan and Local Area Agreement (enforced by the Local Strategic Partnership, which was formed by a conglomeration of different private, public, and third-sector groups in the area) to ensure regeneration would meet a number of different needs (London Borough of Tower Hamlets, 2006, 2007).

The council's cultural policy in the late 1990s and 2000s, was developed in this context and was driven by both a strong regeneration strategy for increasing commercial and economic capital in the area, but also a concern to respond to local needs through providing youth activities, encouraging greater social cohesion, developing community engagement, and placing an emphasis on neighbourhood networks and renewal (London Borough of Tower Hamlets, 2003). A key principle in its model is cultural diversity, which was seen to be a significant social and economic asset of the area and generated a range of benefits. Diversity became regarded as vital for enhancing the appeal of Tower Hamlets to visitors, with vibrant and 'exotic' restaurants and fashion outlets, particularly around Brick Lane in Spitalfields.[2] This echoed the famous assertion made by American academic Richard Florida that cultural diversity is key to urban economic success, in that it helps to attract the creative class by appealing to their lifestyle choices and who in turn bring wealth and innovation to an area (Florida, 2002). Culturally diverse activities may not have become a significant driver for the local economy, but they could help improve 'residents' competitiveness by being a source of training, skills provision, and support for young people making the transition between education and employment. Cultural diversity came to be seen not only in economic terms, but also as an important social tool. It was a way of recognising the different ethnic communities living and working in the area, ensuring that they felt fully included in local decision-making and had a sense of belonging. The council managed this by, amongst other things, providing funding to local voluntary arts groups and over 30 community outdoors festivals and events, which had the aim of engaging with residents from all communities.[3] The principle of diversity also aligned with the council's long-standing engagement with anti-racism and community groups in the area since the 1980s. Tower Hamlets Council was one of the first Labour-led authorities to develop multicultural policies and fund activity along ethnic and cultural lines. As a consequence, many local arts and cultural groups in Tower Hamlets had a strong ethnic dimension, and became committed to cultural diversity as a way to address social problems like racism, inequality, and community participation.[4] Cultural diversity was ostensibly about strengthening particular community identities, but also facilitating connections between different communities too – helping to tackle racial tensions and divisions.

Leaving to one side the council's strategies and approach, it is clear that local arts groups and community activists were also highly committed to the principle of cultural diversity. They felt that the policy of cultural diversity was a way of recognising the enormous influence of different ethnic cultures, which were not so evident in 'high culture' institutions in London like the national museums and galleries. Artists and cultural organisations in the area were proud of the way in which the East End acted as a crucible for exciting new artistic forms. Indeed, the East End in the 1990s was an important site for new culture produced by ethnic minority artists (see, for example, the eclectic and innovative music group, Asian Dub Foundation, which was started in 1993 by a group of participants and tutors involved in a local community music project, or visual artists like the Turner-nominated installation artist and film-maker, Isaac Julien).

Another important idea was that cultural diversity was an appropriate way of thinking about the needs of the local community and the social and economic problems they encountered. Many of these groups, funded by the council, regarded cultural diversity in their work as a tool to promote 'creativity' or self-development. This was thought to be particularly important for socially excluded youth in the Bangladeshi community. The Bangladeshi population in the area traditionally has had the highest rates of unemployment, educational underachievement, and poverty; all of which were seen to contribute to a sense of identity crisis and disillusionment amongst the younger generation, and resulted in widespread prevalence of anti-social behaviour, gang crime, and drugs. Cultural activity was seen as important partly because it gave young people 'something to do' and could divert their energies to productive, safe activity. It also could provide routes into learning new skills and possibly entering the creative sector as a career. Local arts workers felt that one of the problems facing young people was the lack of a coherent identity, and that they should be helped to develop one in a safe, controlled environment, away from the dangerous influence of 'the street'. There was also concern about the added dimension of racial or cultural exclusion that ethnic minority youths may feel. Young people may feel 'alienated' from the mainstream white community, but also from the elders in the Bangladeshi community with quite firm expectations about behaviour, sexuality, education, and choice of career. They therefore might feel unable to find a community – something exacerbated by the instability and displacement brought by a more dynamic economy. One local arts professional who worked with young people said in an interview with me in 2007:

> A lot of the arts stuff that's on offer, sure it's cultural but it's very traditional and it doesn't always match a young person's needs or interests. They're already trapped in this identity of feeling very young but born to much older parents with very traditional lifestyles and life being extremely different on the streets.

In the early 2000s the concern about young Bangladeshis and their sense of identity was also heightened in relation to national and international events: the rise of Islamic identity and Islamophobia following the terrorist attacks on 11 September 2001 and the London bombings of 7 July 2005, plus the perception of racial tension in the country following the 2001 riots by Asian youth in the northern towns of Oldham, Bradford, and Burnley. Cultural diversity therefore came to be seen by many working in the arts and cultural sector as an important principle to help address this crisis of identity and encourage a sense of empowerment amongst young people. However, unlike cultural policy of the past, it was important to relate to young people through their *own culture*, rather than imparting an outside culture to them. The same arts professional noted:

I think if you want to engage with people you have to engage with them from where they are at this particular point in time... It's like sticking with what you know, because that confirms who you are. It's partly fear of the unknown, what you don't know.

This was a clear departure from the liberal-humanist discourse that had shaped much of national arts policy in the post-war period. This approach to cultural policy was less explicitly oriented towards promoting a particular kind of culture ('the best'), and more concerned with using culture to engage with people on their own terms and develop their individual subjectivity for social and economic ends. The choice of culture was based on what engaged the end user, not on any inherent notion of cultural value itself. Indeed, the rhetoric of diversity is self-avowedly *against* 'traditional' models of cultural policy. As a consequence, local cultural professionals emphasised how their approach differed from the exclusory policies of 'the past' and that cultural diversity emerges from the ground – the market place and community centre – so is more in touch with ordinary people.

Culture became seen as a way of developing the individual – their *subjectivity* – and, in turn, triggering a chain of social and economic effects. To illustrate this approach, here is a quote from one person working in an organisation promoting training and advice for residents wishing to work in the cultural and creative sector:

[Culture] can help in terms of community cohesion, in terms of racial understanding, improving the local environment. Just because you do something together around a common cultural form. Whether it's around a festival or event or creating a park – doing something together as a community throws questions up which require answers and if properly managed as an initiative collectively owned by that community, hopefully it throws up questions that can be seriously answered by that community. Whether that's issues around crime, or issues around disharmony, whether it's issues about health or whether it's issues about keeping the streets clean... Now within that participatory set of engagements, you can also work with... individuals, to help 'up skill' people in terms of basic skills such as literacy or numeracy. With some skills, some of those tools can raise expectations around desire for further training and to look at employment options within those kinds of activities, that is, cultural events, community-based activity and for some... it potentially sets up aspirations for wider engagement. Now saying all that, you've also got another set with commercial industries, where it's either music, fashion, lifestyle, ringtones on phones...So by helping a local economy to grow around some of those high ground sectors, whether it's music or fashion or design or whatever, you will then start to create a structure potentially where people if engaged at a local level have an opportunity to create some of those themselves...And for me there's a bigger issue in terms of people talk about local communities, in terms of regions, etcetera, and if you take it from an economic perspective is that what you're trying to do is increase the economic prosperity of the place to drive the quality of the environment and the quality of living which people in society have.

Here, the person being quoted makes a number of claims about the power of cultural activity which link together in a domino effect: assuming that one change, if sustained, will lead to another. Culture can be a trigger to local community debate, it can help train the individual in practical skills and make them more employable, it can nurture a sense of citizenship, it can generate a mechanism for community engagement, and it can improve economic opportunities. The use of the word 'culture' is quite free-floating because it describes quite different types of activities and rather disparate effects. For instance, the macro-economic impact of a cultural industry is quite separate from the re-training of an individual, or the impact of tourists visiting a cultural venue. Yet these separate effects are casually thrown together into the meta-category of 'culture' as if they require little explanation.

This extract is one example of a recurrent feature of cultural policy discourse – what Fairclough (2003) calls the 'logic of appearances', as opposed to 'explanatory logic' (94). The speaker strings together a number of phrases, building up the appearance of a logical, therefore causal and predictable, relation between these effects, yet no explanation is given of how this might happen. In this case, the process assumes that individuals are the locus of change within the community and wider society, and that changing the individual or community mind-set will trigger social effects in relation to the local economy. Hence, a recurrent theme in the economic discourse is a belief that culture can change people's attitudes to their environment and thereby enhance their own social and economic potential.

There were others, particularly artists in Tower Hamlets, who also began to feel uneasy with this economic end-goal and preferred to stress the social value of the arts in promoting creativity, and nurturing a sense of identity or improving personal self-development. As another arts professional stated:

> ... there's a very strong cultural industries argument, there are jobs in the cultural industries, it moves the knowledge economy. On a more generous level, if you want people to work in society, you need people to have confidence and self-esteem. On one level, if you're fundamentally serious about it and not cynical, I'd say releasing people's core identity if that's what you can do.

Cultural policy became seen as important in terms of nurturing a type of subjectivity and engaging with people's mental states. Artists and people in arts organisations felt strongly that diversity should not just be a 'box ticking' exercise driven by the council, but should be 'second nature' to their own creativity and engagement with local communities.

So it would appear that there was a mix of social and economic drivers behind cultural policy. The principle of diversity became seen as vital to encouraging economic success and community identity and cohesion. A more confident, creative person was presumed to be more economically productive and employable. Providing a greater choice of cultures could meet consumer demand and be more inclusive for the various ethnic communities in the area. Above all, the rhetoric of diversity – even when invoked in slightly different ways – was *against* 'traditional' models of cultural policy which were seen as exclusionary, old-fashioned, and out of touch with the needs of people – especially young ethnic minorities – in the area.

Rich Mix Centre – A flagship project

In the late 1990s, Tower Hamlets Council decided to invest in a new flagship project called Rich Mix, as part of its wider regeneration strategy. Funded by a myriad of regional and national public agencies (Arts Council England, the National Lottery, and the Greater London Authority), this new arts and educational centre located in East London was intended to fuse together the many different objectives of culture-led regeneration in the borough, being a new type of organisation that was both culturally high profile and inclusive and would also generate social and economic benefits for the local community.

Rich Mix was cited positively in Tower Hamlets' 2003 cultural strategy, but throughout the rest of the decade the project suffered from cost overruns, delays, and perpetual negative media. Phase I was completed in April 2006 with a three-screen cinema, café and, artist-in-residence workspace, plus a permanent home for the Asian Dub Foundation's community youth music charity, ADFED. Phase II in 2008 saw the unveiling of recording studios, a 200-seater performance venue, an exhibition space, education resources, and workspaces for creative businesses. The BBC also set up a studio in the building. However, the official opening was delayed for years and local opposition politicians frequently criticised the project. In August 2010, Rich Mix attracted further negative media because the council decided to give the centre an additional £2.5m from Section 106 funding, in addition to the £3.9m it received since opening in 2006.

The centre was first conceived in the mid-1990s by a small network of local left-wing activists, artists, and academics, who operated across the political and cultural spheres. Their interest in culture derived in part from the radical left-wing politics of the Greater London Council's Labour leadership in the 1980s. They believed that culture could address political issues, such as racism (exacerbated by the presence of far-right groups in the area), and alienation from private-sector-led regeneration. Their first project was an exhibition in 1992 about local cultural history at Bishopsgate Goods Yard, jointly curated by the University of East London and an arts organisation called Panchayat. Soon afterwards, the organisers developed an idea for a cultural centre in East London that would be at the forefront of celebrating ethnic diversity and contemporary debates about race relations and identity.

It is clear from those who were involved in the project at the time that there were differing accounts about why it was first set up and who it was supposed to be aimed at. One view is that the early influential figures – including local Bangladeshi Labour councillors – wanted it to be a centre to celebrate Bangladeshi culture and history, which would be used first and foremost by the local Bangladeshi community. Another view is that it was supposed to be wider in scope; a kind of 'museum of immigration' that would chart the cultural contribution and heritage of many different migrant communities to the area and privileging none. This would also be a colourful and exciting challenge to a culturally monolithic understanding of 'Britishness'. Another report cited that the centre was an urban regeneration project that would house a museum, exhibition spaces, a market centre for food and artefacts from around the world, audio-visual recording and performing facilities, and even a genealogical centre for visitors to trace their roots (Brownhill and Darke, 2000: 20).

Despite these many seemingly different objectives, what is clear is that there was an overall emphasis on cultural difference in Rich Mix's early years and that this was seen as a way to include excluded groups. The centre was driven more by a principle of diversity – celebrating difference – rather than the desire to prioritise any particular culture or cultural forms, as one might find in a more traditional cultural institution. One slightly vague description of the centre was as a 'museum without objects', so that the cultural space is dedicated to the visitors' diverse identities and interests, not the objects collected and curated by professional 'experts'. This view implicitly attacked mainstream cultural institutions for being preoccupied more with the cultural content in their buildings (i.e. objects) rather than the people who visited and looked. The Rich Mix centre was supposed to be about cultural diversity, not traditional cultural value as in 'high culture' institutions. This thinking amongst the founders was informed by the political ideas and influences of the period. One board member stated in an interview to me:

> [Rich Mix] was meant to be about the cultural politics of the 21st century... All the things that are now ten years out of date but weren't then. Homi Bahaba, Rushdie were writing about, creativity, hybridity... All of that emerges from migration, and the East End should be proud of that.

This model of the cultural centre was very much in line with community arts thinking of the 1970s and 1980s – to value the active participation of people as a cultural product itself, rather than focus on those objects deemed to have value according to what would be known as 'universalist' standards, but in their view were merely Eurocentric. The link between intellectual trends and the practical sphere of local politics was expressed well in the rise of political activists with culture in the borough in the 1980s, of who most were associated with anti-racist and Labour party politics. For example, Professor Michael Keith, a prominent sociology lecturer at Goldsmiths University as well as former Labour leader of the council, was one of the founders of Rich Mix.

The institution of Rich Mix was therefore intended to be a political strategy, and a cultural project in its own right. It was intended to be a site where different cultures might interact and evolve into a community, generating exciting new forms of culture. It was also about reinforcing people's particular cultural identity: 'about valuing your own culture and your roots'.[5]

By 1994 Rich Mix took on another dimension, the original founders became councillors and began actively recruiting the financial backing of Tower Hamlets Council. This added real impetus to the project and marked a shift away from its radical roots as it was no longer operating outside authority, but was becoming institutionalised as part of official local government policy. In 1996 one of the area's publicly funded development agencies, Cityside Regeneration, became responsible for the project and emphasised the potential social and economic value to the area of a new cultural centre that could attract tourists and enhance the 'brand' of the area. This presented a new side to something that was designed initially for local residents. At this stage, the council and regeneration partners began to see the potential of Rich Mix as a way of marketing the cultural life of the area to people outside the borough seeing diversity as an economic asset as well as a political strategy of local engagement. Tower Hamlets Council's involvement loaded new objectives onto Rich Mix: creating new jobs, offering education and training for the creative industries to local residents, nurturing the area's brand and marketability, and delivering a multicultural, community agenda. All the while, the link between identity politics and regeneration was developing, so that one helped shape the other. During this period, the developers began to search for a permanent site, eventually purchasing the former leather factory and showroom at 39–47 Bethnal Green Road. The project team held exhibitions in Bishopsgate Goods Yard and began working with other groups in the area to develop programmes (Rich Mix, 2001: 8).

In 2000, momentum gathered as the new London Mayor, Ken Livingstone, gave his official backing to Rich Mix. It was important to the Mayor's Office as one of a number of 'black projects' within its cultural portfolio, and part of Livingstone's commitment to increasing the presence of ethnically diverse art and culture in the capital's cultural landscape. Rich Mix received the largest single grant from the Greater London Authority for any cultural project, which boosted its political status – this was no longer a small community project but a new London institution. The Greater London Authority also loaned an officer, Anwar Akhtar, to manage the project. He constructed a stronger board with political figures including the then newly elected Labour MP Oona King and the high-profile Labour peer Lord Waheed Ali. These two figures, seen as close to the New Labour government, secured political support for Rich Mix and increased its viability in the eyes of other agencies. The decision of the Millennium Commission to give a major capital grant placed Rich Mix firmly on the map. For another three years, the board and small staff team tried to secure more funds, recruit person-nel, and develop the building. In August 2004, the board appointed Keith Khan to be Chief Executive of Rich Mix. Khan is a British Indian artist (or 'spectacularist', as he describes himself) who had developed an international reputation for his work on large-scale public arts events and carnivals such as the Commonwealth Games in Manchester and the Queen's Golden Jubilee Celebrations in 2002, with his company Motiroti. He was an ideal choice to marry together the diverse strands of Rich Mix, because he worked in ethnically diverse art forms and was known for his commitment to making culture more inclusive and not solely defined around the 'fine arts'. At the same time, Khan was consid-ered to have strong artistic credibility in a mainstream sense; an attribute which board members considered important because of pressure from the Arts Council. Crucially, Khan was an ethnic minority practitioner himself, a fact that some board members felt was important in demon-strating the centre was not run by a middle-class white elite and would feel inclusive to local communities.

From this period onwards, numerous problems beset Rich Mix. The local newspaper, the *East London Advertiser*, ran a number of negative articles about the 'ailing' centre, examining its rising costs (in 2002 it was set at £17m, but had risen to £27m in 2006), delays, and low visitor numbers (2006, 2007a). There were also practical set backs, for instance the centre was refused a 'premises license' in 2006 for live music, which threatened one of the key features of the project. The project attracted significant criticism from local press, politicians, and residents, adding to local disillusionment about the centre's lack of credibility. One councillor branded the project 'scandalous' and a 'bot-tomless pit with no proper business plan'; – claims angrily rejected by the centre's bosses (*East London Advertiser*, 2007b). Keith Khan resigned in February 2007, after a number of months on sick leave which was also reported in the media as signs of further instability (*East London Advertiser*, 2007c). A new Chief Executive was appointed in summer 2007 and oversaw significant improvements to the management of the centre, increasing the occupancy of its creative workspaces and studios from 6 per cent in 2006–7 to 85 per cent. However, she left two years later. In July 2008 *The Times* newspaper ran an article about the various problems, citing the lack of community support:

> ... the centre was originally envisaged as a meeting point for 'City boys, Bangladeshi grandmothers and dungaree-clad students'. But a recent visit on a Saturday afternoon revealed an empty building and

a café without food. A local Bengali women's group appeared not to have heard of the project. 'What is Rich Mix?' asked one woman. 'It's that big fat building up the road that no one ever goes to,' her friend informed her.

(Bartlett, 2008)

The centre finally opened fully in October 2008. According to the centre's annual review for 2008–9, the building was open to the public daily, employed approximately 80 full- and part-time staff (including front-of-house), and ran a regular programme of music and arts events, workshops, talks, and exhibitions. In 2008–9 it attracted over 70,000 visits to the cinema, although it sold only 4124 tickets to arts and cultural events. It also received another life-saving injection of financial support from Tower Hamlets Council of £2.5m in August 2010. Following this, a new interim Chief Executive was appointed and at the time of writing, the management of the centre appears to have finally become more stable. The revenue from approximately 20 creative business occupants sufficiently covers the core running costs. The arts programme in the centre and the number of visitors have also increased, with 80,000 tickets sold in 2010–11 (of which 10,000 are for arts events).[6] Interestingly, the website has toned down the talk of Rich Mix's impact on regeneration and social transformation in East London.

In its early years, Rich Mix presented itself as an entirely new kind of arts centre. In keeping with the multi-faceted nature of Tower Hamlets' wider cultural strategy, it aimed to deliver a range of social and economic objectives – promoting the local cultural and creative industries; improving the brand image of the area; providing training and skills to socially excluded local youth; engaging the local community in the regeneration process; cultivating a global artistic reputation and experimentation; catering for mainstream popular culture; showcasing innovative new media technology; and supporting voluntary and community organisations. It emphasised 'diversity' as its core principle, and in doing so attempted to reconcile various dichotomies of cultural policy discourse: reaching both local and global audiences; engaging amateurs but also professionals; providing skills training for young people but also a platform for established, world-renowned artists; celebrating specific ethnic communities but also a sense of shared identity and community in the borough; and, trying to deliver economic objectives by making local residents more employable and economically active, whilst also adopting a therapeutic approach which is focused on supporting individuals' identity in a fast-changing society.

By trying to fulfil all these various aims, Rich Mix needed to perform a delicate balancing act: it had to be a big flagship project that
would have enough media impact and prestige to improve the global
brand of East London – the former Chair, Oona King, suggested that
it would be 'our very own Tate Modern' (Bartlett, 2008). Yet, at the
same time, it was to maintain its identity as a 'community-focused',
'black' project, working with 'groups on the ground'. Therefore, the
discourse of Rich Mix tried to maintain both the particularistic view
of culture as something embedded in the 'ordinariness' of society and
is 'authentic', with a universalistic approach, whereby culture is something that transcends a locality, and can be judged by standards outside
any particular community. Some figures involved with Rich Mix early
on conceived it as a 'market place', where different audiences could
mix together in the same building to browse the type of cultural offer
that suits their particular interests. Individuals could maintain their own
identity and cultural choices, in a non-judgmental environment, whilst
sampling other options in the market. The model was supposed to satisfy the diversity of funders' requirements (high art, popular culture,
mainstream leisure facilities, education), as well as appeal to different consumers (international commercial art market to local residents,
outside visitors, and tourists).

Underlying this model was an explicit rejection of the claims for artistic authority made by curators and artists themselves. The authority
of the space was not defined by cultural expertise and knowledge, but
whether visitors liked it or not. As one senior staff member explained to
me in an interview:

> I hope that it becomes the first building to house a different rela-
> tionship between communities and culture, so that it ceases to be a
> passive, depository of objects and things and becomes a place that is
> about the interchange of ideas and people ... There are different ways
> we can go about making projects which don't have to be telling or
> teaching people.

Rich Mix also placed a firm emphasis on novelty and change, in reaction
to 'established' or essentialist ideas of 'high culture'. Hence, in the early
stages of the project there was an agreement to try to focus on new
digital technology and innovative media, which were seen to be more
appropriate for this kind of cultural intermixing. In this sense, the Rich
Mix concept was about trying to curate change and flux, rather than
static objects with unassailable cultural value.

We see in these ideas the convergence of the left and right relativist critiques of 'high', universalist cultural policy. The emphasis on outreach and difference meant that cultural authority was put aside in favour of dialogue, flux, and 'conversation', much like James Clifford's notion of the 'cross-cultural contact zone' (Clifford, 1997). Keith Khan stated in an interview to me in 2005:

Me: You're not setting the standards of what the art is.

Respondent: Well we can't set them until we've had the conversations. Because, we can't do it until we set ourselves up in the right way, to be able to reflect what's around us.

The emphasis on diversity also harked back to the need to be seen as 'legitimate' in the eyes of the local community and 'relevant' to their needs. It also linked together the early, left-wing political rationale of the project and Tower Hamlets' community cohesion agenda – to use culture as a way to engage with groups in the locality outside the conventional modes of consultation and political structures. Culture could be an alternative to mainstream politics in engaging with ordinary people. As one of the founders of Rich Mix explained to me, culture is something 'everyone identifies with' and it would not be difficult to get people involved because it is fun and enjoyable, rather than overtly political. Some of the founders of Rich Mix believed that culture offered advantages over conventional forms of politics because it allowed non-directional dialogue and 'ambivalence'. Culture was seen as a way to raise issues inclusively, allowing for conflicting viewpoints to co-exist. A board member told me, 'Creative work at least has ambivalence at the heart of it, or sort of differences and can be quite complicated.'

Contradictions within Rich Mix

Rich Mix was indeed a rich mix of ideas, and an experiment in new thinking about what is 'cultural value'. It might seem unfair to single it out amongst all the other arts centres in the United Kingdom which were being developed at the time, but its evolution and the debate it created illuminates some very important problems in cultural policy more generally. The centre has encountered considerable problems, both organisationally and philosophically, being pulled in different directions and responding to a number of conflicting expectations. The end result was widespread confusion amongst staff, board members, funders, and the public about what it was and who it was for. I will turn to this now.

Confusion of values and aims

The first confusion that emerged for Rich Mix was what culture is and where it should come from: either from within the community itself or outside from expert cultural producers and artists (in other words, whether it is an asset to be exploited, or a threat to be resisted). Many local cultural professionals involved believed that culture had played a key role in regeneration, but were also conscious that the influx of cultural organisations and activity from outside the borough had led to the problem of gentrification and cultural exclusion for local residents. The 2001 business plan (Rich Mix, 2001) itself admitted a 'discernible divide' and how cultural and economic regeneration in the area has 'not greatly benefited the groups that Rich Mix is targeting' (15). Yet, a page later, it described the regeneration of the area as having a 'local' cultural character, and how local cultural activists have contributed to regeneration with a 'new racial dynamic that mixes Asian youth culture with British popular tradition' (16). Although Rich Mix tried to ally itself with the existing processes of cultural regeneration, it also tried to seek legitimacy by claiming to be driven by the groups which have been threatened by this very process.

In this sense, there was always an unacknowledged tension within Rich Mix's definition of culture – whether it was something emerging from the local, particular community or whether it came from outside the community and existed beyond it, and whether indeed this could be a positive thing. In the minds of the founders of Rich Mix, culture *belonged* to groups. This could be contrasted with the liberal notion that culture transcends parochial group identities and is universal in its reach, value, and audience.

How an organisation understands culture is instrumental to the way it operates and how it engages with audiences. In this regard, it is useful to compare Rich Mix's approach to other organisations in the same area. The Whitechapel Gallery, established on Whitechapel Road in 1901, was founded explicitly to bring 'high art' from outside the East End to the local people. It continues to do this today, and although it has an extensive community outreach programme, the gallery's starting point is that it produces world-class art exhibitions of a global reputation. In the same neighbourhood is the council-funded Brady Arts Centre, where the council's arts and music service is based and which runs a diverse range of participatory and community arts activity for residents. Although it pursues high-quality educational and community work, it does not claim to be a space for 'high art' or seek to attract global critical acclaim. Rather, it is a place for the local community to learn and be creative. Both the Whitechapel and the Brady Arts Centre cater to different aspects of culture, and by being clear about their rationale are comfortable in their remit.

Rich Mix, on the other hand, tried to elide differences deliberately. Its board wanted it to be judged in terms of how authentic and relevant it was to the local community by using an anthropological notion of culture which encompasses everyday experiences, social habits, traditions, and values; yet it also spoke in the language of universality, purporting to display the kind of culture that is valued for its aesthetic character and 'excellence'. The result ended up being something of an institutional identity crisis: an ongoing conflict over what kind of activity should be prioritised and what kind of culture was being promoted. Rich Mix could not strive purposefully to be a high-profile arts centre without foregrounding the cultural activity of local artists and community groups as otherwise it would be seen as following conventional notions of excellence and privileging elite art. Conversely, it could not be solely community-led, because this would compromise its prestige (and marketing appeal) as an arts institution selecting work upon aesthetic merit. In its different conceptions of culture, the judgement criteria come into conflict: the 'excellent' art of a flagship institution might not feel accessible to local people; likewise, low-key community workshops would not attract significant profile or praise from the cutting-edge arts community Rich Mix sought to attract and engage. The centre was ambivalent about the idea of expertise, yet alluded to notions of judgement and quality. Indeed, this confusion was recognised quite early on in the project when an internal email dated 18 December 2001 noted that during a meeting there was 'some confusion around the table in terms of content and identity'.[7]

This philosophical conundrum at the heart of the project was exacerbated by the various managerial and financial difficulties that started to emerge from 2002 onwards. These practical problems could be interpreted as specific to the institution of Rich Mix – a combination of circumstance and poor leadership. No doubt some of these problems – growing bureaucracy and administration, building delays, funding gaps, regulatory, and license issues – could have been averted by better decisions and more experienced arts administrators at the helm. However, the problems facing the centre were never solely managerial but arose partly out of contradictory assumptions and confusion over the purpose of the centre. Despite positive rhetoric about the multiple facets of Rich Mix, those involved admitted the difficulty in holding together its contradictory agendas. In trying to be many things to many people, Rich Mix was constantly distracted from developing a coherent artistic vision. One board member explained:

> The project is very complicated, full of contradictions, partly because it is overburdened with a number of agencies having different expectations... there's a heavy layer of decision-making... It's a project set up to fail, I have to say. Because it has so many fingers.

From the inception of the centre, some artists and observers questioned whether it would have enough artistic appeal to attract an arts audience. As one local arts professional observed to me, the project was widely seen to be driven by politics rather than art and that 'it will be a battle to make it an arts space because politicians want to use it to address issues'. By contrast, another board member suggested that it was the Arts Council's criteria of funding which pulled Rich Mix away from its original community focus. Another respondent who had been involved in early planning for the centre felt that there was no core rationale or audience in mind:

> Rich Mix became a phrase that travelled through different hands. It was confusing who was in charge. People had very different ideas about it. The elephant in the room was that it had no shape at all – a lot of money has been thrown at it for consultancy work and to write reports but it is not clear who it is for. Which demographic is it aiming at? The ICA crowd, young Asian professionals, or young Asians who live on Brick Lane? I've widely polled people and there is no grasp of where Rich Mix will go – no-one speaks with belief in the cogency of its artistic policy.

Again and again this confusion resurfaced as the board offered different rationales to different funding bodies, and tried to reconcile them all. The business plan in 2001 affirmed the social agenda of the project and emphasised the regeneration aspects, but in a note to the Arts Council in 2002, it was stated that the project was 'wholly arts driven'.[8] In order to raise more money and gain artistic credibility, the board applied to the Arts Council in London and tried to convince them of the project's artistic rationale. However, in 2002, it was clear that the Arts Council was expressing doubts about the artistic focus of the project, seeing it as a politically oriented project.[9] There was also discussion amongst board members about the need to bring in a high-profile cultural figure that could boost the credibility of the organisation, such as Stuart Hall. The Rich Mix board eventually brought in an external arts consultant – Graham Devlin Associates – to draw up an artistic policy, interestingly only *after* the project had gained momentum. Graham Devlin Associates reported back in 2003 with a short paper about the 'Artistic Purpose of Rich Mix': 'It is difficult at present to identify the sort of central artistic vision that will be necessary if the project is to persuade the Arts Council…that it should be a priority for funding.' It then went on to suggest a focus on digital technology and a range of visual art and music. Yet Rich Mix's stress on artistic quality was not part of the original conception of the project according to some founder members.

There also appeared to be a pull from the council's regeneration department to emphasise the ethnic component of the project, above the artistic side, as some openly expressed concern about the way in which the local Bangladeshi community might feel disengaged from a purely arts-focused centre. After the terrorist attacks of 11 September 2001 in New York, the fundraising applications from Rich Mix made increased reference to problems facing young Asians. In a letter to Gerry Robinson, the Chairman of the Arts Council, dated 14 February 2002, Chair of the Board, Oona King MP, wrote: 'Given the current political climate there has never been a greater need to bring London's diverse communities together in general and, in particular, provide Asian youth with a centre of excellence that they have ownership of.'

Many actors have since blamed the confusion of Rich Mix's objectives on the multiple funding arrangements and the need for Rich Mix to appeal to different sponsors. No doubt, this had a debilitating effect on internal planning and helped lead to the centre's recurrent problems. However, blaming the diversity of funding perhaps reads things the wrong way round. The pressure of different funders arose as a consequence of the diversity of objectives that Rich Mix originally set out to achieve. The board members sought support from organisations as widely set apart as regeneration agencies and the Arts Council, but only because they were themselves pursuing quite different ideas about cultural value. Although this may have been partly a pragmatic strategy to raise funds from multiple sources, it was also integral to the philosophy of the project itself. Furthermore, it is not the case that the project had coherent aims from the start, and had therefore simply become distracted by different agendas; rather, Rich Mix's *raison d'être* was always to marry together diverse aims and overcome perceived dichotomies. Its founders may not have started from a singular artistic purpose, but they certainly had a political agenda regarding the role of culture. The problems over direction did not arise solely from management problems or external circumstances, but rather inherent contradictions relating to the philosophical assumptions of the project itself.

Debate about the need for 'black' projects

A recurrent debate about the principle of cultural diversity in Britain is whether there is a need for specifically 'black' projects. This reflects the tension between the two models of culture within cultural policy discourse – the 'identity' model and the 'universal' model. On the one hand, most artists seem to believe in the need for ethnic involvement and representation, yet on the other hand they dislike being labelled as 'ethnic'. Some bemoan the feeling of being 'pigeon-holed', as ethnic minority artists become defined according to how representative they are of an ethnic or community identity, rather than the quality of their work. There is also a feeling amongst many younger black artists that 'black' projects carry a stigma, and are seen to be driven more by political imperatives and 'box ticking' rather than genuine merit and cultural excellence (see Dyer, 2007). This is seen to damage the reputation of state-led projects and alienate younger artists from ethnic backgrounds.

This tension played out acutely in the development of Rich Mix. The original idea for the centre was that it should be 'black' and represent ethnic cultures, particularly that of the local Bangladeshi population. However, this was quickly undermined by the involvement of younger actors who believed the centre should exist as a high-profile, credible arts organisation in its own right. According to one respondent, the Chair of the Board, Lord Waheed Ali – who himself had a background in broadcast media – insisted that Rich Mix should be about high-quality art and he was concerned about the 'community' aspect of the project, which other founding members continued to maintain was central.[10] Others were uncomfortable about the politicised trajectory of addressing 'difference' with projects such as Rich Mix and felt the project risked being 'worthy' rather than artistically credible. Interestingly, it was younger ethnic professionals involved in the project who seemed most uncomfortable with the older paternalistic paradigm of giving support to ethnic artists. They wanted Rich Mix to be about an *idea* of diversity, rather than devoted to a 'worthy' promotion of Bangladeshi culture which might become creatively restrictive. One person involved in the centre early on explained:

> ...urban London, indigenous culture, that wouldn't be tainted by race as a brownie culture...very fun, vibrant, cutting edge, very provocative...it should have 'brown currents' but not be dominant,

and not just left and right but should show whole diversity of brown culture, which can be conservative in aesthetics, fashion and not just politically...

However, this concern with artistic credibility seemed to conflict with the original purpose of the centre which was to question the notion of 'artistic excellence' itself as the foundation of other arts institutions. Some actors emphasised that Rich Mix should not be defined simply as a prestigious arts space, but show things that 'ordinary' people would appreciate: 'It wouldn't just be like the Tate Gallery, which tends to just be a place to show pictures. But it means the cultural...things that people are interested in, you know, music....' Rich Mix's legitimacy derived from its unique placement of diversity at the heart of the project. One board member stated in an interview:

> What makes us different from the Barbican, or the ICA? And then what makes us different from a community centre? We would say that cultural difference is at the heart of it...Where the Barbican will do the one exhibition on Islam every five years and tick its boxes or do its outreach project, we're not outreach in that sense, because in a way, everything we do is that...

There was a clear aspiration for Rich Mix to move away from conventional criteria for artistic quality and inclusion, and to develop a new basis on which to show culture which was more linked to a particular community. As such, 'artistic quality' was but one factor amongst many in the rationale for Rich Mix. This tension between the community brand and the artistic focus was manifest at the launch event of the Rich Mix project in 2000, where some artists complained that the centre should be more engaged with black artists who represented communities, whilst others insisted that it was too 'black' and should be focused about the arts in a general, less essentialist way. There was clearly a divide amongst black artists about whether they needed a 'black' project.

There was also pressure for Rich Mix to have a black leadership. The Arts Council had earmarked £20m for cultural diversity capital projects, but for Rich Mix to be eligible, it was felt that it needed to be headed up by a black Chair and management that reflected the ethnic diversity aspirations of the project.[11] It is unclear how the black figures involved felt about this requirement, although a number of actors also stated that there was a tension between the management committee and funders about whether this was a 'black' project. As Khan said in his interview with me:

> It's a fascinating project because it's obviously come about because of the cultural shifts in the capital. I would never have taken it if it were a local community project at all. So my interest is that actually it has its roots in local community and in Tower Hamlets but has an international and national reach.

This seems to hint at the argument that some ethnic artists are uncomfortable with 'diversity projects' because they feel it will stigmatise their work and pigeon-hole them (Dyer, 2007; Hylton, 2007). In the case of Rich Mix, there was no clear consensus about whether it was a black project, and indeed it was often ethnic professionals involved who resisted this label, in opposition to their white counterparts within the same organisations. It is somewhat ironic that Rich Mix was originally conceived as a direct response to the racial exclusiveness of the existing arts establishment, yet it was ethnic artists who tried to restore its (and in turn, their own) artistic credibility by seeking endorsement from established bodies such as the Arts Council.

Ambiguity of 'community'

Although there was widespread support for the idea of cultural diversity as a principle in Tower Hamlets when Rich Mix was set up – from policymakers, local arts professionals, and the wider public – there also emerged ambivalence about the idea of engaging with 'communities' and awareness of the failings of such models of representation; what might be classed as the 'corporatist model' of multiculturalism, which treats ethnic groups as monolithic blocks that share similar values, aspirations and problems, and are engaged with through 'community leaders'.[12]

One concern by the late 2000s – during the time I was doing research – was that such an approach in Tower Hamlets was leading to an unhealthy sense of division and competition between groups. This reflected a broader ambivalence about the way in which diverse groups lived in the area. Although people were generally very positive about cultural diversity in the area and saw it as a defining characteristic, some also expressed concern about the division between groups. One local arts professional who had lived and worked in Tower Hamlets over many years stated in an interview:

Cultures tend to live in very small blocks close to one another and they make a bigger picture when you stand back but it's actually not blending that much.

Some actors working in the area were concerned about a territorial attitude over working with ethnic minority people, for instance, that one had to prove one's ethnic credentials or be 'authentic' in order to work with young Bengalis. A local youth arts worker said:

> People who say … who are they, they're not even Bengali, what gives them the right to work with Bengali youth … ? I get the feelings that the organisations almost kind of perpetuate that because they have a very community focus. And I don't mean that in the way that we talk about it in a funding, working way. It's like, it's a bit hard to explain, I know you'll know what I mean, it's parochial. It's like they're from my village, and therefore I'm only going to work with them.[13]

This issue became pronounced in Tower Hamlets as actors would be concerned that the council was driven by 'political correctness' and raised the problem of segregation and division between ethnic groups, feeling that council policies to fund organisations for different groups might encourage that. These apparent divisions seemed to be an endemic issue in Tower Hamlets politics as some felt it was leading to a state of competition between groups. In my own interviews, some respondents would feel that Bangladeshi community organisations were very well supported at grass-roots level, but it was the Somalian community who did not 'know how to play the game'. Whereas others felt that Bangladeshis were still not trusted with political or service delivery responsibility. Despite the rhetoric of community engagement and diversity, it was clear that many respondents working in the borough were sceptical about what benefits ethnic groups really got. One explained:

> So what you would start to see is … a little bit of you know, 'My Somalian community doesn't get as much as your Bengali community.'

Others bemoaned the fact that the political term 'black' was no longer in use because ethnic minorities saw themselves as having separate political interests, rather than being united on the basis of shared experience of racism. A Comedia report commissioned by the council concurred that ethnic division was an issue. The authors noted that whilst the council exceeded the legal requirements for local consultation, they needed to encourage people to communicate 'across ethnic and cultural boundaries' (Comedia, undated: 30).

In the market research commissioned by Rich Mix in 2000, the consultants noted that local respondents felt uncomfortable with the issue of celebrating ethnic difference: 'In order to celebrate difference and different contributions, you have to re-stimulate people's sense of separateness. There is ambivalence over this.' The authors go on to say: 'Although there is a general support for an institution that will recognise the migrant's contribution to society, there does not seem to be a strong desire for a museum to celebrate them as immigrants or "different".'

One criticism with the corporatist multicultural model is that it presumes a degree of homogeneity within groups and the accountability of local community leaders, but ignores how various religious and geographical delineations within a single community can come into conflict, for instance, in the Bangladeshi community (Baumann, 1996; Fremeaux, 2002). Eade and Mele (1998) noted in their study of the area that local opposition to private-sector-led regeneration had been very strong, but was not itself coherent or unified, because it contained conflicting values and visions of the area. Hence, alliances could be superficial and prone to conflict. Furthermore, when diversity is put into practice, it tends to assume a singularity of identity on the part of ethnic minorities. Although black identity exists, using it on an operational level tends to feel restrictive. One arts professional I spoke to said:

[Diversity policies] didn't put across that someone can be black and white, have interests and leanings... it didn't understand that things can become. I am an example of that and I don't feel insecure about not fitting into one identity.

Some of the board members of Rich Mix claimed they did not want to develop Rich Mix along a 'corporate multiculturalist model', which pitted groups against each other and reified differences. They wanted diversity as a principle in its broadest sense, emphasising the inclusion of all ethnic groups, and the hybridity of culture. One stated:

[Rich Mix] is not black... it's equally about Jewish or white working class people... The difficulty is that the council thinks in representational terms. So there's a black constituency, a Somalian constituency, an Asian constituency. And in a way, it wants all that represented. Whereas we're trying to articulate, it's a more conceptual thing, that culture is more hybrid now.

Yet, at the same time, there was an ever-present awareness of the pressure to include different local community representatives on its board and give black individuals senior management positions, or to engage with the local 'movers and shakers'. In my interview with Keith Khan, whilst he was Chief Executive in 2005, this was clear:

MM:... you plan to engage with communities. How do you plan to do this?

KK: Well, by asking them what they would like to see or like to do... we set up peer groups, we set up opportunities for people to come in and be spoken to and listened to. So we do it by outreach, we send in people to find key movers and shakers within the community.

Yet, this seems to be a contradiction – does ethnic representation matter or not, and if so, which ethnicity in Tower Hamlets matters most? Rich Mix at certain points even emphasised the importance of diaspora, to allow it to emphasise particular cultures but at the same time acknowledge its movement and evolution.[14] Yet the notion of diaspora is also problematic because it still asserts that ethnicity is the primary identification or connection between people. As Eagleton (2000) points out, at a basic level, arguments for hybridity and diversity sound progressive but they presuppose cultural purity and the 'contamination' of cultures; otherwise all cultures would be 'hybrid' by definition.

By accepting that communities have 'movers and shakers' who can represent the diversity of local people, Rich Mix ended up accepting the reified notion of community, which it was supposedly set up to reject. These tensions demonstrate a recurrent problem for Rich Mix; it wanted to break out of cultural essentialism and stress the fluidity and change of identity, but by claiming its legitimacy from a particular community, it reproduced this essentialism anew. It wanted to celebrate 'difference' in particularity, but ended up reifying it.

Finally, if connections are presumed to form on the basis of cultural particularism and difference, then the converse must also be true; those who do not share this identity are left out. In the mid-2000s, there started to emerge serious concern that one group was not being considered in local cultural policy – the white working class. However, no-one could work out how it should be integrated:

...what's kind of missing from it is whiteness, actually and white culture – our project is trying to deal with how you think about white working class communities and how they deal with minorities, in fact they're the minority themselves.

(Rich Mix board member)

...almost the most needy young people around here are the white working class young boys. Their identity, is like, they have very little to identify with that isn't black, American, street culture, what I perceive it as somehow, those in the East End.

(local arts worker)

White here in the East End is a fragile notion that just falls apart when you look at it.

(Rich Mix board member)

This discomfort was also raised in the market research conducted by Rich Mix in 2000, which noted that white residents were concerned that the centre would just be for 'immigrants' and concerns that 'white people [are] scared off'. This concern about white exclusion and 'political correctness' became a recurrent theme for the local media. For example, there was some controversy about Tower Hamlets Council's decision to make the theme of the annual Guy Fawkes' Night on 5 November 2006 a Bengali folk tale. The story attracted numerous media reports about 'political correctness', even though the council's arts service had held themed events in previous years.[15] Although local arts professionals were conscious of the breakdown of 'white' culture or a 'white identity', many felt uncomfortable about promoting it because they associated it with racism, nationalism, and exclusion. Whilst the multicultural logic of diversity stressed the particularistic connections between ethnic groups, there was reluctance to apply this to the white population, on the basis that their particular identity has historically appeared exclusive.

Another identity that came to be treated with some ambivalence was the Muslim identity, which grew more visible in East London in the 2000s and was linked to the presence of radical political Islamist organisations and clerics in the area (Eade and Garbin, 2002; Hussain, 2006). Although 'Muslim identity' is diverse and contains a range of opinion – from the politically and culturally conservative, to the moderate, to the radical – there was a restriction placed on the inclusion of these identities in Tower Hamlets' 'cultural' policy. Tower Hamlets did not fund activities which promoted the adoption of a particular faith or religion, and although it did fund religious groups' activities it was with the caveat that they must contribute to promoting mutual understanding and respect between communities. This therefore left Muslim identity in a strange position – being a part of the local 'community' but effectively being treated differently to others in the 'community project' of Rich Mix. Unsurprisingly, local Muslims were not fully convinced that it represented their community.[16]

What these two examples – white working-class culture and a growing Muslim identity – show is that 'the community' which Tower Hamlets' cultural policy referred to, and which Rich Mix was borne of, was not homogenous, and that this diversity could provoke feelings of exclusion, conflict, and resentment. In the end, because cultural activities and projects were touted as 'relevant' to the area and related to the 'local culture', they risked generating resentment about those groups which were excluded. The more 'ordinary' culture was presented to be and the more it was associated with a specific group's experiences, the more differentiated and exclusive it appeared to others.

Cultural communities are inherently fragmentary and fluid, and cannot be easily contained in categories: Tower Hamlets' 'community' breaks down into Asian, white, Somalian, and so on. Likewise, Asian culture breaks down into Indian, Pakistani, or Bangladeshi culture, whilst Muslim culture breaks down into Sunni or Shia, or Muslim men and Muslim women. These apparently stable cultural identities are themselves inherently particular, fragmented, and in constant flux. They cannot account for a whole individual, only general aspects of a group. Hence, it is not surprising that although Rich Mix tried to capture people's 'culture' through these categories, it ended up presenting a cultural form which is not an entirely precise representation. Hence, it reproduced the cultural alienation it was intended to challenge. Ethnic artists and audiences felt 'pigeon-holed' when they feel they were expected to represent something about a community, because the label they were given did not adequately capture who they were.

Lack of community buy-in

As Tower Hamlets began to change in the 1990s, there emerged a strong feeling of disillusionment from locals about the promotion of more commercial or elitist forms of culture in Tower Hamlets, which they perceived to be encouraged by the council. Some respondents complained that the cultural branding of Tower Hamlets excluded ordinary people in the area, and was a waste of public money. One local community volunteer stated in an interview:

> How on earth is [redeveloping] Brick Lane a priority above the needs of people in the area? The estates where people live are disgusting – they do Brick Lane up for the tourists...a bit like the Millennium Dome (unnamed).

The woman complained that the council gave cheap studio space to artists but ignored housing problems on local estates. She also dismissed many of the artists in the area as being 'complete fakes', producing low-quality work, and insisted that her views were 'common'. Some people endorsed the need for the council to encourage cultural activity, but felt that there was already a significant level of cultural life in the area that might be challenged by 'official' cultural strategies, which were too bureaucratic and heavy-handed in their approach.

Rich Mix was intended by the council to be a flagship project that would overcome this scepticism about cultural regeneration and engage local residents in the arts in a new way. Instead of developing cultural content by professional outsiders, it stated that it would put the 'local community' at the heart of its work. However, despite its claim to be 'community-driven', there was profound awareness from people involved that they too were distant from the 'local community' and that its attitudes to them ranged from indifference to outright hostility. Hence, there was a strongly felt need to overcome potential cynicism about 'ownership'. This concern was all the more problematic because the Rich Mix founders had originally sought to overcome the alienation created by previous regeneration policies. In the end, the founders faced the same accusations of distance which they had levelled at the political authorities in the past. A board member admitted in an interview:

> I have to say there's probably a far higher degree of cynicism on the part of the locality in relation to Rich Mix which is probably understood as a kind of top-down, agenda-driven...you know...coming out of central London as well as Tower Hamlets...

Rich Mix staff tried to engage with the community through numerous research and consultation exercises. However, because the 'community' structures in the area were highly professionalised and institutionalised, the groups involved were not necessarily representative. For example, the large community consultation symposium, which Rich Mix held in summer 1997, was attended by 150 individuals who almost all represented local community organisations or quasi-non-governmental agencies, rather than 'ordinary' members of the public.[17] The responses of actors involved in Rich Mix as well as the voices of residents indicated that the project did not emerge organically out of a pre-existing cultural network, but as a political intervention devised primarily by local politicians in relative isolation. Ultimately, it was a project created out of stakeholder interests and various agendas. As one arts professional living in the area said to me, Rich Mix reminded her of a joke: 'What do you call a horse that has been designed by a committee? Answer: a camel.'

There has certainly been local cynicism, resentment and indifference towards Rich Mix, as well as 'official' cultural projects more generally. In 2000, Rich Mix commissioned the Susie Fisher Group to conduct research about local attitudes to the project and their ideas for how cultural projects should develop (Rich Mix, 2000).[18] Eighty-five per cent of respondents were positive about the idea of a 'National Arts Centre' dedicated to cultural diversity and immigration. However, there was concern that the project would be underfunded, of poor quality, 'dominated by moralising middle class white people', and 'promoted by cynical commercial interests'. The focus groups revealed that 'helping artists is a heart-warming idea for many people but not without some cynicism'. In June 2005, I conducted my own casual straw poll of 20 people whilst standing on the corner of Brick Lane and Bethnal Green Road (by the site of the building).[19] Although the building itself was not open to the public, by that time the corporate literature of Rich Mix was stressing the fact that it was 'community-driven'. Only one of the people I stopped had heard about Rich Mix and knew its purpose, and this was because she worked for a regeneration agency in East London. Also, in my regular conversations with people in the borough there were mixed views. Initially, many people seemed positive about the centre, saying that it was always good to have money spent in the area on local cultural projects and the promotion of cultural diversity. However, when probed, people disclosed negative memories of previous cultural projects. There was also a sense that the council was out of touch with the needs of residents – something that was confirmed in Rich Mix's market research.[20] Many of the residents I spoke to were very sceptical about the idea of 'community groups' and 'community leaders', feeling that they too were out of touch with their local constituents. Over the time I conducted my field research, from spring 2005 to summer 2007,

I found that more and more people had heard of the centre, but that there were also increasingly negative comments about its cost, delays, and poor quality of provision.

It is also clear from the market research conducted in 2000 that whilst local residents welcomed a cultural centre, they were not favourable to its artistic focus. In focus groups respondents showed overwhelming support of facilities for live music performances (70 per cent) but far less for educational activities (47 per cent). The researchers said: 'Evidence shows that there is little support for a recording studio and limited interest in community events' (Rich Mix, 2000: unpaginated). The researchers state that 'the artistic agenda is currently alienating. It needs to be more mainstream and inclusive, at least to begin with.' Their findings indicated that the majority of people would prefer more leisure-type activities, and light hobby workshops on aromatherapy or yoga, comedy shows, and entertaining music rather than critical artistic work, which could be 'arty farty', as one respondent put it. Another said, 'It's heading towards opera, not ordinary people. You've got to be careful not to be too high up.' Some of the people I spoke with were positive about new projects, but they did not believe they would use it themselves; rather, they thought it might be good for *other* disadvantaged groups. This suggests an awareness of the social value of cultural projects, but not one that they themselves felt any stake in. The emphasis of residents was on leisure rather than an intense focus on artistic or cultural identity issues; this seems to contradict not only the artistic aims of the Rich Mix project, but also its objective to provide workshops and training for locals.

It is important to note that these responses did not necessarily show an outright rejection of cultural activities, only that cultural services are understood and valued for different reasons by residents, and that the slipperiness of the word 'culture' elided disagreements over the potential value of Rich Mix. Also, local residents did not necessarily regard a swimming pool as a better or worse thing than an art gallery, but they might have preferred to have the former nearby if they had to choose. Early on, Rich Mix promoted its three-screen cinema because this filled an obvious gap in provision (there are no cinemas in the vicinity), and managed to bridge the divide between 'leisure' and 'art', although even this part of the centre struggled to attract residents in the early years. In the end, the market research team concluded: 'the philosophical *raison d'être* proves hard to grasp'.

These responses to Rich Mix reveal a number of points: initially, local people did not necessarily see the centre as relevant to their needs; they felt it has been placed there for the wrong reasons; they saw it as a reflection of the wider ignorance of the council in relation to real problems in the borough; the centre was 'foisted' upon people by artists. In short, the complaints made about Rich Mix were the very same ones made by its own board members about previous regeneration policies. It seems, therefore, that despite its efforts, Rich Mix failed from the start to get any community 'buy-in'. Yet, unlike other artistic centres, Rich Mix's authority did not rest on a 'conventional' artistic rationale; rather, it relied upon having a relationship to a community. Without this relationship, its whole purpose was cast into doubt. Interestingly, the Whitechapel Gallery, by comparison, is less connected to the Tower Hamlets' policy agenda and has a strong artistic rationale, but in my conversations with them during my research, the staff appeared to have greater confidence in engaging with local people. This would suggest that 'high art' is not necessarily a barrier to engagement, as the founders of Rich Mix project may have initially supposed. Indeed, the respondents from the Whitechapel said that they felt that their engagement with local people was much more fruitful if it began from the starting point of the value of the art and the artist, rather than the need to target a specific (invariably 'socially excluded') demographic group, or 'community'.

By 2007, the lack of endorsement for Rich Mix from the local community had led to demoralisation and uncertainty for the staff. One administrator I spoke to told me that many of her colleagues felt disillusioned and she did not think there was much community support for it. Rich Mix asserted its legitimacy on the basis of support from the 'community' soon found that it had none. The centre did not claim the artistic authority or expertise that a more traditional cultural institution would have, but nor could it rest upon its 'authenticity'.[21] In late 2010 the newly appointed interim chief executive finally recognised the seriousness of this failure to develop a strong arts programme and focused attention on this. She even accepted offers to work in partnership with prestigious arts institutions in the locality, which had been refused before. This more 'conventional' approach to arts programming has, to date, led to an increase in visitor numbers, and may even mark a new direction for the centre.

Challenge to artistic authority

As I argued in Chapter 1, both the left, and right-wing political critique of the older model of cultural policy was that it privileged a singular view of what was best and ignored the importance of the end user or consumer. In this sense, the principle of diversity is more consumer-led in its approach to artistic content, which means that something is judged to be worth supporting on the basis of whether it can attract audiences. Furthermore, cultural projects should aim to attract the right kind of audiences to meet the criteria of engaging with diverse 'communities'.

Rich Mix was set up to be self-avowedly consumerist. Although it aspired to be the 'ICA of the East' or 'our very own Tate Modern' and show high art, its programming in the end became highly mixed. For example, the cinema when it first opened showed the standard, populist fare of Hollywood blockbusters (the first film it showed was the multi-million action film *Mission Impossible Three*). The choice of programme was always partly driven by the severe financial pressures of the centre to sustain itself, but also a concern to attract audiences. Some local artists came to see this populism as undermining the credibility of the organisation and its original mission to pursue artistic values and innovation. Others believed that the market philosophy made it difficult to maintain the social focus of the centre and be inclusive.

But the idea of consumer choice in Rich Mix was not solely about showing populist culture (which may well have had its merits, considering the concerns of local residents). The language of consumer choice was also interchangeable with the language of inclusion – giving people 'what they want' was framed in terms of 'giving people what they feel comfortable with'. This philosophy of 'cultural inclusion' leant towards the kinds of culture deemed 'relevant' and familiar, so that people (especially the young) would not feel intimidated but have a ready connection to the culture on offer. More generally, in Tower Hamlets there was longstanding support for arts groups in the borough that provided urban music or new media workshops on the basis that young people might feel 'put off' by something more 'traditional' or unfamiliar. So, Rich Mix was an extension on a larger scale of this approach. Today, it continues to operate successful events like 'Industry Takeover' with music training, seminars, and DJ workshops, which show young people how to succeed in the commercial urban music scene.

It was clear that this consumerist ethic in Rich Mix was seen by many as a positive step away from older, elitist forms of culture which privileged 'the best' and were regarded as insufficiently open to the kinds of culture that young people are interested in. Yet, at the same time, a small minority of people also expressed concern that the mantra of 'inclusion' might narrow the types of cultural experience that young people were being exposed to. As one person noted, it is ironic that for all the talk of 'diversity', young people in Tower Hamlets are generally targeted with a limited range of music and arts activity. One woman who was setting up a youth theatre group in the area in 2006 told me that 'everybody's doing hip-hop because it attracts kids and it's easy', going on to say 'using classical texts and forms is just as valid and the challenge is to get their attention with that stuff'.[22] Culture, particularly for ethnic groups, was not framed at Rich Mix in terms of learning or developing new taste, but rather in terms of identity and community. This supposed that people's tastes are durable and unlikely to change, and some types of culture were more relevant than others. One person I spoke to stated that the word 'community' was often used in the wider arts and cultural sector in quite a reductive way, and ignored the fact that people can belong to many communities at the same time and their relationship with art can be complex and varied.

Another aspect of this 'user-led' approach in Rich Mix was the imperative on the part of cultural practitioners to be sensitive to the needs or tastes of 'the community'. The audience or visitor reaction was seen as paramount, because that was the basis of its legitimacy. Yet this could also mean potential conflict with the artistic impulse to produce work that shocks or upsets conventional thinking. In my interviews between 2005 and 2007, I asked a number of respondents involved with Rich Mix about how they might cope with putting on a piece of work that caused controversy with one or other ethnic group. As an example, I cited the production of the controversial play about a Sikh community in Britain called *Behzti*, by Gurpreet Kaur Bhatti and staged at the Birmingham Repertory Theatre in December 2004. It had caused outrage amongst hundreds of local Sikh residents, who then went on to protest violently outside the theatre on the opening night, causing the play to be cancelled. One board member said:

> I think we initially would probably not do anything like that actually, because you've got to build up confidence. It's about when you do it and how you do it ... If I were in that position, you'd do a lot of other projects, around Islam for instance. But you would start off doing stuff, that would be controversial around other religions ... We probably wouldn't go down that route and provoke ...

Another believed there was no potential conflict at all as long as Rich Mix did everything in partnership:

> ... the thing about that play is that we wouldn't end up in that sort of situation because we would be involving people in our programme

and making decisions…most of those projects will likely be collaborations between either individuals or organisations so we won't ever necessarily be in a position where you have one voice in that sort of way. Because in theory, everything is always a partnership.

This view assumed that local groups could not feel excluded as long as the cultural content was determined through deliberation (in fact, the Birmingham Repertory Theatre did consult with Sikh representatives before the play began, suggesting that this is not a sufficient measure to prevent conflict, or, going further, that such consultation raised the expectation amongst community leaders that they should 'represent' their community and have some influence over the programming).

Despite such optimism, in 2006 Rich Mix encountered its first major controversy, about the wallpaper hanging outside one of the three cinema screens and designed by the cutting-edge Glasgow-based company Timorous Beasties. It was called 'London Toile' and apparently depicted a black man pointing a gun at a woman's head (although the company in fact denied the man was actually black, it was just the shading of the print). The wallpaper, which had been approved by the board, was publicly condemned by 'local community leaders'.

In response, Khan firmly insisted to the local press that the wallpaper was an 'intelligent and humorous' play on society's 'anxieties and stereotypes'. He added, 'I will not bow to McCarthyism. I do not condone the violence in its imagery, but people have to deal with London. It reflects London and is not a sanitised version of it.'

But the same newspaper article in the *Evening Standard* noted that 'he conceded he might have to take the images down if they offend people'. According to the same article, local community leaders were said to be angered and a local Liberal Democrat councillor, John Griffiths, said, 'This depiction can hardly be said to be conducive to the promotion of the community's multiculturalism' (Lefley, 2006).

In the end, the wallpaper was not removed. However, this example shows the inherent tension between the bullish discourse of culture as autonomous ('I will not bow to McCarthyism.') and the softer language of representation and sensitivity ('can hardly be said to be conducive to the promotion of the community's multiculturalism'). What might be seen as offensive for a particular community was seen by some to override Khan's judgement of aesthetic value. Similarly, the aim of Tower Hamlets, cultural strategy – to engender dialogue and consultation within the locality – was hampered by concerns about not offending groups or touching on controversial issues. This brings into doubt the notion that culture and its attention to difference and 'respect' can be conducive to the kind of political debate that cultural policymakers intend.

Conclusion

Clearly, Tower Hamlets Council had hoped to achieve many things with Rich Mix. Its ambition for culture since the 1990s extended far beyond straightforward economic arguments relating to the local cultural industries, and became part of a wider strategy to develop individuals personally, socially, and psychologically. Its arguments for culture tended to emphasise its ameliorative effects on individual subjectivity, and in turn addressed social and community issues. Culture was also presented as a possible way to engage with minority or disadvantaged groups in a way that older forms of politics could not. Such ideas were shaped directly by the political attitudes of people within the cultural left who were involved in Tower Hamlets policy.

In this sense, Rich Mix was, and continues to be, a product of its time, reflecting the political preoccupation with culture and the possibilities of engaging communities for economic and social benefit. However, it was crippled in its early years by its adherence to so much cultural policy and theory. It struggled to overcome its inherent contradiction – striving to be both a celebration of the particularism of culture and 'local identity', yet also aspiring to be universal and gain credibility by being a critically respected arts centre rather than something perceived as 'worthy'. This was played out in the individual personalities involved and the messiness of the funding arrangements, but was not solely attributable to those factors. As the centre evolves it may yet overcome these tensions.

What of the public who have watched passively as millions of pounds have been spent trying to resuscitate the centre? Ironically, for all the efforts to engage them, the community project alienated the community it sought to represent. It remains to be seen whether it can fully rehabilitate its reputation.

By questioning the universalist basis of culture, Rich Mix tried to base its legitimacy on the 'buy-in' of a particular community – by consulting through community leaders and trying to represent their cultural choices in the content of their work. It relied on the identification of a community, rather than a cultural engagement. By communicating with individuals through their identity, Rich Mix also alienated artists and audiences who felt 'pigeon-holed' into ethnic categories, as well as those who did not fit into any category at all. The story of Rich Mix is not over: a clearer analysis of the problems it has faced in its early history might help steer its path in the future.

4
Oldham – A Case Study of Cultural Policy in an Industrial Town in North England

In this case study, I explore how the local authority of the industrial town of Oldham, in the north of England, has used cultural policy to address its social and economic problems, and I examine some of the tensions that have emerged as a result.[1]

Lying amid the Pennine Hills in the north-west of England, the former mill town of Oldham was once famous around the world for being the capital of cotton spinning in Britain. In 2001, however, it gained notoriety for some of the worst race riots in Britain since the 1980s, in which Asian and white youths clashed on the streets. On 26–29 May 2001, around 500 people rioted, injuring two police officers and three members of the public, and causing damage of over £1.4m (Home Office 2001: 7). Riots followed throughout the summer in other neighbouring towns such as Burnley and Bradford.

The eruption of racially linked violence awoke a sudden interest in these largely unnoticed towns as news reporters, columnists, and researchers began to ask what had gone wrong. A number of government-funded reviews and strategy documents were written during this period.[2] They all stressed the social and economic problems arising from deindustrialisation, and the need to build 'community cohesion', improve youth facilities and representation, develop a shared identity, and tackle the segregation between ethnic communities, which was seen as hindering social and economic development of the town. The Cantle Report (Cantle, 2001) in particular found that communities in the northern towns were living 'parallel lives' and rarely met or interacted in any meaningful way.

The town of Oldham has become well known in the media following the riots, unfortunately for negative reasons. It was characterised as a 'race-hate town' and reports of increased racist incidents reinforced the perception that the town was highly segregated. At the same time, there has been much interest from the media and also the local government world in how Oldham has tried to deal with some of the problems raised by the riots – both its economic regeneration and the issue of ethnic division. Oldham has a determined and committed local authority that is trying hard to understand the role culture can play in addressing its social and economic problems. This chapter looks at the history of its approach since the late 1990s and provides some insight into the challenges policymakers face in trying to put cultural diversity into practice at the local level – not in a single cultural institution but in an entire town.

Background

Oldham in the late 1990s experienced a familiar story of economic decline. Although this mill town had played a prominent role in the nineteenth-century textile industry (nicknamed 'King Cotton'), by the mid-twentieth century its mills were struggling to compete in the global market. To maintain productivity in the 1960s, the town encouraged large numbers of migrant labourers from Pakistan and Bangladesh to work in the mills, but this was not enough and in the 1980s the town gradually lost much of its industrial base, with the last mill closing in 1998.

The council sought to diversify the local economy in the 1980s by improving transport links and transforming old mill buildings into spaces for commercial manufacturing and distribution, but the economic problems remained. Oldham continued to have a low-wage, low-skill economy, although manufacturing has remained an important part of the town and is above average for the United Kingdom. On the 2007 Indices of Deprivation Oldham was ranked as the 42nd most deprived local authority area in England. According to the 2001 census, the ethnic population of Oldham was 13.9 per cent and it lived in concentrated areas of the town.

Like many other deindustrialising towns across the United Kingdom, Oldham first began to develop its current local economic policy in the 1990s, focusing on retail, leisure, and culture as new growth areas and ways to make the town more appealing to businesses. The council developed a series of regeneration projects aimed at unlocking public and private investment in the area for new buildings, supporting the relocation of businesses, and improving the transport and road infrastructure. It developed major new capital projects, including two new shopping precincts, the Mumps Enterprise area in Oldham town centre, to attract and nurture creative industries, and the Oldham Sixth Form College.[3] Through these schemes, the council was able to secure grants from central government, the National Lottery, and European Union programmes for major capital development.[4] It was awarded £211 million in special regeneration funding for the 18-year period, 1993–2011 (Ritchie, 2001: 53).

As part of these major capital developments, the council also unveiled plans for the Oldham Cultural Quarter Development. This involved new buildings for the library and gallery and the relocation of the Oldham Coliseum Theatre in the South Union Street Area.[5] Although the town had enjoyed a good reputation for its cultural provision and employed a strong in-house arts and events team, culture had not been regarded as a high political priority up till this point.[6]

Following the riots the council was criticised by external advisers for procuring public funds but not developing a coherent, borough-wide strategy to address deep-seated grass-roots problems (see Ritchie, 2001). Projects had been developed opportunistically in reaction to government pots of funding, rather than according to some meaningful vision for the town. The emphasis on securing funds for capital projects was also said to have shifted attention and resources away from lower-key grass-roots activities which the council had supported previously.

The riots also exposed the geographical segregation between the Asian and the white communities, through housing, schools, and their engagement with local services. Tensions between the local white and Asian population had increased in the 1980s due to the dwindling fortunes of the town. Unemployment following the closure of the mills, combined with poor housing stock and decline in local public services, created widespread disillusionment. This was exacerbated by alleged 'unofficial' council policies of segregation in housing. The resentment deepened in the 1990s through the system of national regeneration funding, which allocated money to area-based initiatives, which invariably fell along ethnic lines. The divisions became a source of intense media scrutiny and as in the weeks running up to the riots there were stories in the national and local press about 'no-go' areas for whites in parts of Glodwick and numerous racially motivated attacks. The police released statistics that showed that the majority of victims reporting racial attacks were white, arguably fuelling the resentment even further. Surveys following the riots suggested a widespread belief that the different communities were divided.[7] Despite the major investment being made in the town, Oldham Council's leadership was seen to be out of touch with emerging issues of cultural identity and division and was urged to think about how it could better support integration between communities and more grass-roots engagement.[8]

Taking on board criticisms, the council began to rethink how culture could play a more integrated role in future regeneration strategies. Crucially, it recruited new staff in a range of areas to bring in outside experience and expertise, and also employed the regeneration consultancy, Comedia, to develop a long-term, borough-wide strategy to look at the economy, community relations, transport and urban design, and culture in the town. *Oldham Beyond* (2004b) contained a detailed audit of the issues facing the borough and set out a vision for future development (Oldham Metropolitan Borough Council, 2004b).[9] This growth of external strategic support meant that Oldham was open to the influential ideas of the national local government sector and the strong emphasis on culture in regeneration. It also brought a greater coherence and integrated 'cultural thinking' into the council's strategy, reflecting the view that one of the causes of Oldham's problems was the council's management.

This re-evaluation led to a renewed interest in grass-roots activity. One of the people who worked in 2003–4 on the *Oldham Beyond* strategy reflected back on how the council's cultural policy at the time 'seemed so hollow. It just seemed like a megalomaniac's dream of men in suits standing around and saying, "Oh yes, a library there, a museum there."...but it's got to come from people at the end of the day, not from a desire to build some nice buildings.'

Oldham Council therefore gradually focused more on people and services, as well as buildings and infrastructure. It received £31m through the Neighbourhood Renewal Fund, and in 2004 it clarified its strategy through a Local Area Agreement (LAA) which channelled £500m of public funds (Oldham Partnership, 2006: 2). The council also focused on the improvement of local collaborative working between agencies such as the council, the Police, local schools, and voluntary groups; modernising the council; focusing on young people through youth and voluntary activities; securing private and public investment in housing, schooling, and local business; a focus on crime and anti-social behaviour; and an effort to combat the rise of extremism and ethnic tensions, through a range of cultural and community-based strategies.

A new cultural policy

Within this wider framework, arts and culture came to be seen as a vital instrument in the council's strategy. They were expected to contribute to the economic revitalisation of the town centre, as well as to the community cohesion agenda (see Cantle, 2001: 6.23). Oldham already had a small number of long-standing cultural and arts organisations in the town, such as the Oldham Coliseum theatre, Gallery Oldham (as part of the Cultural Quarter developments), traditional festivals such as the August Rush Cart Festival in Saddleworth, and smaller, younger arts providers such as Peshkar (a South Asian theatre company). Since the 2001 riots, the council has also supported (and in some cases, received central government funds) annual carnivals (the Spring Bank Holiday Festival and the Lantern Procession in the centre of town). The Oldham Carnival, a very popular event in the early twentieth century, which fell out of favour in the 1990s, was revived in 2006 and renamed the 'People's Carnival'. Because there is limited private provision of cultural activity in the borough (it is the largest borough in the United Kingdom without an in-town cinema, for instance), the local authority's role is quite influential in local cultural life. Interestingly, the council's cultural strategy was mostly oriented towards publicly funded activity – preoccupied as it was with securing public funding – and less interested in the role played by commercial or popular culture amongst communities, which were arguably less divided along community or ethnic lines.

Although Oldham is not a cultural metropolis like Tower Hamlets, it has been recognised nationally for its work in cultural policy; for instance, winning an award for 'Cultural Contribution' in June 2007 from the Academy of Sustainable Communities and hosting various national conferences. The focus of cultural policy in the early 2000s continued to be oriented towards capital projects, particularly the various phases of the Cultural Quarter, but there was also increased concern to encourage cultural participation at grass-roots level. Indeed, Oldham was the first council in the country to include a 'stretch target' for cultural participation, which aimed to increase the number of local people involved in cultural activity.[10]

In its submission to the Academy for Sustainable Communities, Cultural Contribution Award, Oldham Council stated:

> The arts have the power to transform lives and communities, to define and preserve our cultural identity, and to create opportunities for people throughout the borough. They contribute significantly to improving well-being for all, enabling self-expression, delivering basic and specialist skills and celebrating individual, community and national identity.
>
> (Oldham Partnership, 2006)

The meaning of culture also became defined around more abstract concepts, not just particular services. The aim of the cultural services, according to one council employee, was 'to get culture embedded across blocks' and to broaden the role of culture in other departments rather than just in one. Oldham's cultural strategy stated there was a need 'to think beyond traditional departmental and organisational boundaries and delivery mechanisms' (Oldham Metropolitan Borough Council, undated, 2).

The council, in the immediate years following the riots, developed policies in partnership with local organisations through the Oldham Cultural Partnership, a 'local cultural policy elite' composed of a highly networked group with overlapping interests in state-funded and voluntary organisations. The council's in-house arts development team shared a building in the Union Street area with a number of the local arts groups it supported, such as Peshkar, Dreadlions Foundation, and Bang Drum, and was a hub for part-time arts workers in the area.

As Gray (2002) has pointed out, culture can rise in importance as a result of 'policy attachment' – in the case of Oldham, culture became seen as key to regeneration. One of the people involved in the local cultural partnership explained to me in an interview in 2007, 'if the arts weren't in there [regeneration strategy], we wouldn't get the funding. It's expediency'.

One of the regular complaints about arts policy in the United Kingdom today is the growth of bureaucracy and 'box ticking', and a tension between the different aims of the authorities and arts professionals (e.g. Caust, 2003; Tusa, 2007). However, this did not seem to be a particular issue in Oldham. Indeed, there was a strong consensus that culture can and should play a role in addressing social and economic agendas and that the arts had a value in terms that the local authority could appreciate. Few local arts professionals seemed to resent having to 'tick boxes' (at least compared to those in Tower Hamlets around this time) and none of them particularly felt under pressure from the council. Everyone worked proactively with the Cultural Partnership to develop targets they all were comfortable with.

Therefore, local actors developed a relaxed and positive view of the partnership between cultural organisations and the council, feeling they had shared values about the purpose of arts funding in Oldham and enjoyed close high-level relations to the council without compromising the freedom of their programming or how they worked with audiences. Having this sense of purpose and reason clearly gave the arts sector in Oldham self-assurance. Inevitably perhaps, some local professionals felt cynicism about how targets and 'buzz words' like 'identity' can get projects funded, even if they were not very good. As one said:

> ... when you find that every man and his dog is doing a project about identity and what it means to be 'me', I think you should probably be aware really that due to the nature of funding for projects you can find that artistic project ideas are compromised to fit in with the tick box on a funders form.

However, this never amounted to a significant opposition amongst any single group and few individuals felt that the social agenda posed a restraint on artists' creativity. Most professionals involved in cultural policy in Oldham came to accept that the arts should have a social value and address social objectives yet not be too heavily bureaucratised.

Although one of the ostensible reasons for Oldham developing a cultural strategy in the 1990s and 2000s was economic growth and the town had some creative industries potential (particularly because of the strong reputation for creative courses offered at the local sixth form and further education colleges), in truth, this sector was unlikely to be anything more than a minor employer in the town. Comedia's report, *A Survey and Mapping the Cultural Sector in Oldham* (2005), stated that the for-profit cultural sector employed 5,405 people in 998 enterprises, with an annual turnover of £266m, and even 32 per cent of this was the production and distribution of sports equipment (Comedia, 2005: 13). By contrast, manufacturing remains significant, accounting for 23 per cent of employment which is higher than the national average of 17 per cent.

Therefore, Oldham Council's approach following the riots was nuanced, focusing on attracting a creative class of high-skilled, high-waged residents, plus attracting private investors and businesses generally. *Oldham Beyond* stated that 'liveability' was now the most important issue in the town by using culture as a way to attract workers, bring in more spending power, and make the borough more attractive to businesses (5, 14). This approach borrowed directly from arguments made by Richard Florida, who sees the 'creative class' as a key factor in urban renewal. Oldham was even cited as one of Britain's most creative places in his 'Boho Index', largely due to its highly diverse population, which apparently made it more creative.[11]

In the discourse of local economic policy, Oldham Council began to see creativity as key to achieving a number of desirable outcomes in the town – improved liveability, community cohesion, ethnic achievement, engaging young people, and increasing their employability. The social and economic aspects of creativity were joined together and local organisations sought to achieve both. For instance, the local Asian theatre group, Peshkar, was set up in 1991 and funded by the council with the multiple aims of trying to promote careers in the creative industries to local young Asians, but also using cultural activity to address a range of young people's and community issues through participation and audience development initiatives. The creative potential of the Asian population was seen partly in terms of tourism development (branding an area to make it attractive and distinctive), but also in terms of inherent creativity in the town's population (for some reason, young Asians were assumed to be especially creative and interested in innovative culture). Like Tower Hamlets, a local diverse population was seen to offer potential economic benefits.

Creativity and culture were also seen as a way to address the psychological restraints on Oldham's progress, addressing what is seen as a major problem in the town of negative self-perception and a lack of motivation – an 'it's too good for Oldham' mentality . . . '. *Oldham Beyond* identified this psychological challenge, citing 'a loss of *self-confidence* and *pride* in the borough and its future', and saying that 'people feel faintly embarrassed to say that they come from Oldham'. It advocated the need to 'change internal and external perceptions' (11).

In his report following the riots, Cantle (2001) also linked the town's deprivation and racial tensions to psychology, asking 'Why are some groups of white youths so lacking in self-esteem and confidence?' (31). Understandably then, culture became part of Oldham Council's strategy to 're-imagine' the town and address 'low aspirations'. It was used to 'develop personal self-reliance, self-confidence, and flexibility of approach on which an ever changing job market so frequently depends' (Oldham Metropolitan Borough Council, undated: 19). The local courses offered through the arts service and other funded organisations were oriented around confidence building and 'soft skills', which might then go on to increase employability of vulnerable groups such as women and young people in deprived areas. The Oldham Youth Service followed a similar approach, running a number of workshops, summer schools, and programmes designed to use the arts in engaging with young people.[12] The 2005 Comedia report on the cultural sector noted that whilst the commercial cultural sector was small, the non-profit sector was highly important in terms of 'well-being' (Comedia, 2005: 7). The arts were therefore seen explicitly as a way of changing people's attitudes, developing their ability to cope with a changed local economy, and building a sense of community.

Culture was regarded as a 'safe' space in which to engage the local population, as opposed to more conventional types of public engagement, say through politics. Following the riots in 2001, the renowned British playwright David Edgar set about writing a play entitled 'Playing with Fire'. He spent considerable time consulting with people in Oldham about their experiences. In an article in *The Observer* newspaper, Edgar argued that culture was seen in the town as providing a space for divisions to be overcome:

> ...there are efforts in the hardest places to challenge community division. This is not through integrating residence, which will take years, nor by integrating schooling, which follows residence, nor even through the workplace. It is happening through culture. And everyone working in this field agrees that the thing you don't do, when attempting to get groups of young people to know more about each other, is to bring one side into the other's territory.

As Edgar suggests, the arts and culture became seen as a vital part of the council's community cohesion strategy.[13] There was a general consensus that one of the reasons for the highly racialised division in the town was the physical separation between groups and the lack of intersubjective interaction; in other words, people felt divided from others because they did not spend enough time in their company. This sense of division was reinforced spatially, as people chose not to enter territory outside their 'community space'. The arts, in this sense, became seen as a neutral and safe 'hook' to get people together in a neutral space and encourage micro-level interaction. A council official explained to me:

> ...the aims of the bigger festivals and those sort of events...it's actually bringing communities together, and what we've found is that being based here in this area, it's actually considered quite neutral territory for people.

Implicit in this view of the role of culture was a belief that most other types of public activity failed to bring people together, especially politics. The arts were considered particularly good at encouraging interaction because they were accessible, fun, inclusive, and safe. They did not require specialist knowledge and all people of whatever level and ability can participate in them. Culture was also seen as 'primal' and emotional, something appropriate for the state to cultivate. As one person involved in cultural planning explained:

You need to recognise that people have multiple intelligences – people think about their surroundings in different ways, through stories and histories. It's not just a rational world … we bury our emotions. The arts are a way of telling that in a way that people identify with. You can show them as many statistics as you like but for most people you need a story …

Hence, it became a trend to use the arts in Oldham to 'consult' with people on particular council projects and regeneration initiatives, in order to make them feel more emotionally connected to the projects in a way that traditional consultation fails to do. For example, the *Oldham Beyond* team in 2004 used a 'Thought Bubble' to tour around the town and invite responses, sometimes in the form of drawn material. This shift towards a non-political, more emotional mode of engagement reflects the ideas of the political theorists discussed in Chapter 2. As I showed, they linked the decline of party politics to the rise of community groups who desired recognition, esteem, and a more holistic kind of engagement with their feelings. Implicit in this framework of 'cultural' – or, perhaps to put it more accurately, culturally therapeutic engagement – was scepticism that local people could feel connected by an identification with more abstract ideas or principles. This is described as 'old politics' and therefore seen as redundant for most people (especially the young) in the contemporary world.

Culture was thus seen as a way of facilitating micro-level interaction, based on positive, ethical feelings of neighbourliness. The engagement in the cultural space is not rational – on the contrary, it is about a feeling of fun, celebration, and 'joy'. Because the stress was on positive feelings of connection the cultural strategy emphasised those activities perceived to engender this: popular leisure activities, or hobbies or crafts, such as lantern-making, drawing, and music-making. What counted was the opportunity for participation and interaction, not the meaning of the activity or the cultural product itself, which might be relatively banal and uncontroversial.[14]

Many professionals engaged in this work in Oldham saw such low-level interaction as 'healing' and a way of gradually building relationships between communities. One example of this process was a project devised at the Oldham Coliseum, which brought together NEETS (Not In Employment, Education or Training) from different ethnic groups to work on a play for a number of months. The therapeutic value of the arts meant that 'they felt proud of their achievement' and also began to feel a connection. The main basis upon which people are expected to come together in Oldham is the 'ordinary' politeness of everyday interaction. People come together on the basis of their neighbourliness or sense of micro-community, but there is no other notion of 'transcendent' identification based on national sentiment or political identity. This focus on intersubjective interactions has been advocated more widely in academic literature on race and community politics. Lownsbrough and Beunderman (2007) in a Demos report for the Commission for Racial Equality have pointed out that 'banal encounters' in a public space can be important for positive, spontaneous interactions that are focused on common and practical activities. The role of culture is to create such connections in a 'neutral space'. This approach implies that previous forms of political connection and solidarity are inadequate or no longer possible. Paul Gilroy (2004) has used the concept of 'convivial culture' to denote 'the processes of cohabitation and interaction that have made multiculture an ordinary feature of social life in Britain's urban centres and in postcolonial cities elsewhere' (xv). He sees this as a way to avoid the exclusivist tendency of identity politics, which stresses connections based solely on subjective experiences.

Therefore, the neutral space of culture is designed to focus people from different ethnic groups on the process of interaction. They are encouraged to see each other in terms of their unremarkable characteristics as 'neighbours', inhabiting the same physical space. At the same time, the arts can affirm people's different identities and give them cultural pride in a non-judgemental environment.

Another important dimension of cultural policy in Oldham since the early 2000s was the need to make arts and culture themselves more 'relevant' and 'accessible', in line with wider government policy since 1997. The main cultural institutions in the town had a strong history and institutional identity; in the case of Gallery Oldham, it was a well-established, permanent collection of social history, art, and natural science artefacts, which it is legally obliged to display to the public; in the case of the Oldham Coliseum Theatre, it had a loyal season-ticket audience and commercial programming strategy because it relied heavily on box office income. However, the main cultural institutions in the town became concerned after 2001 to target under-represented groups, particularly the local Asian community. Gallery Oldham was keen to bring in a larger number of Asian and other ethnic minority visitors. The concern for cultural institutions to widen and diversify the audience was officially enshrined in the LAA 'stretch target'. The inclusion of the target in Oldham's wider strategy was regarded as testament to the coherence and focus of Oldham's cultural partnership groups.[15]

Whilst public funding was clearly a driver behind this, there was also a very strong personal commitment from local cultural professionals to address diversity and access. These concepts became central to the development of the Cultural Quarter and the desire that the buildings should not be 'off-putting' or intimidating to users. In an interview, one cultural professional at Gallery Oldham said:

> [We] don't want it to be intimidating: we've built that up, but now it's about getting people's trust that when they come to the gallery, that it's not going to be very formal. It's not like that anymore.

Implicit in such statements is a suggestion that cultural provision in the past was exclusive and needed to be changed. This reflects the keen awareness amongst organisations that the majority of people in Oldham felt alienated by 'high culture' and that they needed to prioritise access and inclusion in their work.[16] This led to a particular stress on attracting disadvantaged groups – ethnic minorities and lower socio-economic classes – and shaping the collections in a way that would appeal to their perceived cultural interests or identities. This might range from their support for the local football team (they held an exhibition about Oldham Athletics in 2006) or their ethnic heritage (they held an exhibition about Muslim women wearing veils, called *Sisters* in 2005 and in 2003, an exhibition about Bangladeshi folk art called *Songlines*). Gallery Oldham developed what would become one of the largest collections of Bangladeshi art in the United Kingdom. The Coliseum also sought to attract ethnic audiences by building up South Asian writers, and launched a young Asian playwriting competition. Local events and programmes reflected the issue of cultural diversity; for instance, the theme of the Oldham Literature Festival in October 2007 was 'Identity'. This brief description is not to imply that Gallery Oldham *only* ever hosted exhibitions related to local identity. Indeed, the gallery's activities in the late 2000s included exhibitions on subjects as diverse as Picasso, childhood, and British sculpture. However, the local component began to be more heavily stressed in its work, and they designed regular programmes each year to examine this.

For some professionals, the low level of interest from the local Asian community in cultural institutions was a reflection of the cultural content, which needed to better reflect their culture:

...the celebrating of normal culture has started and has done very well within a couple of museums in Manchester.... If you go to places like that and look at some museums all over the show and you see a crafter's cottage, how their people live, what did it smell like, you know...but now we've got to the realisation...that's not everybody, that history is not how it is. We've got different folk that need their history represented as much as the next man.

(Gallery Oldham employee)

One aspect of the Gallery's audience development work was to show how 'relevant' the collection is and how it reflected the visitors' own cultural background. For instance, it started to run courses for ethnic minority individuals to bring in objects of value to themselves and their families. This was intended partly to assure them that their judgements about what objects were of value were of significance – that a museum is a place which holds 'things that they thought were important to them and their family.' This mirrored the national trend for visitor-led collections and curating.

At the same time, cultural professionals were aware of the risk that 'inclusion' could become mere tokenism, and felt their aim should be to 'integrate' people through their differences, rather than maintaining separation. They wanted to use identity as a 'hook', to bring them into the building and widen their interest in the collection, so that they can be brought in to discover the other exhibitions in the space. To do this, they would hold regular consultations with local community groups to develop exhibition programming. Another way in which the Cultural Partnership tried to boost diversity was through the borough-wide events programme, holding outdoor festivals, and events that would attract families and 'non-traditional' audiences.[17] Thus, it was felt to be very important for cultural institutions in the town to appeal to a diverse range of people, and to engage with their cultural identity.

The aim to widen diversity in cultural organisations also segued with the wider borough commitment to 'community cohesion'.[18] This became a priority following the riots in 2001, when numerous government reviews pointed to the fragmentation and division between Oldham's different ethnic populations. Oldham Council's strategy therefore became oriented towards tackling racism, integrating different ethnic communities, and encouraging greater interaction and feelings of 'togetherness'. On one level, it was widely accepted that structural conditions and material inequality reinforced and exacerbated racial divisions, and the council tried to tackle the physical divisions rein-forced by area-based regeneration funding by moving towards 'theme' based funding, which was spread across geographical areas. Likewise, it became committed to services that brought together a cross-ethnic constituency (such as schooling, health, youth, and community work). But as well as addressing these structural factors, Oldham Council was encouraged to try to 'change attitudes' and address the sense of identity of ethnic but also white communities.

Both Cantle and Ritchie suggested that residential segregation – 'parallel lives' – had been encouraged by certain cultural attitudes within communities that should be tackled. They argued that immi-grant groups had allowed self-segregation to occur by allowing marriage to people abroad, not learning English sufficiently, and choosing to live in the same areas, even when offered homes in non-Asian areas. They also suggested that racist attitudes had been allowed to fester in white communities. Their proposed solutions, therefore, focused not only on addressing material disadvantage, but the 'problem' of strong cultural identification. The existence of strong social capital within communi-ties became presented as a barrier to cohesion with other communities. Cantle even argued that social capital and cultural identity determine economic well-being – inversing the usual sociological truism that it is structural conditions that shape cultural factors.[19]

As a result of these diagnoses, Oldham Council in the mid-2000s focused on 'tackling attitudes' and set upon a series of anti-racism poli-cies and programmes, particularly amongst young people, to encourage behavioural change. The Anti-Discriminatory Practice programme in education 'promotes positive identities in children drawing on black perspectives, also sexuality, religion and culture programmes'.[20] This approach sought to tackle racism through the realm of ethical-social behaviour, seeing it as a type of 'bad attitude' that could be changed through appropriate training and management. Numerous cultural organisations and initiatives were created to encourage inter-racial inter-action. Although established slightly earlier in 1991, the Peacemaker project has been an especially high-profile example of this. Set up by young Asian professionals to target young people and funded by the Youth Justice Board, Community and Young People's Unit, Neighbourhood Support Fund, and the Community Cohesion Facili-tation Grant, Peacemaker worked with young people to tackle 'racist tendencies' by using mentoring programmes, cultural and youth activ-ities, and anti-racism/cultural awareness training sessions for council staff (7).[21] The council also sought to adopt lessons from the experience of Northern Ireland, inviting mediation groups to give training workshops in conflict resolution (Oldham Partnership, 2006: 8). Racism was designated an 'attitude' which needed to be corrected through education, and possibly driven by deeper, psychological issues. As already highlighted, Cantle suggested that young white working-class men suffered from particularly low self-esteem, which might be a cause of tension (39).

In this wider context then, the arts (and sport) came to be seen to be particularly useful as a tool to re-engineer attitudes. Cantle (2001) advocated support for the arts as part of the cohesion agenda (see 6.23). In its response to the Ritchie Report, Oldham emphasised 'the major contribution that Oldham's libraries, museum's theatres and music make in fostering community cohesion.' (Oldham Metropolitan Borough Council, 2002: 35)

Some critics during this time attacked this post-riots emphasis on cultural difference as a way of avoiding harder questions of material deprivation. Bagguley and Hussain (2003) argue that Cantle and Ritchie blame residents (particularly Asians) for wanting to 'live amongst their own kind' rather than the lack of funds invested by central government in places like Oldham (3). The council itself, in its 187-page response to the Ritchie Report, blamed central government funding policies, stating that 'too much emphasis is placed on race as the issue within Oldham and not, as we believe, on poverty, deprivation and social inclusion and the competition for scarce resources' (Oldham Metropolitan Borough Council, 2002: 6). For instance, although Ritchie had called for more funding for housing, the council complained that this had not materialised. Unsurprisingly, central government actors preferred to emphasise better management strategies in relation to existing resources, whereas the council pursued increased funding from central government. Mahamdillie (2002) asserted that cultural difference was touted as a convenient way to avoid harder questions about real material problems; because New Labour 'refuses to enact policies that meet social need, it argues that the only option open to it is to mediate between different ethnic groups while spreading a general message of "tolerance"' (unpaginated). Mahamdillie's statement supposes that culture has become used almost cynically as a 'soft measure' to avoid other political responses, such as increased funding. However, seeing the emphasis on 'soft' factors as a cynical strategy underestimates the degree to which social problems like racism have become gradually redefined in policymaking circles as primarily cultural problems.

As I discussed in Chapter 2, local government is increasingly preoccupied with the decline of 'social capital' and cohesion. Even Oldham Council, which was initially critical of central government's emphasis on 'soft' causes of the riots, conceded that community cohesion was a problem and that they had to address attitudes as well as structural factors.

In his work on multiculturalism in the United Kingdom, Malik (2002b) has argued that councils and activists in the 1980s and 1990s moved from a political assessment of racial division based on structural factors, towards a 'culturalist' explanation. It was assumed that people belonging to different ethnic groups inevitably shared different needs and values, which the state should engage with.

It would be incorrect to overstate the importance Oldham Council attaches to culture in its overall strategy. It has implemented many other policies in order to deal with the problems of poverty and deprivation, for instance investing heavily in new housing developments. However, a brief examination shows how culture occupies a greater significance following the riots and is presumed to play a role in addressing problems of individual attitude and perception. I will now look at how these policies have played out in practice.

Ambiguities

Should cultural difference matter or not?

Oldham Council, following the riots, developed a more coherent cultural strategy which bound together local actors and organisations around the concept of 'diversity'. Arts and cultural activities were geared towards developing individuals and facilitating their economic and social inclusion. The arts were also expected to contribute to a sense of community and identity, and foster relationships between groups divided along ethnic lines.

Yet, despite this coherence of aims, certain tensions also emerged. One of the recurrent tensions was the degree to which cultural activities stressed the diversity or unity of people. On the one hand, culture was intended to provide a 'neutral space' in which people can leave behind their cultural identity and even examine it from a critical angle. David Edgar (2005), in his aforementioned *Observer* article, describes how this 'third space' can encourage people to transcend their cultural identity:

> Rather, you create third spaces, unfamiliar to both, in which different groups can share a similar experience of discovery. Sometimes such spaces allow people to detach aspects of their identity (cultural,

vocational, sexual) from what they have hitherto seen as its essential and dominating character.

The power of the interaction makes them realise their differences are not significant. As one mentor for the Peacemaker project stated in a newspaper interview:

> When you live in Oldham, you see how different people stick together. I didn't like that. It's just the colour of our skin that is making us live apart.
>
> When we got together with the guys from the Holts estate, we noticed we did have a lot of things in common, like the sports and films we liked. And some had the same opinions as myself. Before Peacemaker, I used to see people differently. The project really makes you think about British people.[22]

Yet, conversely, the cultural space is also supposed to remind people of their cultural difference and affirm their ethnic identity. As one council employee stated, 'I think there's room for people to celebrate their own cultures and to demonstrate their cultures to other groups.' Hence, cultural space is not just a place where people 'transcend' cultural differences but it is often where people are encouraged to relate to others *through* their cultural differences. As already shown, institutions like Gallery Oldham and the Coliseum started to engage ethnic groups by emphasising particular ethnic facets in their art. This stressed the particular connection of an individual to their ethnic group identity, as opposed to any another.

The Cantle and Ritchie reports also seemed to repeat this contradiction. Both argued that the emphasis on different cultures had bred divisions in Oldham. Yet both also proposed that an emphasis on culture and identity was a solution. They called for councils to do more to promote greater recognition of diversity and respect for different cultures. In the *Oldham Beyond* report in 2004, the authors criticised previous multicultural policies in the borough, yet advocated a new mode of cultural engagement: 'interculturalism', which focuses on bringing together different communities and encouraging discussion between them.

This ongoing concern with cultural difference and its apparent contradictions made it increasingly hard to know how to judge success. Was an emphasis on different cultures a positive sign or a sign of concern? Whilst there were considerable efforts by cultural providers to create a landscape of diverse practice, it was not always clear that this resulted in more integrated cultural and community activity. Some local ethnic cultural professionals received greater support, they also ended up with their 'own' cultural institutions, which led to a sense of separateness.[23] Peshkar's history is important in this regard: it was created in 1991 out of the Asian Arts workshops run by Oldham Council's Arts Development team. Its intention was to give recognition to South Asian experiences in the mainstream arts sector. Its long-term aim was to integrate South Asians into the theatre by encouraging them to enter the profession and get training ('we intend to become obsolete', as one employee explained to me). Yet, nearly two decades later, Peshkar remains in its own building and organisation, separate to the main theatre. Although it also attracts white audiences, its work largely emphasises the representation and exploration of the black and minority ethnic (BME) experience, appealing to BME audiences and writers. This suggests that whilst the long-term aim may be integration, it is difficult to make such a transition from the current framework of 'diverse' cultural provision.

Likewise, Oldham Coliseum continues today to have a largely white, middle-aged constituency. Although its expanded range of 'participatory' activities attracts large numbers of ethnic minorities, these have not tended to convert into regular theatregoers despite best efforts. It seems that one of the impulses behind expanding participation activities is a realisation that certain ethnic or socio-economic groups will not want to be 'passive' spectators and are extremely difficult to attract. This difference is accommodated by providing different kinds of programming. The Cultural Partnership measures the diversity of audiences through counting participants, but this obscures the underlying differences between how ethnic groups experience local cultural activities. As one local cultural professional admitted, the Partnership reached its 'stretch' target for ethnic minority participation 'basically because we put on the Mela' (a one-day Asian outdoor festival). There seems to be a recognition of the pragmatism to meet funders' requirements, and the difficulty of truly achieving an integrated mix of audiences and programming in cultural institutions. The impulse behind this mode of engagement seems to be based on finding out 'what appeals to people' in order to match targets, but it is much more difficult to connect such audiences to the 'mainstream' programme.

At the same time, despite the efforts of the council and cultural institutions, it seems difficult to break culture out of certain spatial, and therefore ethnic, boundaries. For instance, the more 'Anglo-Saxon' culture of Saddleworth (e.g. the annual folk music festival and brass band contests) is at a distance from the rest of Oldham. Conversely, there are disproportionately fewer visitors from Saddleworth to Gallery Oldham in the town centre.[24] Peshkar today operates mostly in the Asian areas of Oldham and although its workshops attract a mixed ethnic constituency, its work is largely targeted at Asians. One reason for the spatial concentration of cultural experiences is no doubt geographical distance. Furthermore, Saddleworth is said to have its own regional identity, attached to Yorkshire, which it borders.[25] *Oldham Beyond* alludes positively to this geographical diversity, suggesting that each community has its own identity. Yet it might also suggest that despite the rhetoric of 'diversity' cultural experiences do not necessarily bring distinct ethnic or geographical communities together into a common space. It would also appear that for at least a small group of white residents, there is a feeling that local cultural institutions have become too dominated by Asian culture, even though there was little evidence to show this was the case.[26]

Even within the council, there appears to be some disagreement about the extent to which people's ethnic identities should be an issue. One council official mentioned that the Oldham Race Equality Partnership 'wanted us to ask all these questions about religion and race on our library card but we said no. It's too intrusive really.' There is awareness that questions about ethnicity are intrusive, but at the same time the council cannot help but affirm the importance of ethnic identities in their own work. As one respondent at the Gallery (unnamed) suggested to me, in her opinion sometimes activities are funded because they are seen to be 'ethnic'.

In fact, this ambivalence towards cultural identity is evident in the history of policymaking in the area. Both the Cantle and Ritchie reports hovered between wanting to strengthen community identities and wanting to weaken their divisive impact. Part of the problem, they argued, was that the emphasis on diversity had alienated people from each other, making them feel they have different needs and values. The Asian and white communities may have similar aspirations for their town, but they were encouraged to feel culturally separate. This was exacerbated by housing and educational segregation. The dynamic therefore seems to be an acute awareness of difference. Yet at the same time, policymakers advise greater awareness and sensitivity around cultural difference. They assume these differences to be inevitable and in need of 'management'. Although strong ethnic communal identities were viewed as potentially disruptive, there was an overwhelming concern with building 'community leadership' and identities.

Furthermore, the council's cultural strategy, shaped as it was by public funding and government-led agendas in the mid-2000s, was so pre-occupied with managing cultural and ethnic difference that it largely ignored the role played by commercial and popular culture in the town. Oldham today still lacks very few centre-of-town cultural facil-ities like cinemas, bowling alleys, or other popular activities – which might transcend cultural differences more easily – but this did not seem to be a priority for the council officials. One might argue that the political rhetoric of difference blinded them to the fact that most young people in Oldham shared many similar cultural reference points already.

When culture became seen through the prism of ethnicity, it also led to another problem – how to conceptualise 'the white commu-nity'. Cantle suggested in point 6.48: '[the] white community should be encouraged to develop a leadership capacity in the same way as the black and ethnic minority communities' (50). This endorsed the racialisation of politics in Oldham by discussing the 'different' needs of communities and the need for 'cultural awareness'. Yet, for others, the idea of celebrating 'whiteness' had nationalist and racist connota-tions. For example, an employee of a local voluntary group association argued that in his experience ethnic groups in Oldham shared the same problems:

> I suspect that if the communities involved could have seen that they had the same problems, there wouldn't have been riots but there would have been a demonstration outside the community centre. I would have thought that would have ultimately been more whole-some and resulted in more positive outcomes for Oldham in the long term.

Yet, later in the interview he stated that despite these similarities, ethnic groups require different types of support to the white population. He did not believe that white groups should have their own representation like BME groups: 'I don't think there's a respectable group that would say we work for the white community...no, if that's what you're ask-ing, then I don't think so. No, I would have a problem with that....' The exclusion of Asians is interpreted as a problem of cultural differ-ence, whereas it is not for white people. Cultural recognition is seen as a legitimate form of empowerment for Asians and a way for the council to engage with them; however, the notion of a 'white' culture is not accept-able. Therefore, there seems to be some inconsistency in the approach to cultural identity and whether it requires a separate political identity or support.

Another concern was that the stress on diversity might lead to crude stereotypes about ethnic groups, and ignore the internal diversity of attitudes and interests. Interestingly, in my interviews, Asian cultural professionals seemed the most ambivalent about ethnic categories used by policymakers. They were more conscious of the differences *within* Asian communities than their white counterparts, pointing in particular to the gap between generations; for instance, Asian parents sometimes disapprove of letting their children (especially daughters) engage with theatre, dance, and music, fearing that their children might become 'westernised'. Young people also hold cultural attitudes and aspirations that their parents or peers frequently do not share. The rhetoric of diversity, therefore, seems to recognise mostly ethnic differences, but these can belie other, perhaps more significant differences between people. And, as stated earlier, the cultural differences between the Asian and white communities may not be so great in terms of popular or commercial cultural consumption (music, film, video games, food, etc.), as between generations – but official policy remains quite fixed on the former.

Therefore, as the policies of Oldham Council developed, many respondents showed full support for the principle of diversity, but they also felt ambivalence about how it defined groups, excluded others and could be restrictive in its approach. To some extent, it was recognised that the very words of cultural policy – 'diversity', 'access', and 'inclusion' – held little appeal to ordinary people in Oldham. These terms reflected the desires of funders and organisations rather than people at grass-roots level. One cultural professional stated that despite their constant attempts to engage people through identity, it seemed that ethnic groups were not really that interested:

> We've said we've got a project making banners and we'll be working with this group, that group and the other group and it's very difficult and you know you've got to do this to get the money, but the actual... I don't know, but the actual thing of engaging with certain groups is very difficult... But you know it's like with the tick boxes, they've got to be made to come, you've got to engage, you've got to whip them to come!

This suggests that 'diversity' emerged as a policy principle driven by official channels, rather than by demand 'from below', and that the benevolent promotion of difference was not always perceived to be effective by professionals.

Regulating tolerance

In Oldham, local policymakers treated cultural difference as inherently positive and in need of affirmation. For instance, Oldham Council used the phrase 'equal but different' in some of its corporate material.[27] As a result, difference was seen as natural or idealised – something to be accepted, not disagreed over or challenged. On one level, this approach emphasised the importance of tolerance between groups when sharing civic space, attending the same public events, sharing public services (like housing or youth centres), or interacting at a personal level (through polite, neighbourly relations). On another level, this threw up some difficulty in terms of how to deal with differences in viewpoint, attitude, or political perspective. Noticeably, there was little acknowledgement of political difference or debate in the policy literature or among local professionals. Inevitably, the tensions between ethnic groups were not solely based on prejudices and ignorance, but also disagreements about issues such as recent and ongoing immigration, crime, territory, and entitlement. Even if people were polite and tolerant about cultural differences, these disagreements remained present.

The council's emphasis was primarily on cultural interaction and exchange, rather than on political interaction and debate. It chose to support major festivals such as Oldham Carnival, every summer and attracting over 25,000 people, and activities which promoted 'joyous' interaction. In this sense, cultural space was about affirming pride and identity, or bringing people together, and there has been little concern about promoting discussion and exploring disagreements. If people were discussing ideas, it seemed to only be in small, private groups, rather than publicly supported 'cultural space'. Cultural activities did not tend to broach controversial issues in Oldham, but stayed within the realms of leisure, entertainment, or community 'togetherness'.

It is understandable that neither the council nor cultural professionals wished to use cultural activity to provoke disagreement, but this has left the question of how else to address such disagreements in a constructive and open way. Malik (2002b) argues that the promotion of difference is an unsatisfactory way to address political disagreements as it ensures the preservation of competing views, rather than a willingness to develop shared ideas and beliefs: 'A cohesive notion of citizenship cannot be based simply on the idea that we should respect other people's values. It requires a positive articulation of the values to which we should all aspire.' To develop common ideas would require laying out competing ethical, moral, and political principles and asking people to judge them against each other – in other words, to defend positions through debate with the intention of persuading others to agree with them. Conflict and disagreement, therefore, are necessary preconditions for developing a common identity. The stress in community cohesion literature on tolerating or 'respecting' other viewpoints, by contrast, allows difference to remain ever-present. Difference exists as a thing to be managed, rather than overcome. Rather than mixing with an intent to create new beliefs, ideas, and loyalties, it is just mixing for its own sake.

As a result, the council (albeit perhaps unwittingly) developed an impulse to regulate discussion and enforce the idea of 'respect' in Oldham. 'Respect' was a term that was never properly defined but indicated a sensitivity to, and positive acceptance of, a way of life or set of attitudes. This was illustrated in the way in which the council espoused open debate, yet deemed certain views to be inappropriate – particularly any comments that were racist, and therefore illegitimate or 'misrepresentative':

> We believe that community cohesion can only come about through people freely choosing to increase mutual understanding, interaction and participation in the life of the Borough, and that the process must be characterised by an honest, fair, frank and open debate using language that is shared and widely understood.
>
> (Oldham Metropolitan Borough Council, 2002: 15)

Yet, at the same time, Oldham Council felt compelled on a number of occasions to silence controversial opinion or confrontational discussion in the name of safety or community relations. In the 2001 local elections, the far-right British National Party (BNP) gained its strongest electoral result in the United Kingdom in more than a decade. In Oldham West and Royton, BNP leader Nick Griffin won 6552 votes (16.4 per cent), and in Oldham East and Saddleworth, the BNP candidate Mick Treacy won 5091 votes, almost 11 per cent of the total vote. Aware that the national media was watching, and concerned that the BNP would have a public platform, the council banned all political parties from speaking that evening, including the BNP winner, thereby refusing them their chance to speak to the electorate. This 'ban' was seen as a necessary way of alleviating tension in the town; a precedent had already been set by the Commission for Racial Equality which had made an official request to all three political parties not to play the 'race card' that year (O'Neill, 2001). In September 2001, the Home Secretary banned all public marches in Oldham until October on grounds of safety. Cantle (2001) pointed out that there were complaints from the public about the police's over-zealous restrictions on political marches against racism in the town, and festivals to celebrate cultural diversity (60). Both the Ritchie and the Cantle Reports advocated that political parties work together to agree common rules over how to discuss race – implying that such debate required policing for inappropriate language and statements. This approach coincided with a growth in anti-racism/cultural sensitivity training and schemes and an acceptance that Oldham Council had a role in presenting the 'correct' attitudes and ideas about race.

Culture also came to be seen around this time as a way to conduct this type of regulation and behavioural modification, allowing the authorities to train the way in which people engage with one another. This was particularly the case with young people, who were regarded somewhat anxiously by the authorities as being unable to engage with each other safely. They were thought to require interpersonal training, to insulate themselves from the cultural prejudices of their community, as well as being victims of the prejudices of others. For instance, a senior employee in the Oldham Youth Service explained about a project they had initiated in the late 2000s called 'Fusion': a week-long residential school for children which was designed to use culture and interaction to 'shift attitudes':

> ...because it's quite an intense experience it really does allow us to get into those underlying beliefs and values, and by experiencing being with other young people and other workers of different communities and cultures and taking part in workshops which are geared to raising awareness you can really shift their attitudes... By its nature, music's one of the key mechanisms we can use in terms of creating awareness and understanding and challenging attitudes and changing behaviour, we do a hell of a lot of music.

In this environment of tolerance and discussion, the youth service was expected to draw the line on certain 'inappropriate comments', or follow the racism incident procedure which all educational establishments must follow by law. But the line itself could be difficult to draw when matters of religion and politics were under discussion. As one youth worker explained to me, 'we're not allowed to promote any particular political belief or religion, though we wouldn't tolerate any behaviour or views that would oppress anyone because of their religion'. This raises the question: at what point does 'respect' for cultural difference become suppression of disagreement? And what is the appropriate role for the authorities in allowing debate to flow or not? The framework of culture seems inadequate to the task.

This is not to suggest that youth workers in Oldham could not discuss political issues with young people – no doubt many did – but their responsibility was set by official policy, was to discuss the issues at the level of personal ethics and individual behaviour, rather than engaging with the arguments such opinions represent. It would appear that the imperative was to avoid confrontation by invoking the need to respect cultural difference, even though there may be political disagreements underlying such attitudes. 'Common values' are assumed, rather than debated.

The stress on safety also led to some attempts to regulate public space and prevent potentially dangerous interaction between groups. 'The Wall' is a wrought-iron fence that was put up between Royle Close and Honeywell Lane in Hathershaw, following the riots. It effectively put a protective barrier between a predominantly white and a predominantly Asian community. Although welcomed by some locals in 2001, three years later locals interviewed in a newspaper said they wanted it to be removed as it felt divisive for locals (*The Asian News*, 2004). In September 2001, the police were also reported to have looked into applying to the Home Secretary for permission to instigate curfew laws in Oldham for young people in areas where there was likely to be 'trouble' (*The Asian News*, 2001a). Some of the council's tactics were borrowed directly from Northern Ireland, where community divisions along religious and territorial lines are notorious. In 2002 the council initiated the 'Building Good Relations' programme and employed Mediation Ireland to give mediation training to council staff (Institute of Community Cohesion, 2006). Interestingly, the local police also took on an arbitration role, insisting on their right to designate other people's actions and behaviour as racist, even in some cases where the individuals concerned (victims and aggressors) deny this to be the case (O'Neill, 2001; *The Asian News*, 2001b).

These examples show that although there emerged a discourse of shared space and unity in Oldham's cultural and community strategies, it coexisted with a concern to manage difference and even, to some extent, regulate public space and interaction. This is not to suggest failure on the part of the local authorities necessarily, but instead to point to the limitations of cultural discourse in addressing socio-political tensions. The reification of difference as something beyond scrutiny or intellectual debate leaves it as a source of potential tension that requires official monitoring.

Role of state and official recognition of culture

Policymakers in Oldham started to take an interest in culture not only for its measurable economic and social outcomes, but also as part of an attempt to re-engineer attitudes of citizens and minimise confrontation. One aspect of this was to use culture to promote tolerance and diversity amongst different groups. Oldham Council and its funded bodies took on the function of bestowing recognition upon certain cultural identities, symbols, or attitudes, as well as censoring or criticising others. This primarily played out through stories in the local media, whereby Oldham Council tried to demonstrate its credentials as an inclusive organisation that respects difference. For instance, in March 2002, council leaders publicised their decision to fly the Union Jack flag at all times at the Civic Centre, as a way to reclaim it as a symbol from the extreme right. It also stated it would fly the Pakistani, Indian, and Bangladeshi flags for the duration of official visits from those countries (*The Asian News*, 2002). These measures were clearly driven by a desire to positively value difference in order to make local ethnic populations feel included.

However, there was also concern that certain identities are confrontational and therefore should not be valorised in public. An example of this, which I came across in 2007, was a recurrent rumour from local people that the council had banned the flying of the English national flag. Although this is not really a well-established tradition in the town (nor, arguably in England), it has become a political issue in recent years through the local and national media, particularly since the European Football Championships in 1996, when England hosted the competition and the flag was visibly popular throughout the country. No-one I spoke to (Asian or white) seemed to know why or when this had happened, although they believed it was 'typical'. One respondent suggested it might be because of health and safety issues, whereas another suggested it was probably to prevent causing offence to local Asians. It transpired that, according to the Ritchie Report, the flag had been removed from some town lamp posts because permission had not been sought and they were considered a road hazard. The incident grew into an urban myth, possibly spread by the local BNP and exacerbated by other stories of bans and 'political correctness' in the national media. However, the willingness of some people to believe it was real pointed to a very genuine feeling that white culture was regarded as harmful by the authorities. The message of this widely accepted urban myth was clear: Oldham Council did not want white people to celebrate their identity in this way because it was a risk to local community relations.

The truth was far more complex. On the one hand, the council stated that white culture needs recognition in some way. In its report, *Forward Together*, Oldham Council echoed comments by a Government Neighbourhood Renewal Advisor that highlighted the need for white communities to be given opportunities to express and celebrate their culture alongside the other communities of Oldham. 'An important issue is the need to recognise and value the culture and heritage of Oldham's white, working class communities' (Oldham Metropolitan Borough Council, 2004b: 9).

At the same time, local policymakers were anxious about affirming 'white' or 'English' identity as this could lead to tensions. For instance, although Oldham Council supported St George's Day events in the town, particularly in predominantly white areas such as Royton and Saddleworth, one official admitted there was little demand for it elsewhere, and went on to explain, 'I think I would be concerned about getting too involved in something that was billed as something that was particularly English event. Yes, I would be concerned about that really, because I'd rather be promoting an event that was all inclusive.' When I asked why an 'English' event was considered to be more 'exclusive' than, say, Bangladeshi cultural events, she responded: 'Because I think St George's Day has particular connotations. Because in a way it's been hijacked for political purposes and I think that's something that we'd want to avoid. I know that one of the big parades as part of Streets Ahead in Manchester falls on St George's Day and there was a bit of trouble at that with the BNP.'

This would suggest that the council is aware that certain cultural symbols and identifications are politically charged and therefore 'off-limits'. In particular, there is awareness that extreme right groups have seized upon the importance of culture and are using symbols like the St George's flag to express their own grievances. Despite the ethic to celebrate all cultures and identities, Oldham Council is in a precarious position, because some cultures and identities are inherently confrontational and politicised.

Therefore, although the council does not have a policy to exclude white culture, its politicised approach to cultural symbols and the anxiety people feel about 'white culture' means that there is a widespread perception that it does. In this sense, there is a paradox in the council's strategy: it has sought to use ethnic culture and identity as a way to promote diversity and inclusion but has potentially fuelled a sense of exclusion from other groups. White groups feel disenfranchised, but also resentful at what is perceived to be special treatment of Asians. A senior figure in the local cultural partnership said:

> It's an issue, it's a real issue. These economically disadvantaged communities look at the Millennium Centre [owned by the Oldham Bangladeshi Association]... I can understand if you live in squalor.... Ignorance breeds resentment.

Indeed, the flag has become a way not only of expressing a benevolent English or 'white identity', it has also become symbolic of a sense of grievance and loss, which is aggressive in character. The problem with 'white culture' is the more potent and aggressive it becomes, the more reluctant the authorities are to incorporate it, creating a vicious cycle.

Whilst the council did not appear to recognise or acknowledge the problems about 'white culture' in its policy literature, this seems to surface in other, unofficial discourse, such as rumours and newspaper articles which may or may not be substantiated. For instance, one story that circulated was about how the council had not included Christmas in its official diaries and calendars (*The Asian News*, 2007). A majority of the people I interviewed during my fieldwork expressed concern about 'political correctness' in the town. Although few people believed that words or arguments were actually banned (indeed, there was a sort of light-hearted mocking sense in their statements), there was a belief that certain criticisms could not be made. Some regarded the efforts of anti-racism advocates as unnecessary and self-congratulatory, rather than helpful. One respondent felt that anti-racist groups from outside Oldham overplayed the influence of the BNP and were just 'stirring up trouble' rather than dealing with the 'real' issues of poverty and education. Another Asian person echoed this by saying that he thought the issue of racism had been exaggerated and that there was too much 'political correctness':

> I think it's silly... people are entitled to their own culture. Asian people think it's a bit barmy sometimes. That's down to councillors who aren't in touch with the communities they serve. It sends out a dangerous message – we're a special case, we're really easy to offend,

we're not chilled out like white people, and others then might say we don't want a mosque in our street...It's bureaucrats making these decisions.

Even if the council was not regularly banning activities or censoring speech, it seemed to be deploying culture instrumentally as a tool to change attitudes, and therefore its decisions were seen to be driven by political imperatives, such as avoiding controversy or offence to particular groups. The flipside to regulating tolerance is mistrust on the part of those who feel they are being regulated or those who feel their own views are not also being taken into account. This seems to them to be a zero-sum game. One group's claim to victimisation detracts from another's victim status. In this context, it is difficult for authorities to intervene and give recognition to cultural symbols whilst maintaining credibility as impartial regulators. The lack of trust in its authority to bestow recognition leads to a circular pressure: to consult further with the communities, and thus to invite further resentment from those communities that have not been properly consulted.

In her study of racial tensions in the United States, Terry Ann Knopf (2006) explains how the pervasiveness of race rumours indicates an underlying social conflict. They thrive where situations are ambiguous and officials do not make their positions on particular issues clear. Lack of transparency can lead to suspicion and the loss of trust in official channels. Fine and Turner (2001) suggest that rumours serve an expressive function in a climate where more public channels are censored or closed to certain opinions:

> What happens when we dare not speak these beliefs? What happens when we deny – to ourselves and to others – that we hold them because we have come to accept that they are morally illegitimate? We believe that two responses are common. First, we become ashamed; we withdraw from dialogue...Second, following from this, we become too willing to accept claims of 'actual happenings' that support these hidden beliefs. (16)

This reaction seems evident in the United Kingdom in recent years. Hewitt (2005) describes how a white backlash developed in South East London in response to race equality measures and the intense media interest following the racially motivated murder of the young black youth Stephen Lawrence. He describes how racism was 'tucked away' amongst the politically powerless white working class, who had festering grievances – their rumours grew through neighbourhood talk, rumour, narrative, and counter-narrative (34). The authorities' tactics to silence these views by 'scary and oblique references' to the BNP ended up reinforcing the sense of shame people felt, and further drove these views underground without proper scrutiny. Likewise, stories about 'political correctness gone mad' in the media have been shown in newspaper reports to be urban myths (Taylor, D., 2002; Burkeman, 2006). However, the point is that such stories only have credence amongst the public because they reflect the widespread suspicion that cultural policy decisions are driven by political motives.

It would be impossible without further research to speculate on the extent to which such rumours have become widespread in Oldham, but local cultural professionals at least acknowledge that some white people feel frustrated in or excluded from the cultural space. Diversity policies seem to fuel their resentment, and furthermore their identification with 'whiteness'. This becomes a vicious circle, because as the white identity becomes more politicised and controversial, the harder it is for the council to incorporate it into the non-confrontational discourse of diversity.

Hence, there is a contradictory tension between, on the one hand, a reaction against overbearing, intrusive regulation and 'political correctness' and, on the other hand, a demand for more official management of diversity and recognition of identity. For instance, Cantle noted critically in his 2006 report that people in Oldham 'wanted to ask questions around faith and culture, but were afraid to do so because it might be thought "politically incorrect"' (Institute of Community Cohesion, 2006: 49). He argued that a more honest and open debate was needed to broach difficult issues. Yet he then pointed out the need for the council to institute more cultural awareness training within the voluntary and community sector, suggesting that people required guidance from the authorities in how to approach culturally sensitive subjects. As long as difference is reified and cannot be properly debated, it haunts social interactions as a potential source of tension that requires official management. Yet increasingly, the council struggles to maintain the credibility required to play this role.

Trying to move on from the riots

It is very difficult to judge the extent to which social divisions have increased or decreased in Oldham since the council implemented its post-2001 riots strategy. As such, it is hard to assess whether its cultural strategy achieved its objectives except through anecdotal evidence and abstract statistics. At the extreme level of violent or verbal confrontation, there has been a substantial reduction in the number of racist incidents reported to the police – from 1300 a month in 2001 to 360 in 2011. Indicators such as racial incident reporting can only give a partial account of wider attitudes towards race, and it would be unlikely for personal beliefs and community relations to change overnight. In 2006, the Cantle Report noted that Oldham had taken important practical steps in addressing racial segregation and achieved some short-term successes.[28] Yet he expressed concern that the problems of division remained pertinent. He suggested, furthermore, that regardless of how much structural change was put in place, division would continue to be a problem as long as communities were stuck in their attitudes about difference:

> This is as much in the minds of people as in neighbourhood structures and is at odds with experience in many other areas of the country. Hence our view that if you want to change a community, the community must want to change. In short, polarised communities continue to be a significant feature of relations across all sections of Oldham society.[29]

Yet, although Cantle calls on the people of Oldham to change their 'attitudes', it is worth considering how official policy was itself deeply ambivalent and confused about how to 'manage' difference. Policy initiatives and advice (including Cantle's) often made a paradoxical case; asking people to 'celebrate' and 'respect' their differences, whilst at the same time berating people for feeling that they are different. It may even be possible that such confusion served to reinforce existing tensions in the town, so that the subtle nuances and confusions of the policy discourse mediate ethnic division anew.

Overall, the stress on cultural difference reflected how Oldham is caught between two contradictory impulses – to forget the riots altogether or to focus on ethnic division as the central cause of the town's problems. In 2004, Oldham MP, Phil Woolas, and former Oldham Mayor, Councillor Riaz Ahmed, reacted angrily to news that a former student of the Oldham Sixth Form College was planning a production of *Romeo and Juliet* set in Oldham, at the Manchester Royal Exchange Theatre. The play was intended to examine some of the tensions arising out of the riots. But Woolas said it was time for the town to 'move on', and 'unfortunately we just can't seem to stop people talking about the riots' (*The Asian News*, 2004). This criticism seems unfair, considering that the council itself has placed so much emphasis on ethnic divisions and community cohesion, particularly in its own cultural strategy. It is difficult for the town to 'move on' from the riots and race-related troubles when they became a defining element in Oldham's cultural policy. It was not simply the people of Oldham who remained caught in the prison of 'cultural difference', but the council itself.

Yet, there are signs that more recently Oldham Council has recognised this problem and has adopted a slightly different language when talking about its plans by reaching for a language beyond cultural difference. Rather than looking to develop projects in reaction to public funding and in isolation, the council has tried to frame Oldham's growth in relation to the Greater Manchester 'city-region'. This shift brings a fresh perspective on addressing economic problems and there is a strong emphasis on improving education for young people who can participate in this wider economy. This approach also seems to be less dominated by the concern to manage cultural difference and ethnic division in the town, possibly even accepting that identities will change and evolve in the context of a more dynamic social context.

In 2010, Oldham Council merged two failing secondary schools in the town: Breeze Hill, with a predominantly Asian intake, and Counthill, with a predominantly white intake. The result is the new Waterhead Academy, sponsored by Oldham College, a local further education college. The intention is to bring together young people into a shared environment, overcoming the entrenched segregation that exists in most Oldham schools, but also improve school achievement (although the creation of the new single campus will not be complete until 2012). Most importantly, the school authorities have placed the emphasis firmly on raising attainment and educational outcomes, rather than on community cohesion or mixing. They have focused on articulating a language of shared goals and aspirations, which see community cohesion as a secondary or indirect result, not the primary aim. In a special feature on BBC 2's *Newsnight* television programme, the Principal of the Waterhead Academy, David Yates, was asked by the interviewer, 'What do you think comes first, academic achievement or mixing?' He replied:

> Academic achievement . . . schools are a place of learning . . . that is a dictionary definition of the word 'school'. I strongly believe if we can switch the students on to learning and achievement and progress then – not the rest takes care of itself, that's far too simplistic – but when students are put together who all need to add fractions

together it doesn't matter somebody's skin colour, we're all there for a common purpose we're all here to improve our maths grade.

In other words, a focus on the shared aspiration for educational improvement allows people to come together, regardless of ethnic divisions. This comment indicates awareness of the complexities of bringing together divided communities and the need to find a common ground beyond 'difference' and ethnicity.

Conclusion

In this case study I have examined how culture was used to address a set of social problems in Oldham following the 2001 riots. There was initially a strong economic motive behind the local cultural strategy along the lines of stimulating creative industries, attracting the 'creative class', and improving individual employability, but also an emphasis on the value of culture in addressing community divisions and 'healing' psychological issues.

Overall, 'diversity' became a guiding principle, which led to the main arts institutions in Oldham developing inclusive strategies to celebrate cultural difference. Culture became seen as a way to bring people together in a way that politics cannot. However, over time, there has emerged some ambivalence about the principle of diversity, and the extent to which difference can bring people together or not. Furthermore, the stress on cultural identity can be exclusive as well as inclusive, and can mask differences within groups. And whilst culture is useful for bringing people together through ethical or 'joyous' connections, it has been unable to address the need for political argument and debate.

The turn to culture following the 2001 riots encouraged the local council to take on a new role in managing local attitudes and regulating tolerance. However, the politicised nature of cultural policy and the principle of 'diversity' meant that the council's cultural authority eventually came to be treated locally with some scepticism. Cultural policy therefore became a source of contention as well as a tool for achieving harmony.

More recently again, there are signs that Oldham Council is trying to shift its approach and focus on new ways of engaging the local population, for instance through more integrated schooling and a new emphasis on participating in the wider city-region of Manchester. As policymaking evolves, it will be interesting to see how far the council can move on from the language of difference which was so dominant in the immediate aftermath of the riots.

5
Analysis: The Case for Universalism

It is clear from the previous chapters that local government, arts organisations, and arts agencies have in recent years become re-oriented around the notions of diversity and identity – a new set of values which underpin cultural policymaking in the twenty-first century. The previous two chapters explored the lived reality of cultural policy – examining the rationales by which cultural projects are enacted and some of the conflicts that arise. Of course, not all cultural projects and schemes are alike, and not all will encounter the same extent of problems. The case studies take into account the unique political, social, and economic circumstances, plus the motivations and actions of organisations and actors involved. Yet, by investigating these examples in depth, we can begin to see some of the broader faultiness that runs through cultural policymaking today and ideas of 'cultural diversity'. These studies show us how the confusion and ambivalence about cultural value at a philosophical level manifests itself in day-to-day operations.

As I explained in Chapter 1, cultural policy in the modern era has, historically, relied on a notion of 'universalism' for its legitimacy. The public nature of cultural policy means that its authority cannot rest merely on the arbitrary, private taste of individuals, but upon more objective criteria of judgement, derived from knowledge or critical insight that is (theoretically at least) available to everyone. Internally related to this are aesthetic concepts of standards, quality, and judgement, that is, that certain things are 'good enough' to be in an art museum or gallery. In this mode, culture is presumed to be something one cultivates through learning, reason, and imaginative or intellectual engagement, rather than something one is born with or 'absorbs' from living within a local or particular community. The appreciation

155

of culture is seen to be something that transcends the different relative experiences of human beings and, therefore, can belong to humanity as a whole. The implied purpose of a universalist cultural policy is to impart 'the best' of culture, even though 'the best' might be constantly changing, and even contested. Implicit in these assumptions is also a view of human beings as sharing a universal quality – an ability to transcend differences and make connections beyond ethnic or cultural groupings.

In the early twenty-first century, this model is under serious challenge. The notion of 'cultural authority' has been undermined and, along with it, the type of subjectivity that characterised the Modernist project. The 'postmodern' project offers a new principle of 'cultural diversity', based on a new model of subjectivity. This has been promoted and institutionalised over the past three decades through the New Left/community arts movement, and self-consciously rejects the older model of cultural policy.

The new model of cultural policy does not regard culture as having universal value or aspiring to this claim, but presents a view of culture as something that is inherently differentiated according to the identities of end users (or consumers). As such, this approach not only argues that the cultural 'canon' is outdated or irrelevant, but that its very premise – the ability to judge cultural products through aesthetic or historical categories – is flawed. The value of culture is presumed to be relative, resting upon its authenticity and representativeness. Implicit in this reading of culture is a view of human beings as being determined by their cultural identity and inherently differentiated. The emphasis on diversity is also ethically instructive about the nature of citizenship and behaviour in social life, teaching people to accept and tolerate differences, rather than see them as mutable. The individual person is also regarded as vulnerable and lacking in agency – their group cultural identity being seen as something core to their self-worth and in need of preservation and recognition. Culture is a useful tool to fashion a new kind of citizen and help him or her to deal with a range of problems, urban decline, unemployment, lack of identity, community fragmentation, and so on. This new kind of engagement with the individual subject results in an emphasis on the economic and social or therapeutic value of culture in the discourse of cultural policy.

The focus of much cultural policy is about making socially excluded individuals employable and responsible in a new, flexible labour market and generating economic opportunities by changing individual behaviour. One could argue that this is still articulated in the conventional economic language of 'upskilling'. However, there is also a tendency in this skills discourse to refer to 'soft skills', such as communication, creative-thinking, and empathy, which all have a clear psychological emphasis. Cultural projects and participation enable people to gain 'confidence', 'self-esteem', and 'well-being', which in turn are supposed to help them become productive and entrepreneurial. Furthermore, cultural policy helps individuals deal with the emotional effects of structural problems which they feel little control over, and can bind them to a community.

This emphasis on psychological factors supports Furedi's description of a 'therapy culture' in broader society and its promotion and perpetuation by the state (albeit incoherent at times and not always effectively managed). Policymakers have turned to cultural policy as a way to address the presumed demand for and identity from ordinary citizens. As I have already suggested, the rhetoric of cultural policy reflects the dominance of the ideas of the New Left, which Stuart Hall states was partly about recognising 'the return of the subjective' in social and political analyses (Hall, S., 1989: 120–1). Terry Eagleton (2000) argues that the turn to culture in this way is fundamentally utopian, a desire to achieve in the realm of the imagination a resolution of the fundamental structural contradictions of capital. For him, the post-structuralist turn to culture attributes historical agency to individuated, culturised strategies of representation at the realm of consumption, thus abandoning collective strategies at the level of production.

The use of culture to change attitudes also has a strong political dimension. As I showed in Chapter 2, culture has become regarded by the local state as an alternative way to engage individuals and mediate the contradictions of social experience – alienation – under capitalism today. The Rich Mix centre is expected to engage the local community in the regeneration process and help nurture their cultural identity. In Oldham, arts and cultural activities are valued for encouraging participation in a way that more conventional modes of political engagement seem unable to. It is accepted wisdom that culture offers a new, updated approach to engaging with citizens, particularly minority groups. Culture allows room for emotional engagement and subjective experience. It is not 'rational' and therefore, based on judgements between one type of idea over another, but rather, it allows differences and competing value systems to co-exist. This approach focuses on people's different and particular cultural identities as members of communities (being black, Asian, female, gay, disabled, and so on) rather than on the ideal of the colour-blind, 'universal' citizen who is engaged with abstract ideas and argument. The concept of diversity is also part of a desire to change attitudes about difference and teach people to be more 'tolerant' and 'respectful'. In this sense, cultural policy has both a practical/instrumental dimension, but also a moral/ethical one.

It is clear from the case studies that this new cultural policy discourse is not simply imposed by the state; rather, it is fashioned by actors in state and non-state organisations working in 'partnership': artists, arts organisations, community and voluntary groups, regeneration agencies, private and public funding bodies. Despite tensions and disagreements between actors, there is a degree of consensus about the social and instrumental value of culture. Indeed, it is often cultural practitioners who are driving the 'cultural turn' and trying to integrate culture into regeneration issues, often 'attaching' themselves to increase their influence, as Gray (2002) suggests. This ideology is also something that cross-fertilises across regions, institutions, and agencies, creating 'stereotyped ideological responses' (Dunleavy, 1980). 'Issue entrepreneurs' like Comedia have spread ideas about cultural policy widely.

As I have suggested, many of the artists, activists, and community organisations in both Tower Hamlets and Oldham accepted the economic, instrumentalist objectives for cultural policy, although they tended to combine it with broader arguments about personal development. Thus, whilst there are differences and, to some extent, antagonisms between how groups rationalise cultural policy, they largely share an instrumentalist view of culture and there is a mixing of economic and social/community discourses.

However, whilst there is a clear consistency about the overall importance of culture to social life, actors in different sectors articulated the rationales for this slightly differently, and sometimes, self-consciously, in opposition to each other.

In Tower Hamlets, for example, local cultural organisations worked 'in partnership' with the council, but within their own network they expressed cynicism and resentment about the council's policies. The community-based artists' network, which was self-avowedly 'radical' and anti-establishment in character, was fairly critical about what it saw as the economically driven nature of Tower Hamlets' cultural policy. This did not tend to translate into practical opposition of much consequence, but resulted in a widespread feeling of suspicion. In Oldham there was greater consensus between the local political and cultural elite, and a degree of partnership oriented around using culture for social goals. But tensions arose in the way in which the local population perceive cultural interventions as being politically motivated. There has also been confusion in policymaking generally about the appropriate emphasis on difference. The Arts Council's cultural diversity projects have been criticised widely for being ill-judged and failing to address underlying problems. The result is a feeling of suspicion and cynicism from the artists who are supposed to benefit. In all these cases, the trust in cultural decisions is weakened by a suspicion that people with an ulterior motive are using culture for their own purposes.

This shift in cultural policy goes beyond questions of culture in the narrower, artistic sense, and points to a shift in attitudes towards the human subject itself, particularly the idea that individual humans can transcend their subjective experience and acquire a more objective position from which to view the world and their place in it. The meaning of culture is emptied of the dialectical tension which Williams (2000) captured in his two-fold definition of culture as something that is 'ordinary' and also reflective and critical. Calcutt (2005) explains that by privileging the 'ordinary' cultural thinking inevitably stops at the level of surface appearance and meaning, and its potential for critique remains rather limited. Culturalism, he argues, is an expression of conventionalism, and a circular emphasis on intersubjective relations rather than social relations (104, 118). It ceases to have any penetrative power; that is, it is 'nothing special' or transcendent and everyone has their own 'cultures'. It also loses its critical, transformative power, merely mirroring or representing social relations as they are. The emphasis on culture today is not a celebration of its universality, but rather a rejection of abstract thinking and the ability to distinguish the merits of certain truth claims against others. This, I suggest, has implications for the cultural sector, but also reflects changes in broader political life today. If culture is just what we experience subjectively, it loses its power to change our world view, and thus our power to change the world.

To clarify, I present here two models of cultural policy relating to Universalism and Identity, in order to draw out their distinct characteristics. These are 'ideal types' in the Weberian sense, and have never existed in pure form in reality. They distil the essential features of competing ideological models of culture.

Two 'ideal' models of cultural policy

Universalist cultural policy	Identity-based cultural policy
Assumes a stable and unified subject. Capable of transcending subjective realm through abstraction.	Assumes an unstable, fragmented subject. Perspective is inevitably particular.
Possibility of objective knowledge.	Subjective knowledge. Partial insights are the limits of truth.
Culture as critique.	Culture as affirmation.
Subject can mediate ideas through reason and argument.	Subject can mediate subjective experience through emotion and empathy.
Unifies the general and the particular.	Splits the general and particular.
Robust, autonomous individual who determines own identity.	Vulnerable individual, dependent on recognition by others.
Culture is open to development and change.	Culture requires protection and continuity.
Subject shapes culture.	Subject shaped by culture.
'Nothing human is alien to me'.	'Relevance'.
Hierarchy of judgements.	Relativisation of judgements.
Autonomy: trusted to form relations with others.	Invites regulation: inherent differences can lead to conflict.
Social subject.	Atomised subject.

There are a number of 'clashes' which can be discerned. The first is about the nature of authority and cultural value.

I would suggest that there is a contradictory tension within the diversity model of cultural policy – the cultural institution necessarily gives value to its chosen display of objects, but at the same time it must seek to show this value as relative. Stuart Hall (2001) describes this as the need 'to destabilise its own stabilities'. This contradictory pull in the discourse is not acknowledged in official cultural policy literature, yet it tugs at the foundational premise of the cultural institution.

The *raison d'être* of the cultural institution – taking objects, words, or images out of ordinary life and placing them in a special, public space – means that it *cannot but* make a claim to universal value. The meaning of this gesture is to make a statement about the worthiness of the object as cultural, which deems it appropriate for public esteem, rather than private preference or mere monetary value. Conversely, if cultural institutions are expected to recognise all people as being equally creative and capable of producing great culture, it reduces all creativity – all culture – to being ordinary. What, then, is the point of the special space of the museum? Why should it have any value that distinguishes it from the everyday street? With what authority does the cultural institution choose, display, or perform particular cultural forms if the only criterion is that it is authentically 'ordinary'? The recognition of culture cannot be empowering if a body without any transcendental authority bestows it.

This fact is most exemplified in the early problems of the Rich Mix project. On the one hand, Rich Mix rejected the notion of universality, which historically guided the work of older galleries (for instance, its neighbour, the Whitechapel Art Gallery), and claimed that culture is always bound to the logic of particular community traditions, that is, 'identity'. Hence 'high art' inevitably excludes minority cultures. However, the project had no other authority upon which to build its prestige. It was not sufficiently 'authentic' and by privileging artistic excellence over leisure, it did not provide the 'community' with what it wanted. According to people involved in Rich Mix and the wider cultural network, many local residents either resented the centre for being too 'arty', too 'populist', or being 'too ethnic', and 'not for them'. This tension is unsurprising when artists involved in the project at a senior level also expressed ambivalence about it being a 'community project'. Whilst they supported the idea of diversity in principle, they personally did not want to be seen as 'black' artists, or judged on the basis of how 'authentic' or representative they were of a particular community. Interestingly, whilst Rich Mix began its life as a critique of the arts establishment, it ended up seeking its legitimacy and credibility from it.

Connected to this was considerable ambivalence amongst artists in the area of Tower Hamlets about the pragmatic instrumentalism of cultural policy, and a concern that this might impede a 'pure' artistic rationale with 'box ticking' and tokenism. This tension between competing notions of value – authenticity and aesthetic excellence, instrumentalism, and artistic autonomy – no doubt represent two very different strands of influence – a strong independent artistic community, and a strong community/voluntary sector – and many artists co-exist within both.

Rich Mix struggled to combine universal and particularistic conceptions of value, and was unable to satisfy either. Its lack of coherence resulted in anxiety about the content and purpose of exhibitions or performances. Without a regular visiting public or founding vision to guide the centre, it became free-floating, unstable, and infinitely malleable to diverse expectations. Actors involved in Rich Mix believed the problems it faces arise from conflicting partners, lack of funding, or local cynicism, but they actually resided in the philosophical contradictions of the project itself. These contradictions then amplified the institutional problems of securing an audience, funding, and credibility.

Oldham, by contrast, did not have this same clash of values or confusion about the purpose of culture. This was partly because the notion of 'art for art's sake' was less pronounced, but also because there was a greater degree of consensus around its instrumentalism. Arguably, the existence of a historical collection also gave certain cultural institutions like Gallery Oldham a much stronger sense of identity and purpose. However, there was a tension within Oldham about the authority of cultural policy choices and how things were decided upon. It is clear that cultural choices were not based solely on objective artistic or cultural principles, but on the basis of what is authentic or politically desirable; in other words, culture was *politicised*. Oldham Council's cultural policy was visibly expedient, and concerned with addressing the wishes of certain parts of the 'local community'. Whilst recognition through benevolent symbolic gestures might 'reassure' members of minority groups, it can result in anger from others. That this resentment came to be expressed in anger about cultural symbols (rumours about flag flying, and so on) was not surprising as this was how inclusion issues were often discussed in the area. From my interviews with local actors, it appeared that there was an attitude amongst some residents that cultural institutions like the gallery and theatre were being run by people who are not 'like us'. To what extent this was actually true is not the point – the politicisation of culture opens up the possibility for mistrust. If art is being privileged because of its value as a tool of community cohesion, there is suspicion that it is not 'good enough' in artistic terms. There was also, on the part of some members of the white community at least, a suspicion that *their* culture was politically too disruptive. Indeed, even the nature of a politicised or ethnicised art policy opens up the possibility for communities to talk about 'their art'.

The evacuation of universalism undermines cultural authority. This means that there is a less clear and transparent basis upon which cultural institutions can carry out their work. Brighton (1999) makes the point that managerial expertise has replaced cultural experts as the basis of authority, and that despite the claims to being more democratic and participatory, this allows a creeping authoritarianism. Cultural policy is determined by the arbitrary wishes of a political elite and non-artistic objectives, such as boosting visitor numbers, increasing the ethnic diversity of the audiences, addressing social problems, and cutting costs. Without the claim to the impartiality of aesthetic criteria, the cultural institution exposes its political agenda explicitly, depleting its own moral authority and claim to accountability. It is paradoxical that whilst cultural policy is presented as a spur to greater participation from the citizenry, in reality, there is evidence to suggest that citizens feel disengaged from cultural policies in their area.

The politicisation of culture as a tool of the state has potentially anti-democratic implications. The state presumes that culture should be used as a tool, almost like marketing or advertising, to re-engineer the citizen's attitudes and behaviour. This approach expects people to engage with culture passively, as uncritical consumers. Adorno's critique of 'the culture industry' seems pertinent here:

> Although the culture industry undeniably speculates on the conscious and unconscious state of the millions towards which it is directed, the masses are not primary, but secondary, they are an object of calculation; an appendage of the machinery. The customer is not king, as the culture industry would have us believe, not its subject but its object... The culture industry misuses its concern for the masses in order to duplicate, reinforce and strengthen their mentality, which it presumes is given and unchangeable. How this mentality might be changed is excluded throughout.
>
> (Adorno, 2001: 99)

Although Adorno's critique here focuses on commercial culture, his critique of a consumerised relationship between individual and culture might be just as well applied to state support for culture. Individuals are presumed unable to develop their taste beyond the familiar and comfortable. In this way, the consumerist approach also reduces the worth of cultural content to whether people like it; that is, if it can attract an audience. If the cultural content is controversial or offends a particular ethnic group, it is deemed to be of less value. Again, in Tower Hamlets, there was some discomfort amongst artists about self-censorship for this purpose, yet at the same time a clear desire to gain legitimacy by showing more 'sensitivity' to a particular ethnic community. This concern about the offensiveness of culture meant Rich Mix risked submitting to more policing by so-called community leaders or local politicians. The artist's freedom to explore the 'truth' is compromised by political sensitivity to the feelings of the local community. The principle of consumer choice further relativises the authority of cultural institutions such as museums and galleries, because it maintains that the worth of art on display can only ever be based on subjective judgement or 'taste'.

Yet, if the stress on diversity and consumerism cannot deliver the required cultural authority for an institution to operate, is it desirable to return to some more traditional notion of 'universalism' in art? Clearly, the idea of absolute, dehistoricised value seems naïve to us today. The period of modernity has brought with it a greater understanding of the contingency of value and its relative nature to society.

Yet, because cultural value is not absolute or 'divine', this does not mean, *prima facie,* that it is entirely fluid, insubstantial, or 'unreal'. The value of culture is not inherent to the material particles of the object, but rather it lies within its relationship to human society. As such, culture emerges as a concrete product of a particular society at a particular time, but is also something which can be viewed and appreciated in abstraction, from another period. Culture has its own internal, constantly unfolding logic – which allows us to appreciate it outside the immediate context in which it was created. This internal value relies on the capacity of humans to abstract an object from its particular society and judge it in relation to other cultures and knowledge. Such an approach presumes that all cultural products have – at some level – a degree of commensurability. This does not mean sameness; rather, it means we are able to view them through the use of methods and critical understanding. Of course, cultural judgements are rarely static and change constantly throughout history due to fashion and taste. But in making the truth claim 'this object is of cultural value', we implicitly reach for a definition of value that exists beyond the mere subjective and temporary.

Art historian Steven Edwards (1999) explains that the canon is not intended to be an unchanging collection of paintings or texts defined by an eternal standard. Indeed, the point about the endless contestation of the canon is that it is dynamic and exists in tension with its own critique. He argues that it is the self-critical contingency of the canon that signifies its universality – feminist and post-colonial negations can only exist in relation to the assertion of the Eurocentric body. An essential paradox therefore exists when those who believe that value judgements are only historical then assert the value of other, less recognised, works:

> Some recent art historians seem to believe that judgements about works of art can be avoided in a kind of happy pluralism where any interpretation, and any object of investigation is as good as any other. Interpretation, however, always establishes kinds of critical hierarchies that we call value judgement ... This does not mean that it is possible to return to transcendental judgements: judgements

are always made by social actors who carry their specific invest-
ments with them, but neither can the issue of value be dissolved into
historical explanation.

(Edwards, 1999: 14)

When people disagree about the value of a poem or the significance of
a painting, they do so on the basis that concepts such as 'excellence',
'value', and 'best' have some durability. Without this claim to universality, there is no basis upon which cultural authority can be legitimately
exercised. By default, the claim that all cultures are valuable becomes
meaningless because value itself is without basis.

Ultimately, the museum or gallery is an artificial contrivance,
designed to momentarily 'remove' culture from its particularity and
place it in a neutral context. By doing this, it presents the artefact as
something to be studied in isolation, according to certain rules and
standards of judgement. The modern museum and art gallery creates a
rupture by abstracting the cultural product from its 'ordinariness' and
ascribing it with a new, 'otherworldly' value. For example, a Yoruba
mask in a museum is no longer an artefact invested with mystical powers
as its Nigerian tribal owners believed; it is a cultural object that signifies a whole system of meaning and belief. It has value because it may
have beauty, or is explanatory in some way of its society. Its value is
something that exists beyond its particular use value in a particular culture. Likewise, the representation of religious narratives in Renaissance
altarpieces can be treated as instrumental tools of devotion, but in the
context of the art museum they can also function as texts of social or aesthetic history or objects of beauty to be consumed, in and of themselves.
This does not mean that cultural artefacts do not belong to particular traditions and cannot be understood in that way, only that in the
gallery the object's relationship to the particular society from whence
it came does not determine its value in relation to the sum of human
knowledge.

Of course, an object's value may change over time and in relation to
the evolution of human criticism and appreciation. It may deepen with
knowledge and become re-evaluated in light of new thinking. However,
what does not change is the ability to analyse and assess the art work in
cultural and historic terms, and to submit it to judgement. We seek to
test its significance according to criteria which are set by the museum,
not by the people who produced it or the heterogeneous tastes of the
visitors who look at it as they are passing through on a brief visit. In this
sense, the value of the object is not contained solely within the work

itself (although it cannot exist without it), but in humanity's relationship to it. This leads us back, whether we like it or not, to the idea of the historical canon. Through purely logical deduction, we must assume there is someone making a judgement about culture, even if we ourselves accept that this position needs to be treated with scepticism at all times. We are making a truth claim and admitting the possibility that it may be wrong, but are making a truth claim nonetheless. It is not a paradox one can ignore, but rather something one has to resolve with constant vigilance and defence of one's position. I cannot say simply that the Mona Lisa is a great work of art and expect you to believe it. I have to make the argument again and again to viewers and be prepared to engage in whatever contestation might ensue.

In this sense, it is absolutely right that art historians and curators commit to pursuing a truer picture of the development of art, and aspire to unite the various strands of knowledge about art traditions in the world. This would require us to stretch the canon, and expand the history of art in the world, rather than to deconstruct it completely or say it has no relevance. Modernism is a project that has failed to live up to its promise, but that might lead us to conclude it needs to try harder, rather than we should give up altogether.

What I am presenting is a case for the universalist orientation in art. The word 'universalism' is much derided these days, associated with an outlook that privileges Euro-centric views and has, historically at least, been used as a cover to denigrate other, non-European cultures. Universalism or the notion of a 'universal' man is portrayed as a simplistic portrayal of human subjectivity which presumes we are all the same in some banal sense (we all eat, drink, need clothes, or like Leonardo da Vinci's Vitruvian Man share the same physical proportions), or else, we should all be striving to be the same (our ideas, customs and beliefs will eventually one day become the same; that is western). This is a profound misunderstanding of the term and sets up a false dichotomy between an outlook which is inclusive and one which is exclusive.

To clarify, a universalist orientation means simply that human beings have the capacity to transcend differences. Whilst we may all be born in particular times, places, and cultures, we are not bound by these influences and our ability to think, reason, or use our imagination is an act of transcendence. In the words of the Roman playwright Terence: 'I am a human being. I consider nothing human alien to me.'

Of course, it would be true to say that no individual can ever completely escape their particularity, or their individual subjectivity. When we make art, or when we study it, we are looking from a particular perspective and place in human history, with all the personal and social baggage that comes with that. Even when we strive to look with a more neutral eye, and attempt to abstract ourselves from our own circumstances, there is always the possibility that our view is constricted by our position. Like someone sitting in the restricted seat in a theatre, we are bound by the space we inhabit. Our 'truth claim' is one of many truth claims which are often in competition if not conflict. Yet the quality of being human and of having language is that we do not merely look from this limited individual perspective, in competition with other limited perspectives. We can communicate what we see to others, and they can communicate back to us. In other words, we have the capacity to develop a collective subjectivity which transcends the individual truth claim. We can build upon this limited picture, and, to extend the analogy, ask other people sitting in other seats in the theatre what they can see. It is a necessarily complicated business, but the end goal is to strive to understand the complete picture before us – one that is more accurate and revealing than if we were to do it alone.

This universalist outlook is vital for assessing and understanding culture of the past. In science it would seem odd to separate off the contribution that black scientists have made as a 'different science'; rather, we see their knowledge in the context of the wider 'western' scientific tradition, drawing on similar methods and processes of investigation. So too, it would be strange to separate off black artists, writers, dramatists, and musicians to a different cultural category, rather than understanding them within the development of human culture as a whole. Indeed, if the history of culture and art shows us anything, it is that ethnicity is rarely the most useful way to define cultural traditions. C.L.R. James (1969), the radical black historian, expressed this sentiment when he said: 'I, a man of the Caribbean, have found that it is in the study of Western literature, Western philosophy and Western history that I have found out the things that I have found out, even about the underdeveloped countries.' James was a pioneer in the academic discipline of black studies, but whilst he believed the subject was a pragmatic way to bring attention to black writers, historians, and artists, he did not feel it was possible to separate black studies from white studies 'in any theoretical point of view' (James, 1984).

Of course, that does not mean that distinct national or cultural traditions do not matter or are not useful at all – certainly we talk about the German romantic tradition, or the unique development of Islamic art, as having their own internal logic and integrity which it is important to understand – but we have to appreciate two things: first, that ethnic traditions, at least from the sixteenth century onwards, have been subject to international and intra-cultural influences.[1] Secondly, the insights, beauty, and cultural value of these works in their particular context are revealing about the human condition to those who seek to understand and appreciate them. When European painters of the nineteenth century discovered Japanese print-making and the use of different, non-naturalistic perspective, did they not see the value of representing the world in this new way and borrow such techniques themselves? Is it not true that the innovation of jazz music pioneered by black musicians in early twentieth-century America shaped not only popular and classical music in the western tradition, but also its poetry and visual art? When Liz Lochead, one of Scotland's greatest living dramatists, talked about her play *Thebans* (an adaptation of a series of Greek plays), she insisted, 'It's not an easy watch, you know, but the stories are so good. They talk about things that are so important to us all' (Batten, 2003).

In this sense, the contemporary concern amongst educators and cultural institutions to find 'relevance' in art from the past is something of a tautology; the art itself, from the moment of creation, was a profound act of 'making relevant' to others something which was at one point in time only relevant to the individual creator. We might need help in understanding language, decoding symbolism, or appreciating the historical context (for which cultural education is crucial), but after such effort it is a source of continual amazement that we are made familiar by this human connection – that which is not alien to us.

This does not mean that the canon has not been shaped by political and social expediency. It has shamefully excluded artists and intellectuals on grounds of ethnicity, political orientation, sexuality, gender, and many other factors. Yet, this is an argument then to make our canon better, understand our history better, and ensure we continue to do so for contemporary cultural practice. We do make choices about what is great art, but we must recognise the limitations and be open to revision. Such an approach would lead us to a more 'truthful' canon, albeit never complete.

Why should it matter that the notion of cultural value is under attack? For cultural institutions it is the basis of their legitimacy and value.[2] For sociologists, it indicates a profound change in the way we understand human subjectivity. The shift towards an identity-based approach to culture – one with a therapeutic turn – indicates a set of attitudes and ideas which view the human being in a particular way. The subject of cultural policy is – like the subject of many other areas of policy such as health, education, law, housing – perceived differently than in the past and assumed to have certain features. In culture, this perception strains against the institutional forms and practices that we have inherited from the past. This clash creates a conflict which is manifest on a day-to-day basis. As the case studies show, there is a tension between actors when they are not sure which cultural values should dominate and what expectations they ought to have of themselves or their audiences.

Naturally, we cannot go back in time and return to a period when cultural value was merely taken as given. There are too many questions and contestations about what is good and what is not. However, we do need to appreciate the edifice upon which cultural organisations are constructed, and recognise that unless we acknowledge cultural value and try to understand it better we will continue to experience the same tensions in the exercise of cultural policy.

Reification of difference

A second contradiction is the way in which culture is perceived to be something that both transcends difference and yet is itself a product of difference.

As I argued in Chapter 3, the rise of identity politics emphasises the given nature of the individual, as opposed to its self-constitutive nature: the individual's 'being' as opposed to its 'becoming'. This mode of subjectivity is passive and inherited. Related to this passivity, the individual is always situated within subjective experience (ordinary, everyday 'culture'), which is inevitably different to that of other people's. This approach rejects the possibility that humans might transcend their subjective experience and develop a more abstract perspective of their world through their imagination and intellect. There is no such thing as universal reason, or universal culture, as proposed by liberal-humanist discourse.

The concept of identity presented here runs counter to the Enlightenment model of subjectivity. The former views human beings as determined by their cultural experience and constituted by something beyond their control. Yet, if culture is all-determining, how can we explain the ability of humans to transcend their cultural perspective and develop new understandings of their world? In short, how can we explain the human *creation of* culture, as well as human creation *by culture*? The essentialist view of culture has been criticised for reifying identity and treating it as though it were fixed, monolithic, and stable (Kuper, 1999). Bayart (2005) writes that 'the culturalist argument does not allow itself to reflect on the ways in which social actors produce their history in a conflictual manner, by defining themselves both in relation to their perception of the past and in relation to their conception of the future' (71). Malik (2002a) also emphasises this active, creative side of culture:

> Clearly no human can live outside of culture. But to say this is not to say they have to live inside a particular one. To view humans as culture-bearing is to view them as social beings, and hence as transformative beings. It suggests that humans have the capacity for change, for progress, and for the creation of universal moral and political forms through reason and dialogue.
>
> (unpaginated)

There are a number of consequences which arise from the identity model. The first is that without the notion of transcendence, human cultural difference is naturalised and reified. Culture is not something that one acquires actively through self-development and 'cultivation', but something that one imbues through passive consumption. The impulse of this approach within the context of a cultural institution is to make art 'relevant' to cultural groups and engage them with 'their culture', that is, what is presumed to be familiar to their way of life. Whilst cultural policy borrows the universalist rhetoric of showing new worlds and cultures, it is in fact also concerned to 'give them what they want or know'. Hence, as we have seen in the case studies, cultural activity is often oriented towards exhibitions, performances, or events that people are presumed to 'identify' with through a durable, coherent ethnicity. This arguably leads to a kind of essentialism, which presumes a limitation on what cultural content people are likely to enjoy. It is an irony that some respondents in the case studies complained about the 'lack of diversity' in local cultural provision, because it was 'all hip hop, and giving kids what they want'.[3] As we have seen in relation to Rich Mix and the Arts Council's diversity schemes, ethnic artists are particularly conscious of the 'burden of representation' they are under. On the one hand, they recognised the label of being 'black', yet on the other, they rejected the way it closed their identity in official discourse.

Anthony Appiah (1994) has accused multiculturalism of the desire to 'freeze' cultures and deny individuals the autonomy to criticise others within the same culture or choose alternative identities (157). The fixed categories of identity proposed in official policy can often jar with the messier identifications and fluidity of people's identities in lived reality. Baumann (1996) believes that public discourse about ethnic minorities in Britain has become dominated by a notion of a reified, homogenous cultural identity, which belies the underlying diversity and conflict in any 'community'. Eade and Mele (1998) also point to the internal conflicts and diversity within the East London Bangladeshi community and question the validity of even calling it a 'community' at all. In the United Kingdom (and London especially), the era of 'super-diversity' in which ethnic difference and cosmopolitan mixing is immense, the narrow focus on single ethnicities would seem out of date.

As well as freezing individuals into a prison of identity, the policy of 'cultural diversity' (or identity politics) risks undermining social and political solidarity between groups of different ethnicities. In his critical study of the UNESCO *Our Creative Diversity* report, Hylland Eriksen (2001) detects a romantic view of culture which is bound to identity and belonging to a society. Whilst the report argues for greater tolerance between cultures, he points out that it also insists on their inevitable difference: 'Cultures need to talk to each other and tolerate each other as it were, but they remain bounded cultures nonetheless' (unpaginated). Such a view, he suggests, leads to an unresolved tension between difference and the desire to achieve a global identity or set of values that might bring nations and ethnic groups together.

In a compelling reading of Stuart Hall's work, Chris Rojek (2003) argues that the foremost theorist of cultural diversity is himself bound by this contradiction between anti-essentialist arguments and a basis for solidarity. Much of Hall's work has been a repudiation of the Marxist privileging of class as the primary difference, stating that it has no greater objective basis than cultural difference. For him, there is no such thing as the 'universal subject' – working class or not – and, hence, no basis for transcendent solidarity in the structures of capitalist society. He treats the individual as a post-Cartesian subject that is fundamentally dialogically constructed. Yet, at the same time as Hall wishes to reject essentialism, he seeks to ground identity in something that is more substantial than mere lifestyle. Whilst he desires the fluidity and multiplicity of identity, he seeks the unity that can allow subjects to form durable connections. Rojek states that because Hall rejects universalism, and specifically class, he has nothing else to fall back on except culture. However, this is unsatisfactory because it always leads to 'Otherness' and divisiveness rather than the possibility of unity. Hall himself has admitted that he is uncertain of how to construct solidarity from the particular (Hall, S., 1992).

At a more concrete level, high-profile advocates of cultural diversity policies have noted this tension in practice between connectedness and division. Franco Bianchini has warned that the promotion of cultural diversity in public discourse risks entrenching 'community' divisions and ethnic differentiation along spatial lines (Bianchini, 2004: 220ff, cited in Cochrane, 2007: 119). The desire to bring people together through cultural identity is simultaneously undermined by the exclusive nature of cultural difference. The more recent stress on 'interculturalism' by some authors is an explicit recognition of the limits of multiculturalist discourse, yet which also reveals the extent to which cultural difference remains firmly embedded as a way of viewing the citizenry.

This raises the question of whether culture, with its inevitable emphasis on difference, can be a successful way of forging meaningful unity between groups. In Tower Hamlets respondents complained that it was difficult to satisfy one group's needs without creating tensions with another. In Oldham, the gallery tried to attract people from an Asian background by showing displays of 'their culture', but this was interpreted by non-Asian people that such culture is not theirs. Although both authorities sought to use culture to bring communities together, the logic of diversity raised sensitivity to differences and risked entrenching the primacy of ethnic identity.

In the case of the white working class, it is no surprise perhaps that right-wing groups like the BNP have transformed their essentialist, racist discourse into a new language of 'white identity'. Like Frankenstein's monster, their particularly pernicious brand of racism is given new life. The language of identity and cultural diversity inevitably excludes one group – white people. Whilst black and Asian communities are supported in their difference, there is no similar level of support for white communities, even though people in both areas often agreed that white working-class people were often as disadvantaged. Whilst ethnic identities are seen as positive, enriching, and to be celebrated, white identity is seen as threatening and confrontational, representing grievance and exclusion. This means at the heart of cultural policy discourse there is a constant ambivalence about difference. It exists as a fact, but the authorities hover between celebrating it and seeing it as an inevitable source of tension.

In light of this inherent divisiveness of culture, it seems unrealistic to expect cultural policy – or, more accurately, *identity politics* – to deliver social cohesion or consensus. In conventional politics, the individual is required to have the ability to abstract from his or her immediate personal interests in order to develop solidarity with other people, based on shared interests. This solidarity is not simply about pragmatic alliance of objectives (supporting one group in order to gain privileges for another). It also relies on a shared vision for wider society – something which rests on the exercise of reason, critical judgment, and political world view. The system of democracy is premised upon an equality and potential universality of interest, mediated through elected politicians and parties. Cultural politics, by contrast, presumes that people cannot escape their identities and so tries to build new political alliances around them. Yet, without a universalist orientation, this solidarity surely falls away. Emphasising cultural identity as a form of political engagement inevitably shores up the existence of separate communities and reinforces the view that they have different, fixed, and even conflicting interests.

Although cultural difference is benign in the social realm (indeed, desirable), it is pretty unsatisfactory as the basis of political engagement. Cultural identity is, by its nature, exclusive, being open only to those who have directly experienced particular traditions, lifestyles, or 'heritage'. Being a woman, or ethnic minority, or disabled, inevitably involves different cultural and lifestyle experiences to being a white, middle-class male. Political identities are supposed to transcend these subjective experiences, and allow us to identify with others on the basis of a shared set of ideas and values. Whilst individuals cannot vanquish their cultural identity, it is reasonable to expect that they exercise more control over what they think than over the culture in which they have been brought up. I have not chosen to be an Asian-British woman with a particular upbringing, but I have chosen my beliefs over time and take responsibility for them. This capacity for transcendence allows us to not only reassess our culturally inherited values, but also to identify with other values and ideas which are initially unfamiliar.

Without the notion of universalism in politics, differences are also depoliticised. To call a value or idea 'cultural' is to relativise it and mark it out for special immunity from scrutiny. For this reason, Brown (2006) argues that cultural politics ignores rather than resolves political disagreements. The reification of difference leads to a belief that cultures are 'simply there' and should be tolerated: 'there is no suggestion that the differences at issue, or the identities through which those differences are negotiated have been socially or historically constituted and are themselves the effect of power and hegemonic norms...' (16). By framing cultural identities in terms of 'respect', they are endowed with cogency and insulated from critique.

Writing about Northern Ireland, a territory torn by decades of conflict between the resident Catholic and Protestant populations, Savaric (2001) argues that multicultural policies since the 1980s have failed to address the deep-seated political disagreements between people. In the Good Friday Agreement in 1998, the authorities enshrined the principle of 'parity of esteem'[4] – the recognition and support of different cultural identities. However this has only reinforced segregation because it leaves untouched the political conditions that led to division in the first place. By asserting the importance of cultural difference in only a positive way, it refuses to acknowledge the problematic basis of such division, which may be political. The Cultural Traditions Group, set up in 1988 to support community relations, states its support for multicultural engagement by asserting that 'conflict [is] more likely to be contained in a multi-cultural society with pluralist values' (Savaric, 2001: unpaginated). Yet Savaric cites the theorist Michel Wieviorka in order to claim the opposite:

> To think [of] the conflictuality culture implies, even if it is not necessarily built practically, put in shape on the ground, expressed and lived as such, enables us to overcome the simplistic or partial conceptions of what a politics of alterity or an acknowledgement of otherness could be. Indeed, if such an acknowledgement is nothing but a mere ethical operation, or is reduced to the a-sociological, a-historical, or a-political idea of a moral exigency to learn to live together with our differences, it ignores the necessarily conflicting reality of social life.
>
> (Wieviorka, 1997, cited in Savaric, 2001: unpaginated)

Instead of seeking to engage with differences of opinion and belief through rational debate, cultural politics avoids debate altogether. Differences are left to continue, rather than be resolved. Primarily, people are urged to 'set aside' differences and forge connections on the basis of common feelings and empathy, or an ethical responsibility. There is a focus on the banal, 'joyful' encounters around food, dress, cultural activity, and leisure.

Yet, whilst these are presented as ways of developing 'togetherness', in fact, they denote a shallow kind of connection which places questions of substance and meaning in parentheses. A result of this shift is that people are left to try to resolve political conflict through intersubjective interaction. In Oldham, this means the state takes on the role of retraining individuals to educate them in the positive notion of diversity.[5] In Tower Hamlets, there is also a desire to use culture to educate the population in the value of diversity. Both councils aspire to train citizens in order to 'manage' their differences. Brown (2006) points out that the invocation of tolerance as a political strategy means that a 'justice project is replaced with a therapeutic or behavioural one' (16). Whilst conviviality between groups can be the basis of a genuine social solidarity and even draw attention to shared interests, it is rarely sufficient, and clearly not something the state is adept at doing.

Intersubjectivity leads to a focus on emotion and psychology; so instead of racism being an ideology which one can argue against, it is viewed as a pathology, a psychological disposition that needs to be trained. It is purely subjective and needs to be managed. 'Cultural awareness training' is intended to educate people that differences are inherently positive and need not be questioned (note the word 'aware-ness', suggesting passive observation of a phenomenon). In his book, *After Identity*, Jonathan Rutherford (2007) endorses this ethics of inter-personal relationships as a way to forge a more 'social identity'. Drawing on the writings of the French philosopher, Paul Ricoer, he states, 'There is nothing more in the world than individuals and what is between us. After identity, there is ethical life, which is what we make out of what lies between' (36). How we interact with others on a daily basis and the emotional connections forged through friendship and compassion are, Rutherford argues, the foundations of solidarity. This focus on interper-sonal relations through ethical behaviour and training is presented as a new moral consensus which can form the basis of a collective, shared identity in the absence of universal truth claims. However, the problem with this approach is that as long as cultural diversity policies insist that individuals, groups, and communities all have their own separate truth regimes which are incommensurate, there is no basis on which we can expect them to develop mutual regard.

In the nineteenth century, Matthew Arnold pointed to the essential relationship between truth and social solidarity. *Culture and Anarchy* warns the reader of the fragmentation of society against the dissipating force of market logic. Arnold believed that the philosophy of cultural relativism, which espoused that 'every man may say what he likes' (38), would diminish the collective spiritual project to pursue perfec-tion. A society that lacked a desire to develop a shared, universal culture would inevitably tend towards fragmentation, relativism, and mutual disregard and come to believe that:

> ... there is no such thing at all as a best self and a right reason having
> claim to paramount authority ... that there is nothing but an infinite

number of ideas and words of our ordinary selves, and suggestions of our natural taste for the bathos, pretty equal in value, which are doomed either to an irreconcilable conflict, or else to a perpetual give and take; and that wisdom consists in choosing the give and take rather than the conflict, and in sticking to our choice with patience and good humour (89).

He goes on to draw out the relationship between the idea of truth and social solidarity: '...without order there can be no society, and without society, there can be no human perfection' (149). Although Arnold is somewhat out of favour these days, we should heed his caution that when people no longer feel it appropriate to challenge or question the moral/ethical/political views of others, they cut themselves off from serious engagement. The 'Self' and 'Other' remain as distant as before.

The concepts of cultural authority and expertise, and Truth and Perfection, are no longer as customary as they once were. Whilst cultural institutions invoke them in their work, they also challenge their own rationale by using the language of diversity and difference. The attempt to use culture to create community cohesion is undermined when policymakers stress at the same time the fragmentary, particularised nature of culture itself. Also, as the case studies show, attempts to short-circuit this problem are received with ambivalence. The moral enforcement of 'respect for diversity' does not automatically lead to stronger feelings of solidarity. Indeed the opposite may be the case; moralising programmes may provoke resentment and feelings of division.

Regulation of consensus

In his critique of the Beamish Museum in the North of England, Tony Bennett (1995) attacks its unified, sentimentalised and depoliticised portrayal of the past. By trying to show history as a singular narrative, he argues, the museum denies the possibility of ambivalence and disagreement. Bennett not only criticises the particular representation of the past offered by the museum (which is romantic and unsatisfactory) but the very notion of a singular, universalised narrative; a destabilised perspective would, he argues, be inherently more political because it allows a plurality of truths to co-exist.

Bennett makes an important point about the need to recognise disagreement in cultural institutions, and that they are more often places of debate than consensus. The opening up of museum and gallery exhibitions to new voices and lines of scholarly inquiry can benefit the wider pursuit of knowledge. However, debate and disagreement is the journey, not the endpoint. The drive must be, at least in the back of our minds, an ongoing ambition to unify and bring together a shared understanding which rings true for others, not just ourselves. Without this aspiration, the museum becomes merely a collection of subjective opinions, not a pursuit of truth.[6]

In contrast to Bennett, I suggest that the endpoint of ambivalence (which is at the heart of the strategy to foreground cultural diversity in the political realm) renders difference inscrutable and fixed. I have suggested through my research that cultural policy discourse treats differences as worthy of 'respect' because they are seen as the defining features of people's identity. In this sense, they are associated with people's sense of self-worth and put beyond the reach of critical scrutiny. If you challenge a group's opinion of something, you are offending them. In the case of Rich Mix, for instance, if an artwork offended a community it was deemed to be off limits. Ambivalence obviates disagreement because it allows the 'safe' co-existence of contradictory and conflicting arguments, none of which need to be tested in the heat of debate. Culture is celebrated as non-confrontational and 'safe', whereas politics is seen as divisive. Culture privileges consensus at the level of behaving well towards each other but preserves differences as immutable.

In this way, both case study areas regard culture as a way to forge consensus and connectedness. 'You have your opinions, I have mine.' Yet, the reality is that disagreements and conflicts cannot be submerged under politeness for long, and conflicting opinions surface. Without the political means to resolve disagreements, they are, by implication, seen as a source of disruption and require regulation.

This is particularly pronounced in Oldham, where the official rhetoric of cultural diversity espouses open and honest debate, but the actions of the council suggest fear of any debate that may lead to conflict. In Tower Hamlets the pressure to avoid offending the local community means that certain subjects can be deemed off limits.

In this sense, diversity as a principle privileges the regulation of consensus above the notion of truth, which is central to liberal-humanist discourse. Beng-Huat (2005) provides a useful illustration of this dilemma in his description of the highly institutionalised multicultural regime in Singapore. He notes how the preservation of 'race harmony' through legislation, policies, and cultural influence, overrides any meaningful debate about cultural differences and possible discrimination between the Chinese, Malay, and Indian populations. Public voicing of grievances about race are suppressed by the authorities and even criminalised on the basis that such discussion may threaten racial harmony (18). For all the talk of accepting difference, it is a difference which is clearly set out by authorities, rather than from the active engagement of debate.

Wendy Brown (2006) also exposes the regulation of consensus in the name of tolerance. In her study of the Los Angeles Museum of Tolerance (MOT), opened by the Simon Wiesenthal Centre (a museum devoted to racism and remembrance of the Holocaust), she exposes the strictly authoritarian character of 'tolerance talk' in practice. Opinions are deemed appropriate or inappropriate, and questions posed to the visitors are highly moralised, making it impossible to discuss moral statements made by museum authorities throughout the visit. The set-up of the museum is to privilege consensus but through moralised enforcement rather than rational persuasion. Of course, she says, it is a tricky balancing act. The MOT makes contrived attempts to ask visitors' for their opinions and encourage them to think, but overall 'it is hard not to conclude that in urging its visitors to "think", it is actually urging something closer to the opposite: namely to accept without question the MOT's version of reality and its values' (127).

The prescriptive character of contemporary cultural policy – deciding what are appropriate and inappropriate attitudes – bears some resemblance to the Victorian moralism of the nineteenth century, which regarded culture as a tool to fashion correct behaviour and attitudes. Yet the use of cultural authority today is significantly different because it did not even claim any special legitimacy on the basis of cultural value. It is more explicitly politicised. This in turn leads to greater scepticism amongst the subjects of cultural policy, leading them to regard the local state's decisions as 'politically correct'. Savaric argues that in Northern Ireland, paradoxically, cultural politics does not tackle underlying conflicts but reproduces them in new form through debates over culture (such as the legitimacy of Orange Marches or Gaelic language teaching). Hewitt (2005) argues that multicultural policies at the national and local level have led to an 'unfairness to whites discourse' in places like South East London (128). He describes in detail how young white people in Greenwich in the 1980s, for instance, appropriated English cultural symbols like the Union Jack flag. Instead of viewing this as a merely racist gesture, Hewitt regards it as a complex attempt to resist stigmatisation and counter the perceived double standards of the authorities against their 'white community'.

In this sense, whilst the local state tries to defuse conflicts by pushing them into the cultural sphere, it ends up doing the opposite: politicising culture and creating further conditions of mistrust. The divisions and tensions between groups are not properly resolved, so require further management and mediation by the state. As the inclusion of one group inevitably leads to the exclusion of another, this constant motion of providing recognition brings the state further into the workings of the cultural sector, undermining the universal rationale for cultural policy and the legitimacy of decisions as 'aesthetic' rather than politicised.

Most importantly, the hollowing out of cultural value and authority denudes it of its moral force. Cultural institutions are expected to play an increasingly political role at a time when they lack legitimacy in their own sphere. This tension lends a certain anxiety amongst cultural policymakers, who are seeking connections with the public but can no longer rely on the moral force of the values that had once made such connections meaningful.

If cultural policy is to restore its legitimacy we need to see it in universal terms. With this comes a belief in the robust individual and a genuinely tolerant society which can engage meaningfully in debate and ideas, in the pursuit of truth, standards, and excellence. Such an approach, rather than being 'elitist', is democratic in the truest sense, as it requires us to trust people to make up their own mind. It accepts that culture can be offensive and upsetting. The ideas bound up with the universalist conception of culture are also those which underlie a universalist politics. Although they create the conditions for instability and disagreement, they also allow for the possibility of open debate, open-mindedness, and solidarity.

Epilogue

'Excellence, excellence, excellence', said Ruth Mackenzie, the Director of Culture for the London 2012 Olympic and Paralympic Games, when asked at a press briefing at the Royal Opera House in 2010 about the defining theme of the artistic celebrations in the city that year. The answer, she said, reflected her aspiration that just as sportsmen and sportswomen from around the world would gather together in London to achieve their personal best, so too should artists. Mackenzie was appointed in early 2010 to organise the cultural component of the Olympics and Paralympics in London, following much media criticism that the programme lacked credibility and would not match London's reputation as a world city for culture. Her answer, at least from where I sat in the audience, seemed to reassure arts journalists that Britain would manage to put on a fine show.

The word 'excellence' remains a necessary part of our cultural vocabulary, however much some critics question it. We use notions of excellence to make judgements in the cultural sector and, of course, to spend money. We also seek to persuade audiences to do the same when choosing which exhibition to attend or which play to see. We raise money from philanthropists and government to build museums and galleries which will house what are deemed to be important artefacts or artworks. Unlike the excellence of sportsmen and women, cultural excellence is not always so easy to judge. It is not about spotting the fastest, highest, or farthest, but about exercising a different kind of judgement and measure.

In the first two chapters, I suggested that culture has – at least historically – been judged according to some measure of cultural value – representing some aspect of human experience, in all its rich intensity, emotion, complexity, beauty, ugliness, and more. It is also, as I have tried to show, bound up with a view of human beings as capable of transcending their subjective experience. For the most part, our system of cultural subsidy in the United Kingdom has grown up around the idea of such judgement. Yet politically the word excellence has become tainted with connotations of elitism and exclusivity. It is seen as the territory of a single group rather than for all. The cultural sector is perhaps the most deeply suspicious and uncomfortable about referring to cultural value, perhaps afraid that they will be asked to define it according to a formula or that they will sound snobbish for doing so. Historically, people have good reason to be suspicious of the way in which excellence has been used to ignore or marginalise some artists.

But by arguing against the ideas of excellence and of universalism, we throw out the baby with the bathwater. Cultural professionals are now under pressure to prove their usefulness, even when their immediate social or economic impacts are fairly hard to measure. It is not good enough simply to be good; cultural organisations have to provide other benefits. In some cases, these so-called benefits may be non-existent or, at least, far less valuable than those of other policy interventions. But the attitude is ingrained now. At the time of writing, the trend of instrumentalism may become even more pronounced as local authorities in the United Kingdom cut funding for culture and move towards commissioning cultural organisations to 'delivering' services.

All this has happened, ironically, at a time when culture has become much more important publicly and part of mainstream political discourse. There has been a steady growth of funding, policy measures, legislation, and institutions relating to culture, driven partly by economics of course, but just as importantly, by widespread political and social changes in the second half of the twentieth century. We value culture for instrumental reasons but still feel sheepish about saying it is a good thing for its own sake. We particularly value culture because we think it will nurture a sense of cultural identity. In the past two decades, this has been seen as particularly important for ethnic minorities who may feel disempowered by the way culture operates.

In this book I have tried to show how this new kind of cultural policy operates in practice and some of the contradictions that arise. Although I have outlined some of the tensions in cultural policy today, I have not been narrowly pre-scriptive about how cultural organisations should manage these in their daily operations. It would be impossible to write a manual for such a thing – each organisation is different and must grapple with unique issues. The historical con-text and local feeling towards an organisation, or the kind of work and collection an institution might have, can make all the difference in how they deal with these issues.

Of course, many cultural professionals and organisations will try to be both diverse and inclusive, whilst also keeping cultural expertise central to what they do. Naturally, many will be interested in producing excellent cultural work whilst also keeping an eye on their social and economic outcomes. They will value what they bring to their communities as public spaces, places to meet, even as places to keep warm or enjoy a nice meal. They value engaging with new audiences and visitors, and, quite rightly, want to be open to the possibilities of new creative exploration that such encounters could bring.

But they will not be able to manage these different needs and values unless they are anchored by a belief in cultural value, and by this I mean an intrinsic value in their own cultural production. This means at times a degree of single-mindedness and willingness to do things alone and without immediate public or political support. It means valuing certain activity which is not necessarily socially beneficial in the immediate short term, but which may have public value in the longer term. It also means having confidence in the universal power of the culture one is producing and the possibility that individuals regardless of their background can identify with it. Paradoxically, without this independence to do what is culturally important and to believe in their own universal value, organisations will struggle to engage a diverse public in the longer term.

The implications also go beyond the cultural sector. Museums and galleries have, it is true, been useful tools for social and political messages, so the impli-cations today are no less profound than when they were performing this role in the nineteenth century. Today, cultural policy reinforces a political view of indi-viduals as vulnerable, anxious, in need of protection, and fixed in their identity.

What does all this mean for the many diversity policies which have grown up in the last 20 or so years? These policies were intended to increase the engagement of ethnic minorities in particular in the cultural sector and help them to feel part of a conversation. Such policies are also supposed to bring different ethnic groups together through an emphasis on identity. They are predicated on a belief that somehow cultural organisations lack the capacity to engage with diverse groups and artists and need to be re-organised around new principles.

In my view, it is extremely positive that artists and cultural organisations have become more open to new influences and are committed to engaging with all people. This can lead to exciting new creative possibilities, and enable more people to enjoy cultural activity as well as contribute to it themselves. However, we also need to question the relevance and effectiveness of asking an artist or cultural organisation to define themselves through their ethnicity. In an increasingly diverse society (especially in a super-diverse metropolis like London), emphasising specific identities seems somewhat out of date and counterproductive. The idea of a specific 'black' or 'black and minority ethnic' strand of funding or support risks reinforcing a sense of ghettoisation, and also alienating other groups. Importantly for cultural organisations, it can undermine the confidence in the relevance of their work to all audiences and visitors. On a political level, the message this sends out can also create discomfort.

In late 2010, another event took place which has some bearing on this issue. One of Britain's most famous contemporary artists, Anish Kapoor, opened his first exhibition in India. Kapoor, born and schooled in India, went to art college in London and made his name in Britain in the 1980s and 1990s. His global success and reputation has transcended any obvious categories like 'black' or 'Asian'. Although his early works were inspired by aspects of India, such as the spice markets or the unusual architecture of the eighteenth century Jantar Mantar astronomical observatory of New Delhi, his beautiful abstract pieces which explore shape and sensation are not easily defined by his cultural background. He says of himself:

> I grew up here, so of course India is one of the contexts for me. But I want the work to be looked at for what it is, and not for the fact that I'm Indian. Think of any artist: you don't refer to Picasso in terms of his Spanishness, because it attributes too much of the creative energy in the work to a background culture.
>
> (cited in Sooke, 2010)

Kapoor's reputation as an artist is more often seen in the context of 1980s British sculptors, rather than an Indian tradition, and he draws inspiration for abstract art as much as anything to do with his individual upbringing. His global success with major art commissions in Chicago, New York, and Berlin, and his considerable status in Britain (he was selected to represent Britain at the 1990 Venice Biennale, had the first solo show by any living artist at the Royal Academy of Art in 2010, and was recently commissioned by the Mayor of London to build a flagship sculpture in the Queen Elizabeth Olympic Park in London for 2012) makes one ask whether one needs diversity policies which are so preoccupied with the ethnicity of the artist. Indeed, we might ask whether such policies might actually hold an ethnic minority artist back. Of course, some artists may choose to explore their ethnic identity as part of their practice, which is their perfect right to do – but this should come from their own creative choices and not be imposed on them by funding structures or policy. This also allows them to weigh up the relative influences on them, whether ethnic, mainstream, or otherwise.

The shift towards cultural diversity – as a principle in both politics and culture – challenges the foundational premises of politics and culture by extinguishing the idea of universality. Although advocates of diversity see it as a way to make politics and culture more inclusive and democratic, it actually rubs up against these ideals by posing the individual person in a different way. Diversity undermines a range of desirable objectives, such as social solidarity, equality, free expression, autonomy, and aesthetic standards – objectives which are still supported in principle by many actors operating in the cultural sphere today. Cultural diversity policies do not (indeed, cannot) evacuate these ideas from discourse explicitly, but they threaten the basis of their existence, and with it the foundations of cultural institutions and political democracy. Although the concept of universalism is not without tensions or problems of its own, its conception of human beings, I believe, is more able to accommodate the dialectical relationships between culture and politics, and the individual and society.

Notes

Introduction

1. http://www.richmix.org.uk/about.htm (website last accessed 30 January 2011).
2. At different points in this paper, I refer to either Arts Council of Great Britain and Arts Council England, as it was devolved into separate national bodies after 1994. Where appropriate, I have used the name of the institution as it existed at the time.
3. Interview for 'National Treasures', BBC Radio 4, 5 September 2007.
4. For instance, Noel Gallagher, Damon Albarn, Margaret Drabble, Joseph Azagury (Buckwell, 2007).
5. In one of his first speeches as Secretary of State for Culture, Jeremy Hunt MP stated on 19 May 2010: 'I am totally passionate about arts and culture in our country. It is the most incredible privilege to do what I am doing and I am unbelievably excited. For me culture is not just about the economic value of our creative industries – it is what defines us as a civilisation. Culture helps us understand the world around us, explain it, and sometimes escape from it – as Picasso put it: "washing the dust of daily life from our souls"...I want you to know that the government's commitment to the arts goes right to the top.' In an interview in 2009 Ed Vaizey MP said, as Shadow Minister for the Arts, that Conservative arts policy would not be very different to Labour's, in ideological terms: 'Yes, there will be changes, but I am not pretending that they are massive ideological changes. I admit they are detailed points, and I am not going to pretend that an equally committed Labour minister wouldn't get them sorted if they had the same application' (Higgins, 2009).
6. Gerry Robinson, former Chairman of the Arts Council, in his keynote address in 1998, cited in Stallabrass (2006: 298).
7. Total spending on arts, culture, and heritage is approximately 0.1 per cent of annual Treasury expenditure.
8. Although this book makes claims about the changing nature of cultural policy in the UK, it does not explore in detail the important variations between England, Scotland, Wales, and Northern Ireland. For instance, the historical context presented in Chapter 2 focuses largely on England. However, because the broader sociological arguments presented here are relevant to all these countries, I have decided to keep the claim that this book is about cultural policy in the UK.
9. The case study approach allows a rich empirical study of the policy process within a specific social, economic, and political context over a period of time. It is regarded as a suitable tool for open-ended research where questions are exploratory in nature and demand a degree of flexibility in design (Yin, 2003). I used a 'grounded theory' approach, oscillating between the concrete findings of my fieldwork and developing tentative conceptual

structures throughout (Strauss and Corbin, 1998). My methods included document analysis (textual statements and archive material); qualitative, semi-structured interviews with key actors; and observation of buildings and events, and participation during events and meetings where my own input was appropriate to encourage responses from others. The combination of interviews, documents, and observation allowed me to cross-check evidence and construct a reliable chronological account of policy developments and differences of opinion – in the text I do not refer to individual interviews to allow the account to read more smoothly. I used ATLAS. ti. software to analyse the data.

10. See for example, U40 'Cultural Diversity 2030' – an international capacity building programme for cultural diversity – initiated by the German Commission for UNESCO in 2007 as part of the German EU Council Presidency.

11. For example, Looseley (2001) describes the evolution of France's cultural policy since 1959 which, although quite different to Britain's emphasis on the 'arm's-length principle', bears some resemblance in more recent years.

1 From Confidence to Uncertainty – Cultural Value and What It Means to Be Human

1. In their classic study of definitions of culture Kroeber and Kluckhohn (1952) state that the romantic, anthropological definition only began to rise to prominence much later. In the mid-nineteenth century Edward Tylor's famous work, *Primitive Culture* [1871] elaborated on the notion that culture was 'ethnographic' and included 'knowledge, belief, art, morals, law, custom, and any other capabilities and habits acquired by man as a member of society'. However, it was the Webster's *New International Dictionary* of 1929 that 'seems the first to recognise the anthropological and scientific meaning which the word had acquired' (63).

2. Although the history I present here focuses on the emergence of Enlightenment philosophy in the 'western' art tradition, this need not exclude the experiences and contributions of non-western artists. 'Western', in this sense, is not a geographical category. In post-war Britain, for example, Rasheed Araeen has argued that artists from the Caribbean, Africa, and Asia played an important role in shaping Modernism and that this should be more fully recognised. This is just one historical period in which artists from different social and cultural traditions might be said to participate in a wider, unified narrative of art history, albeit one which might study together different strands that have evolved from distant and separate points in the past. For discussion on the issues arising from constructing a unified world art history, see Carrier (2008).

3. See, for instance, John Barrell's study of the debates in English visual arts during this period (Barrell, 1990).

4. In America, this paradox was particularly pronounced. At the height of the Cold War in the USA, the political authorities through the Central Intelligence Agency (CIA) recruited members of the cultural elite to fight a 'propaganda war' against the Soviet Union, promoting art forms such as Abstract Expressionism, which were presumed to be devoid of the radical content of

social realism and therefore an advertisement for artistic autonomy in the west. Stonor Saunders (1999) points out in her detailed account of this period, 'One of the extraordinary features of the role that American painting played in the cultural Cold War is not the fact that it became part of the enterprise, but that a movement which so deliberately declared itself to be apolitical could become so intensely politicised' (275).

5. Fairclough (2003) defines an 'order of discourse' as the point when particular representations develop a coherence of ideological meaning and internal logic (3).

6. Other academics influenced by Bennett include Ian Hunter, Toby Miller, and George Yudice (see Rothfield, 1999).

2 The Development of Cultural Policy in the United Kingdom

1. UNESCO has published papers about culture since the 1950s. Article 22 in the Universal Declaration of Human Rights in 1948 enshrined a respect for cultural rights and UNESCO commissioned the influential anthropological theorist, Claude Levi Strauss, to write Race et histoire (1952), whose ideas about cultural relativism had a profound influence on the organisation. However, UNESCO was not always consistent in its theoretical approach to culture and its interest really only grew from the late 1970s onwards when it commissioned more reports (Hylland Eriksen, 2001).

2. In its 'World Conference on Cultural Policies' in Mexico City, 1982, culture was defined as '...not in the restricted sense of belles-lettres, the fine arts, literature and philosophy but as the distinctive and specific features and ways of thinking and organising the lives of every individual and every community' (cited in Wallach, 2000: 4).

3. This document would have a subsequent influence on cultural policy in the United Kingdom – see Meredyth and Minson, 2000.

4. Significant academic publications today include: *Journal of Arts Management*, *International Journal of Cultural Policy*, and *Cultural Trends*. Annual conferences include the Conference on Social Theory, Politics and the Arts, Association for Cultural Economics, and the International Conference of Cultural Policy Research. Europe's first university department for Arts Policy and Management (today Cultural Policy and Management) is based at City University in London. Other major departments include the Centre for Cultural Policy Studies based at the University of Warwick, and Centre for Cultural Policy Research at the University of Glasgow. Outside academia, think tanks across the political spectrum in Britain have published extensively on cultural policy issues since the early 2000s, for instance: Demos (Landry and Bianchini, 1995; Holden, 2007, 2004), the Institute of Public Policy Research (Keaney, 2006b; Cowling, 2004), and Policy Exchange (Mirza, 2006). Bennett (2001b) provides a European overview of the state of cultural policy research and argues that it has increased in significance (21). In America, the National Endowment of the Arts published policy reports from the late 1970s onwards.

5. Due to the recession there has been a slight decline to £157.3m in 2008–9

6. The DCMS subsidy to Arts Council England increased by 73 per cent over ten years in real terms, from £187m in 1997–8 to £412m in 2006–7 (DCMS, 2007). As part of this, theatre funding more than doubled, from £47.9m in 1996–7 to an estimated £97.5m in 2006–7. In 2003 DCMS gave an extra £75m to Arts Council England (which included doubling of funds for individual artists) and also £40m to Creative Partnerships, the flagship arts and education scheme administered by Arts Council England (ACE, 2003). Added to this funding boost, the Labour government introduced a policy of free admission to the national museums and galleries. Although institutions have complained that this policy has not been fully compensated for by increased subsidy, the overall perception in the mid-2000s was that times had improved for culture. This excitement was tempered somewhat when lottery funding for the arts was diverted to the London 2012 Olympics, and even further still with the onset of the economic recession from 2008 onwards. The October spending review awarded 30 per cent cuts to Arts Council England and 15 per cent to national museums and galleries. Despite these cuts, all three political parties support public subsidy and agree that culture offers considerable social and economic value to society.

7. (Higgins, 2009). See also the answer to Parliamentary question 13999 in September 2010 by Hugh Robertson MP, in Hansard.

8. This was exemplified in an essay by the former Secretary of State for Culture, Tessa Jowell MP, who complained that the arts were too often measured according to their social function, yet only a few paragraphs later, called for the arts to address 'the poverty of aspiration', in order to deal with social exclusion (Jowell, 2004).

9. There are 410 local authorities in England and Wales. Although the arts and culture are not a statutory obligation, local government is the second largest funder of the arts after Arts Council subsidy. DCMS guidance in the past decade has urged all authorities to develop a cultural strategy and there are various mechanisms to measure their delivery in this area, such as the Audit Commission's Best Value Performance Indicators and the Comprehensive Performance Assessment for all local government services. Consequently, the local government sector as a whole has embraced the social and economic value of culture wholeheartedly, generating what the sociologist Patrick Dunleavy (1980) would term 'stereotyped ideological responses' (156). The Local Government Association (LGA) has initiated numerous reports, conferences, guidelines, and best practice guides for local authorities in this area (LGA, 1993, 2001a, 2001b, 2002, 2004). Numerous cultural policy associations and networks have also come into existence, including the National Association of Local Government Arts Officers (NALGAO), which was set up in 2002 as an amalgamation of two local government arts organisations that were established in the early 1980s. Of course, rhetoric is not the same as funding. Bond and Roberts (1998) in their evaluation of local authority arts policies point out that, on an individual authority basis, a strong policy does not necessarily lead to enhanced funding, or vice versa. But there is clearly proof of institutional commitment, as well as greater coherence and status for culture within local government.

10. There is now a considerable volume of literature analysing how policy-making is mediated by ideas, assumptions, and actors. Hannigan (1995)

highlights the influence of 'rhetorical idioms' in sensitising people to particular social phenomenon and shaping their behavioural responses to problems, as well as the impact of 'issues entrepreneurs' who vocalise concerns, raise awareness, and point to specific examples to build a case for change. Collyer (2003) stresses the importance of 'policy networks' in articulating and propagating ideas, in order to gradually effect structural and institutional change. It is also important to recognise that there is rarely a single, coherent rationale driving policy development, but a mix of competing and sometimes conflicting drivers. Policies can hide compromises and problems, or respond to the 'feedback' of previous policies and actors' reactions (Hill, 2005: 180). Policy development is also restricted within structural limits and institutions and actors might pursue a particular course of action based on ideological assumptions and institutional routines that have developed over time (Pierson, 2004: 15).

11. In 1981, in an exhibition at the Institute of Contemporary Art (ICA) entitled *A Continuing Process: The New Creativity in British Arts Education 1955–1965*, the exhibitions director, Sandy Nairne, acknowledged the ideas of these educators as 'the sources of most secondary school and art colleges today' (cited in Thistlewood, 1981).

12. Tony Bennett (2005) cites Comedia's edited volume, *The Museum Time-Machine* (Lumley, 1988) as highly influential in the cultural sector when it was published in 1988, bringing together many of the arguments of the 'new museology', including his own (17). Francois Matarasso's *Use or Ornament?* (1997) became a constant reference for councils, arts organisations, and funding bodies who were keen to demonstrate the social impact of the arts, even though it has since been argued that the methodologies were dubious and accepted rather too uncritically (Belfiore, 2002; Merli, 2002). Charles Landry and Franco Bianchini's *The Creative City* in 1995 foreshadowed Richard Florida's work on creativity and was frequently referenced by local authority planners. Writing in 1998, one of Comedia's early figures, Ken Worpole, stated that since the 1980s they had produced 500 studies and worked in over 20 countries.

13. For example, in 2006, the NMDC jointly commissioned a report with Museums Libraries Archives (MLA) by Tony Travers of the LSE, to explore the economic impact of Britain's leading museums and galleries. In 2004, Arts Council England commissioned a similar exercise exploring the economic impact of theatre in the UK. In 2010, in response to the impending cuts during the recession, an alliance of major arts and cultural agencies and organisations launched *Cultural Capital: A Manifesto for the Future* which argued that investing in culture will build Britain's social and economic recovery.

14. An interesting example of the inconclusiveness of the evidence is Coalter's (2001) discussion of the educational value of the arts. He asserts that the research evidence indicates the positive educational value of including the arts in schooling and play. However, the actual body of evidence he cites is far less convincing. A study of GCSE results in all subjects between 1994 and 1996 comparing attainment levels showed that those students taking one arts-related subject (visual arts, music, drama) had better overall results than those not taking an arts-related subject. However, students taking more than one of the three subjects had lower academic attainment than those

students taking no arts-related subjects at all (Harland et al., 1998, cited in Coalter, 2001: 15). The possibility that including the arts in education might have a *negative* impact on attainment levels, as the evidence suggests, is not further explored by Coalter.

15. Higgins (2009).
16. A key turning point in the debate recently is that the Arts Council in 2010 commissioned a series of essays by *Third Text* called *Beyond Cultural Diversity: The Case for Creativity* (2010) which expanded on these points, and signal a possible shift in direction in the agency at least.
17. 'I think we have to resist being pigeonholed,' he says. 'I'm not interested in being an Indian artist. I don't need that as a peg to hang on.' Interview on 30 October 2008 (Nayeri, 2008).

3 Rich Mix Centre – A Case Study of a New Arts Centre in East London

1. This case study draws on a mixture of source material including face-to-face hour-long interviews, media reports, email correspondence with respondents, and records or reports published by the London Borough of Tower Hamlets. The interviews took place between January 2005 and December 2007. I have chosen to keep the names of interview respondents anonymous, unless I am using quotes published previously.
2. A report commissioned by Comedia, stated that the council saw diversity as 'the major asset for economic comparative advantage' (Comedia, undated). It suggests that the commitment to diversity focuses on the 'skills, talents and ambitions of people' – implying, of course, that ethnic populations are inherently more cultural or creative (12).
3. The council's focus is towards community-led projects and groups, such as the Oxford House arts and community centre, around 30 festivals a year (the highest number in any UK borough), and its in-house arts team, plus approximately 30–40 ethnically-focused cultural groups in the borough, ranging from well-established centres such as the Kobi Nazrul Centre, the Bangladeshi Welfare Association, and the East London Chinese Centre, to smaller organisations such as the Swadhinata Trust and Nzinga Dance. There are also community-based organisations that offer multi-ethnic cultural provision, such as Friends of Arnold Circus and Oxford House. The council also funds public indoor and outdoor events and festivals which are intended to reach as wide a constituency of residents as possible. Although it gives smaller grants to local 'high art' institutions like the Whitechapel Art Gallery, this tends to be earmarked for education work.
4. Most community groups were formed during the peak of immigration from the Bengali community in the 1960s and 1970s to help newcomers settle. It is difficult to estimate the number of groups currently operating. One respondent at the Bangladeshi Youth Movement told me there were approximately 400 'paper' groups, but only 45–50 were 'real', i.e. operated at a regular and sustainable level of activity.
5. Interview with unnamed respondent.
6. Email to author from Interim Chief Executive of Rich Mix, Jane Earl, on 28 January 2011.

7. To protect the identity of the sender, I have not named them here.
8. Archive material, dated 21 June 2002. I have chosen not to name the correspondents.
9. Minutes from a Rich Mix board meeting on 20 May 2002.
10. Unnamed interview respondent.
11. Notes from a Rich Mix meeting with Arts Council England on 23 August 2000, reporting comments by Chief Executive, Peter Hewitt.
12. The Comedia intercultural report into Tower Hamlets said: 'Corporate approach to community engagement is currently managed along a multicultural approach of demarcating community by ethnicity and celebrating difference on these terms' (Comedia, undated: 26).
13. Interview with Sonia Mehti.
14. Diaspora was also a key theme of Arts Council England's 'Connecting Flights' conference about diversity policy in the arts in 2002.
15. Media articles about the story include: 'Tower Hamlets replaces Guy Fawkes with Bengali Festival', 2 November 2006 (*Evening Standard*, 2006) and 'Fury over "PC" Guy Fawkes Ban', 2 November 2006 (*Sun*, 2006), and ' "Bengali Bonfire Night" defended', 2 November 2006 (*BBC Online*, 2006).
16. Some young Muslims I spoke to in the area complained that the Rich Mix centre was imposed from outside and did not factor in the needs of the religious community. Knowing that Rich Mix was framed in terms of being a 'community centre', they suggested that it was not 'their' community. By contrast, they suggested that their mosque, which had been funded by donations from the local Bangladeshi population, was more in tune with local need than a council project.
17. Details of attendees given in the 25 October 2001 Business Plan (Rich Mix, 2001).
18. The research involved interviews with 103 respondents and 12 focus groups, including local school children.
19. I actually stopped many more people, but most were visitors to the area. I wanted to ask only local residents, i.e. those who would be designated in official terms as part of the 'community'.
20. 'Just another half-hearted, under-funded community regeneration project', as one respondent said in the focus groups commissioned by Rich Mix (2000).
21. This was my impression during the summer months of 2007 when it proved quite difficult to retrieve information about the project. There were no publicly available annual reports to examine, and there was confusion when I rang personally to enquire about where information might be kept.
22. Conversation with unnamed youth worker at an event for youth workers at the Rich Mix centre on 15 May 2007, where I heard similar expressions.

4   Oldham – A Case Study of Cultural Policy in an Industrial Town in North England

1. This case study draws on a range of source material, including face-to-face interviews, media reports, email correspondence with respondents, and reports, policy papers, and records from Oldham Metropolitan Borough. The

interviews took place between October 2005 and June 2007. I have chosen to keep the names of interview respondents anonymous, unless I am using quotes published previously.

2. Most influential were: the *Independent Review* (the 'Ritchie Report') (Ritchie, 2001), commissioned by Oldham Council and the Greater Manchester Police Authority; Oldham Council's own response to the Ritchie Report (Oldham Metropolitan Borough Council, 2002); and the Community Cohesion Review Team report (known as 'the Cantle Report') (Cantle, 2001).

3. In 2005, the University Centre Oldham was opened. This was a collaboration with Huddersfield University to provide higher education opportunities for local residents.

4. It received £53m funding from the New Deal for Communities, £37m from European and lottery funding for businesses and to create jobs, £20m from the Single Regeneration Budget, and it awarded £9m to build the award-winning Gallery Oldham. Oldham Council also sought to develop its tourism industry, which attracts 6m visitors each year, spending £100m (Oldham Metropolitan Borough Council, 2004a: 20–21).

5. The Cultural Quarter has been completed in four phases since 2002, and it incorporates a new state-of-the-art library and lifelong learning centre, the refurbishment of the Victorian library into a local archive and museum space, and a new performing arts space which will be home for the Oldham Coliseum in the Union Street Area. The development has been funded by various sources including the European Regional Development Fund and Oldham Council, and Arts Council England.

6. This brief history is based on a combination of verbal reports by individuals working for the council, council-funded organisations, and Comedia, as well as archive documents and newspaper articles from the local *Oldham Evening Chronicle*.

7. The 2003 Citizens' Survey asked panellists questions about whether they felt a sense of identification with their local neighbourhood, whether people in their area could be trusted and shared the same values, and whether people from different ethnic and cultural backgrounds got on well together in their area. Whilst some areas (noticeably the more prosperous Saddleworth and Lees) felt a strong sense of community identity, the majority of participants' responses suggested that levels of community cohesion were low in parts of Oldham. This was more likely to be expressed by younger residents and ethnic minorities. Eighty-three per cent believed that Oldham was not a place where residents respected ethnic and cultural differences between people (ORC International, 2003: 31).

8. Thomas (2007) argues that throughout the 1980s and early 1990s an 'anti-racist' approach dominated youth service provision, leading youth workers to believe that different ethnic groups required their own services. Following the riots, the community cohesion approach began to take over and youth workers focused more on encouraging young people to mix across ethnic lines and interact meaningfully – a 'critical multiculturalism'.

9. *Oldham Beyond* was produced by a team of consultants and regeneration specialists (Comedia, URBED, S333, King Sturge and WSP). Its aim was to devise a borough-wide strategy on a range of issues. It was published in April 2004

and produced through consultation with over 2000 people in the borough, through work with schools, workshops, working groups, focus groups, and a travelling 'Thought Bubble' – an inflatable room that toured different venues in the borough.

10. Their target in 2007 was to increase active participation of adult residents (+16 years) by 14,000 (22,000 in total) and BME participants by 2000.

11. Demos's 'Boho Britain' study ranked 40 of the UK's largest cities according to three indicators: ethnic diversity, proportion of gay residents, and the number of patent applications per head. It ranked Oldham 36th out of 40th in terms of population but 22nd in terms of creativity and diversity – the relatively high ranking seems to be based on the presence of ethnic communities in Oldham (Oldham Metropolitan Borough Council, 2004b: 18; Demos 2003).

12. Interviews with employees at Oldham Youth Service and also First Choice Homes.

13. In Oldham Council's document, *Forward Together – Building Community Cohesion in Oldham*, it states: 'Doing, seeing, hearing and feeling are powerful vehicles for creating understanding, and celebration provides an "X Factor" which explains why communities respond so well to artistic, cultural and sporting initiatives' (Oldham Metropolitan Borough Council, 2004c: 89).

14. For example, Oldham Council's response to the Ritchie Report, highlighted a quote from one participant to show how the arts and leisure can break down 'the language and cultural barriers': 'I don't really like talking on stage, but we say everything through the shadow puppets and the images in the scenes' (Jameelun Begum, participant in the youth production) (cited in Oldham Metropolitan Borough Council, 2002: 36).

15. Full details of the LAA 'stretch' target, and the *Art for All; All for Art scheme* can be found on Oldham Council's application for the Academy of Sustainable Communities, available online (Oldham Partnership, 2006).

16. The Comedia report on Oldham's cultural sector cites a survey that states 41 per cent of young people said they would feel out of place in an art gallery or theatre; 24.7 per cent said they would feel out of place in a sports centre.

17. For instance, the 2006 Festival of Diversity involved over 92 voluntary and community groups, and over 19,000 residents.

18. Definitions of 'community cohesion' vary. The Oldham Community Cohesion Strategy states it as: 'people share a sense of belonging and a common identity; people are strong in their own identities and respect others; a more equal Borough; people relate to each other; people play their part and; resilience to threats and conflict' (Oldham Metropolitan Borough Council, 2007: 3). There is cross-party support for the Oldham Partnership's work on community cohesion. The Leader of the Council holds the Cabinet portfolio for community cohesion and the Chief Executive is the lead officer. The theme was chosen for Oldham Council's 2003 Citizens' Survey.

19. 'It is accepted that in societies where there is a high degree of community cohesion, there is greater economic growth and strong development. Areas lacking in community cohesion are usually identified as economically deprived' (Cantle 2001: 75).

20. Other schemes and programmes include: 'There's No Place for Racism in Oldham' campaign; 'Celebrating Diversity' competition at Oldham College;

'Unity in the Community' project; and various sports programmes run by Oldham Athletics Football Club, Oldham Fire Service, Oldham Metropolitan Police. Also see *Report on Community Cohesion Initiatives in Oldham Primary Schools* (Haddock, 2003). The anti-racism education also extends to the borough's employees. *Forward Together* outlines a three-year Equalities and Diversity Training Plan for staff and the range of race and cultural awareness schemes designed to promote 'cultural sensitivity', training, and literature being used in the borough (Oldham Metropolitan Borough Council, 2004c: 8–9, 31,45).

21. For instance, Raja Miah, a senior officer at Peacemaker and two school students who are part of Peacemaker gave evidence to the Select Committee on Home Affairs on 14 December 2004. Josie Tyas, said, 'I think it is important to tell what is right in primary schools especially, because as a young person myself, by the time we get to senior school if you are racist, most people do not want to change their views, but if you teach them when they are young, when the generations come through, eventually, I think, Britain will become more anti-racist, full stop.'

22. James (2003).

23. Interview with unnamed respondent.

24. Interview with unnamed Gallery official.

25. They do not necessarily think of themselves as belonging to the town of Oldham – a point reinforced by some of the respondents I spoke to.

26. One council official recounted to me in an interview how she had overheard a local resident outside the gallery saying to someone else, 'that's where they put all the Asian art'. Without further research it would be impossible to know how widespread this view is amongst local white residents.

27. For instance, the phrase was repeated throughout a film commissioned by Oldham Race Equality Partnership called 'Celebrating Diversity', about the run-up to the Festival of Diversity in the town in 2005 and featured young people preparing performances for the finale event at the Queen Elizabeth Hall.

28. In 2004 no BNP councillors were elected, although they had achieved some success in nine other districts nearby. There was also improved ethnic representation on the council staff – 5.7 per cent of the total.

29. Ritchie and Cantle made similar points in 2001. Ritchie said: 'There is a willingness to put responsibility onto the shoulders of officialdom, which too easily can be a reason for people not to shape up to their own responsibilities, beginning with their own attitudes. People must be prepared to look hard and honestly at these and where they need to change to decide to change them and then do so' (Ritchie, 2001: 4). Cantle, 2001: 'It is easy to focus on systems, processes and institutions and to forget that community cohesion fundamentally depends on people and their values' (18).

5 Analysis: The Case for Universalism

1. See Carrier (2008) on the challenge of creating a 'world art history' and his argument that after the sixteenth century art history traditions from Asia, Africa, and Europe began to interact.

2. The following exchange between the artist Antony Gormley and late art historian E.H. Gombrich is illustrative of this point:

AG: You have always been concerned with finding a value in art, the application of rational principles to the understanding of an emerging language, and I think that art – certainly in the earlier part of the twentieth century – took a view of that history in order to validate its own vision. I think that it is more difficult to do that now. All of us are aware that western history is one history among many histories, and in some way there now has to be a reappraisal of where value has to come from. Subjective experience exists within a broader frame of reference. When you think about what happens next in art, it is very hard not to ask the question: what happens next in the development of global civilisation?
EG: I agree with you in that the value of our civilisation and the values of art are linked. One cannot have an art in a civilisation which believes in no value whatever… (Gormley, Gombrich, 1996).

3. Interview with unnamed respondent at a youth arts event at Rich Mix, 15 May 2007.

4. This phrase appears in Article 1 of the Good Friday Agreement 1998 and also as a defining principle of the Cultural Traditions Group, set up in 1988 and absorbed into the Community Relations Council in 1990 (Thompson, 2006: 68).

5. Michel Foucault's theory of 'governmentality' is pertinent here: 'In its simplest terms, governmentality refers to the arts and rationalities of governing, where the conduct of conduct is the key activity. It is an attempt to reformulate the governor-governed relationship, one that does not make the relation dependent upon administrative machines, juridical institutions, or other apparatuses that usually get grouped under the rubric of the State. Rather… the conduct of conduct takes place at innumerable sites, through an array of techniques and programs that are usually defined as cultural' (Bratich et al., 2003: 4).

6. An interesting example of this ambition is *A History of the World in 100 Objects* project, run by the BBC and the British Museum in 2010, and published as a book in the same year. Neil MacGregor, the director of the museum, picked 100 objects from the museum's collection that might tell a unified historical story of the world, working with scholars from many different countries. Whilst recognising the inherent limitations of the collection and the possibility of bias, he explains that his approach is underpinned by a belief in the Enlightenment pursuit of truth and the need to develop a shared understanding of our common heritage (MacGregor, 2010).

Bibliography

Abercrombie, N. (1982) *Cultural Policy in the UK*. Paris: UNESCO.

Adorno, T. (2001) *The Culture Industry. Selected Essays on Mass Culture*. London/New York: Routledge.

Ang, I. (2005) 'The Predicament of Diversity: Multiculturalism in Practice at the Art Museum' *Ethnicities*, 5(3), 305–320.

Appiah, K.A. (1994) 'Identity, Authenticity, Survival: Multicultural Societies and Social Production' in Gutman, A. ed. *Multiculturalism: Examining the Politics of Recognition*. Princeton: Princeton University Press.

Appiah, K.A. (2006) 'The Case For Contamination' *The New York Times*, 1 January 2006. http://www.nytimes.com/2006/01/01/magazine/01cosmopolitan.html (last accessed 29 December 2010).

Appignanesi, R. (ed.) (2010) *Beyond Cultural Diversity. The Case for Creativity*. London: Third Text.

Appleton, J. (2001) 'Museums for "The People"?' *Spiked online* [internet site]. 8 November. Available online: http://www.spiked-online.com/Articles/00000002D2BA.htm (last accessed 22 December 2010).

Araeen, R. (2004) 'A History on the Margins' *Spiked online* [internet site]. 26 February. Available online: http://www.spiked-online.com/Articles/0000000CA421.htm (last accessed 29 December 2010).

Araeen, R. (2010) 'Ethnic Minorities, Multiculturalism and Celebration of the Postcolonial Other' in Appignenesi, R. ed. *Beyond Cultural Diversity. The Case for Creativity*. London: Third Text.

Arendt, H. (2006) *Between Past and Future*. London: Penguin.

Arnold, M. (2006) [1869] *Culture and Anarchy*. Oxford: Oxford University Press.

Art Fund (2006) Art Fund Museum Survey Reveals Collecting Crisis. Art Fund Website [internet site]. 11 May. Available online: http://www.artfund.org/news/428 (last accessed 29 December 2010).

Arts Council England (ACE) (1998) *Correcting the Picture*. London: ACE.

—— (2001) *Eclipse Report: Developing Strategies to Combat Racism in Theatre*. London: ACE.

—— (2002a) *The Shared Space: Cultural Diversity and The Public Domain*. London: ACE.

—— (2002b) *Towards a Greater Diversity*. London: ACE.

—— (2003) 'Arts Enter New Era of Growth'. Press Release. 25 March. London: ACE.

—— (2004) *The Art of Inclusion*. London: ACE.

—— (2006a) *Turning Point: A Strategy for the Contemporary Visual Arts in England*. London: Arts Council England.

—— (2006b) *Arts Matters*. London: ACE.

Arts Council of Great Britain (1984) *The Glory of the Garden*. London: Arts Council.

—— (1989) *An Urban Renaissance*. London: Arts Council.

—— (undateda) unpublished archive material. Arts Council/32/22. London. Victoria and Albert Museum Archives.

—— (undatedb) 'The Cultural Underpinning – Final Report' (unpublished archive material). Arts Council of Great Britain/32/22. London. Victoria and Albert Museum Archives.

Ayton-Shenker, D. (1995) United Nations 'The Challenge of Human Rights and Cultural Diversity' Background Note [internet site]. Available at: http://www.un.org/rights/dpi1627e.htm (last accessed 29 December 2010).

Bagguley, P. and Hussain, Y. (2003) 'Conflict and Cohesion: Constructions of "Community" around the 2001 "Riots"'. Paper presented to the *Communities Conference* on 18–20 September 2003. Available online: http://www.leeds.ac.uk/sociology/people/pbdocs/Conflict%20and%20Cohesion%204%20conference.doc (last accessed 29 December 2010).

Barrell, J. (1990) 'Sir Joshua Reynolds and the Englishness of English Art' in Bhabha, H.K. ed. *Nation and Narration*. London: Routledge.

Barthes, R. (1997) *The Eiffel Tower and Other Mythologies*. California: University of California Press.

Bartlett, K. (2008) 'A Rich Mix of Politics in East London' *The Times*, 15 July 2008.

Batten, R. (2003) 'Liz Lochead: The Light Relief of Tragedy' *The Independent*, 22 August 2003.

Baumann, G. (1996) *Contesting Culture. Discourses of Identity in Multi-Ethnic London*. Cambridge: Cambridge University Press.

Bayart, J. (2005) *The Illusion of Cultural Identity*, 2nd edn. London: C. Hurst & Co (Publishers) Ltd.

BBC Online (2006) ' "Bengali Bonfire Night" Defended', 2 November, BBC Online.

Belfiore, E. (2002) 'Art as a Means of Alleviating Social Exclusion: Does it Really Work?' *International Journal of Cultural Policy*, 8(1), 91–106.

Belfiore, E. and Bennett, O. (2006) 'Rethinking the Social Impact of the Arts: A Critical-Historical Review'. Centre for Policy Studies Research Paper no. 9.

Beng-Huat (2005) 'Taking Group Rights Seriously: Multiculturalism in Singapore'. Working Paper No.124, Perth: Asia Research Centre, Murdoch University. Available online: http://wwwarc.murdoch.edu.au/wp/wp124.pdf (last accessed 29 December 2010).

Bennett, O. (1996) *Cultural Policy and the Crisis of Legitimacy: Entrepreneurial Answers in the UK*. Centre for the Study of Cultural Policy, Warwick.

—— (2004) 'The Two Halves of Cultural Policy Research' *International Journal of Cultural Policy*, 10(2), 237–248.

—— (2005) 'Beyond Machinery: The Cultural Policies of Matthew Arnold' *History of Political Economy*, 37(3), 455–482.

—— (2007) 'Intellectuals, Romantics and Cultural Policy' in Bennett, O. and Ahearne, J. eds. *Intellectuals and Cultural Policy*. Oxon/New York: Routledge.

Bennett, T. (1992) 'Putting Policy into Cultural Studies' in Grossberg, L., Nelson, C., and Treichler, P. eds. *Cultural Studies*. New York: Routledge.

—— (1995) *The Birth of the Museum*, 2nd edn. Oxon/New York: Routledge.

—— (1998) *Culture: A Reformer's Science*. London: Sage.

———— (2001a) *Cultural Policy and Cultural Diversity: Mapping the Policy Domain.* Policy Note 7. Cultural Policies Research and Development Unit, Council of Europe, Strasbourg: Council of Europe Publishing.

———— (2001b) 'European Overview' in Williams, J. ed. *Research in the Arts and Cultural Industries: Towards New Policy Alliances.* A Transatlantic workshop co-organized by Division of Arts and Culture Enterprise, UNESCO, National Arts Journalism Program, Columbia University, Centre for Arts and Cultural Policy Studies at Princeton University, with the cooperation of the Council of Europe. Appendix 49–60, UNESCO Headquarters, Paris [internet site]. Available online: http://unesdoc.unesco.org/images/0012/001261/126114e.pdf (last accessed 29 December 2010).

———— (2003) 'The Political Rationality of the Museum' in Lewis, J. and Miller, T. eds. *Critical Cultural Policy Studies: A Reader.* Oxford: Blackwell Publishing Ltd.

———— (2005) 'Civic Laboratories: Museums, Cultural Objecthood, and the Governance of the Social'. CRESC Working Paper Series. Centre for Research on Socio-Cultural Change, The Open University.

Berger, P. and Luckmann, T. (1966) *The Social Construction of Reality.* London: Penguin Books.

Bianchini, F. and Ghilardi, L. (1997) *Culture and Neighbourhoods: A Comparative Report.* Strasbourg: Council of Europe.

Bianchini, F. and Parkinson, M. (1993) *Culture and Urban Regeneration: The West European Experience.* Manchester: Manchester University Press.

Blair, T. (1997) Speech for the Launch of the Social Exclusion Unit, 8 December.

Blandina-Quinn, R. (1998) *Public Policy & the Arts: A Comparative Study of Great Britain and Ireland.* Aldershot, Hants: Ashgate Publishing.

Bond, A. and Roberts, S. (1998) *Evaluation of Local Authority Arts Policies: A Report by Artservice for the Arts Council of England.* London: Arts Council England.

Bourdieu, P (1986) *Distinction: Towards a Social Critique of The Judgement of Taste.* London/ New York: Routledge.

Braden, S. (1978) *Artists and People.* London: Routledge & Kegan Paul Ltd.

Bratich, J.Z., Packer, J., and McCarthy, C. (2003) 'Governing the Present' in Bratich, J.Z., Packer, J., and McCarthy, C. eds. *Foucault, Cultural Studies, and Governmentality.* Albany: State University of New York Press.

Briers, D. (2001) 'Shared Terrain? Urban Regeneration' in *Making Places – Working with Art in the Public Realm.* Wakefield: Public Arts.

Brighton, A. (1999) 'Towards a Command Culture: New Labour's Cultural Policy and Soviet Socialist Realism' in Warnock, M. and Wallinger, M. eds. (2000) *Art for All? Their Policies and Our Culture.* London: Peer.

———— (2007) 'The Managerial State' in Mirza, M. ed. *Printed Project.* Dublin: Visual Arts Ireland, 8, 75–89.

Britton, L. and Casebourne, J. (2002) *Defining Social Inclusion.* London: Centre for Economic and Social Inclusion.

Brown, W. (2006) *Regulating Aversion: Tolerance in the Age of Identity and Empire.* Princeton and Oxford: Princeton University Press.

Brownhill, S. and Darke, J. (2000) *'Rich Mix'. Inclusive Strategies for Urban Regeneration.* (reprint) Bristol: The Policy Press.

Buckingham, D. and Jones, K. (2001) 'New Labour's Cultural Turn: Some Tensions in Contemporary Educational and Cultural Policy' *Journal of Education Policy*, 16(1), 1–14.

Buckwell, A. (2007) 'Cool Britannia Dumps Blair' *The Daily Mail*, 1 May.

Burkeman, O. (2006) 'The Phoney War on Christmas' *The Guardian*, 8 December.

Calcutt, A. (2005) *Creative Britain: The Role of Culture in the Re-mediation of Social Relations*. DPhil thesis, submitted to the University of East London.

Cantle, T. (2001) *Community Cohesion. A Report of the Independent Review Team*. London: Home Office.

Carey, J. (1992) *The Intellectuals and the Masses: Pride and Prejudice Among the Literary Intelligentsia, 1800–1939*. London: Penguin.

Carrier, D. (2008) *A World Art History and Its Objects*. The Pennsylvania State University Press: University Park, Pennsylvania.

Caust, J. (2003) 'Putting the "Art" Back into Arts Policy-Making: How arts Policy has been "Captured" by The Economists and The Marketers' *International Journal of Cultural Policy*, 9(1), 51–63.

Christiansen, R. (2008) 'The Arts Column', *Daily Telegraph*, 16 January 2008.

Clifford, J. (1997) *Travel and Translation in the Late Twentieth Century*. New Haven: Harvard University Press.

Coalter, F. (2001) *Realising the Potential of Cultural Services*. London: Local Government Association.

Cochrane, A. (2007) *Understanding Urban Policy. A Critical Approach*. Massachusetts/Oxon/Victoria: Blackwell Publishing.

Cockburn, C. (1977) *The Local State: Management of Cities and People*. London: Pluto Press.

Cohen, P. (1998) 'Urban Regeneration and the Polyversity Dual Market: The Road to Beckton Pier?' *Rising East – Journal of East London Studies*, 1(3), 24–51.

Collyer, F. (2003) 'Theorising Privatisation: Policy, Network Analysis, and Class' *Electronic Journal of Sociology*, 7(3). Available online: http://www.sociology.org/content/vol7.3/01_collyer.html (last accessed 29 December 2010).

Comedia (2002) *Releasing the Cultural Potential of our Core Cities*. Stroud: Comedia.

——— (2004) *Culture and Regeneration. An evaluation of the Evidence*. Stroud: Comedia.

——— (2005) 'A Survey and Mapping of the Cultural Sector in Oldham. A Report for the Oldham Cultural Partnership' (unpublished), in association with Knight, Kavanagh and Page and Burns Collett.

——— (undated) *London Borough of Tower Hamlets. Intercultural Consultation for a Global City*. Stroud: Comedia.

Commission on the Future of Multi-Ethnic Britain (2000) *The Future of Multi-Ethnic Britain (The Parekh Report)*. London: Profile Books Ltd.

Cowling, J. (2004) *For Art's Sake*. London: Institute for Public Policy Research.

Creigh-Tyte, S. and Stiven, G. (2001) 'Why Does Government Fund the Cultural Sector?' in Selwood, S. ed. *The UK Cultural Sector*. London: Policy Studies Institute.

Cubitt (2009) 'Bringing it Home: Making Local Meaning in 2007 Bicentenary Exhibitions in Slavery and Abolition' *Slavery and Abolition*, 30(2), 259–275.

Delingpole, J. (2006) 'What are Museums For?' *The Times*, 17 March.

Demos (2003) 'Manchester is Favourite with New Bohemians' [Internet site]. Available online: http://www.demos.co.uk/press_releases/bohobritain (last accessed 29 December 2010).

Department of Communications and the Arts (1994) *Creative Nation. The Role of the Commonwealth in Australia's Cultural Development Policy*, DOCA.

Department of Culture, Media and Sport (DCMS) (1998a) *A New Cultural Framework*. London: DCMS.

—— (1998b) *Creative Industries Mapping Document 1998*. London: DCMS.

—— (1999) *Social Exclusion: A New Framework for Action*. London: DCMS.

—— (2000) *Centres for Social Change. Museums, Galleries and Archives for All*. London: DCMS.

—— (2004a) *DCMS Evidence Toolkit*. London: DCMS.

—— (2004b) *Guidance on Integrating Cultural and Community Strategies – Consultation Draft*. London: DCMS.

—— (2007) *Culture and Creativity in the UK*. London: DCMS.

De Duve, T. (1994) 'When Form Becomes Attitude' in Ville, D. and Foster, S. eds. *The Artist and the Academy: Issues in Fine Art Education and the Wider Cultural Context*. Southampton: John Hansard Gallery, University of Southampton.

Dodd, J. (2002) 'Interactivity and Social Inclusion'. Paper given to Interactive Learning in Museums of Art and Design conference, 17–18 May 2002. Available online: http://www.vam.ac.uk/files/file_upload/5761_file.pdf (last accessed 29 December 2010).

Driver, S. and Martell, L. (1999) 'New Labour: Culture and Economy' in Ray, L. and Sayer, A. eds. *Culture and Economy after the Cultural Turn*. London: Sage Publications Ltd.

Dunleavy, P. (1980) *Urban Political Analysis*. London and Basingstoke: The Macmillan Press Ltd.

Dyer, S. (2007) *Boxed In: How Cultural Diversity Policies Restrict Black Artists*. London: Manifesto Club.

Eade, J. (1989) *The Politics of Community: The Bangladeshi Community in East London*. Aldershot: Avebury.

Eade, J. and Garbin, D. (2002) 'Changing Narratives of Violence, Struggle and Resistance: Bangladeshis and the Competition for Resources in the Global City' *Oxford Development Studies*, 30(2), 137–149.

Eade, J. and Mele, C. (1998) 'Global Processes and Customised Landscapes: The "Eastern Promise" of New York and London' *Rising East – Journal of East London Studies*, 1(3), 52–73.

Eagleton, T. (2000) *The Idea of Culture*. Oxford: Blackwell Publishers Ltd.

East London Advertiser (2006) 'Rich Mix Costs Still Rising', 12 June.

—— (2007a) 'Town Hall Splashes Out on a "Rich" Mix of Cash on "Away" Days', 13 July.

—— (2007b) 'Rich Mix or Money Pit?' 18 January.

—— (2007c) 'Rich Mix Boss Quits Troubled Centre', 26 February.

Edelman, M. (1967) *The Symbolic Uses of Politics*. Urbana and Chicago: University of Illinois.

Edgar, D. (2005) 'My Fight with the Front' *The Observer*, 14 September.

Edwards, S. (ed.) (1999) *Art and its Histories: A Reader*. New Haven and London: Yale University Press in association with The Open University.

Eliot, T.S. (1962) *Notes Towards the Definition of Culture*, 2nd edn. London: Faber & Faber Ltd.

Elliott, A. (2006) *Concepts of the Self*, 3rd edn. Cambridge/Massachusetts: Polity Press.

Elliott, L. and Atkinson, D. (2007) *Fantasy Island. Waking Up to the Incredible Economic, Political and Social Illusions of the Blair Legacy*. London: Constable.

Ellis, A. (2003) *Valuing Culture*. London: AEA Consulting. Available online: http://www.aeaconsulting.com/site/assets/pdf/valuingculturepdf.pdf   (last accessed 21 November 2007).

Evening Standard (2006) 'Tower Hamlets Replaces Guy Fawkes with Bengali Festival', 2 November.

Fairclough, N. (2000) *New Labour, New Language?* London: Routledge.

—— (2003) *Analysing Discourse. Textual Analysis for Social Research*. London/ New York: Routledge.

Fine, G.A. and Turner, P. (2001) *Whispers on the Color Line. Rumours and Race in America*. Berkeley: University of California Press.

Florida, R. (2002) *The Rise of the Creative Class and How It's Transforming Work, Leisure and Everyday Life*. London: Basic Books.

Ford, S. and Davies, A. (1998) 'Art Capital' *Art Monthly*, 213 (February), 1–4.

Fraser, N. (1995) 'From Redistribution to Recognition? Dilemmas of Justice in a "Post-Socialist" Age' *New Left Review*, 212, 68–92.

Freeman, A. (2007) *London's Creative Sector 2007 Update, Working Paper 22*. London: Greater London Authority.

Fremeaux, I. (2002) *The Strategic Dimension of the Concept of Community in Cultural Projects within Urban Regeneration Schemes*. DPhil thesis submitted to London Guildhall University.

Fukuyama, F. (1992) *The End of History and The Last Man*. New York: Free Press.

Furedi, F. (2003) *Therapy Culture: Cultivating Vulnerability in an Uncertain Age*. London: Routledge.

Garcia, B. (2004) 'Cultural Policy and Urban Regeneration in Western European Cities: Lessons from Experience, Prospects for the Future' *Local Economy*, 19(4), 312–326.

Garnham, N. (2001) 'Afterword: The Cultural Commodity and Cultural Policy' in Selwood, S. ed. *The UK Cultural Sector: Profile and Policy Issues*. London: Policy Studies Institute.

Giddens, A. (1991) *Modernity and Self-Identity. Self and Society in the Late Modern Age*. Cambridge: The Polity Press in Association with Blackwell Publishing Ltd.

—— (1994) *Beyond Left and Right. The Future of Radical Politics*. Cambridge: Polity Press.

Gilroy, P. (2004) *After Empire: Melancholia or Convivial Culture*. London: Routledge.

Gitlin, T. (1994) 'From Universality to Difference: Notes on the Fragmentation of the Idea of the Left' in Calhoun, C. ed. *Social Theory and the Politics of Identity*. Cambridge, Massachussetts/Oxford: Blackwell.

Gomez, M. (1998) 'Reflective Images: The Case of Urban Regeneration in Glasgow and Bilbao' *International Journal of Urban and Regional Research*, 22(1), 106–121.

Goodison, N. (2004) *Securing the Best for Museums: Private Giving and Government Support*. London: HM Treasury.

Gormley, A. and Gombrich, E. (1996) 'Gormley and Gombrich in Conversation' *Prospect Magazine*, 20 August 1996. Available online: http://

www.prospectmagazine.co.uk/1996/08/gormleyandgombrichinconversation/ (last accessed 29 December 2010).

Gray, C. (2000) *The Politics of the Arts in Britain*. Basingstoke: Macmillan Press Ltd.

—— (2002) 'Local Government and the Arts' *Local Government Studies*, 28(1) 77–90.

—— (2004) 'Joining Up or Tagging On? The Arts, "Cultural Planning" and the View from Below' *Public Policy and Administration*, 19(2), 38–49.

—— (2006) 'Managing the Unmanageable: The Politics of Cultural Planning' *Public Policy and Administration*, 21(2), 101–113.

Greater London Authority (2004) *The London Plan*. London: Greater London Authority.

—— (2010) *Cultural Metropolis: The Mayor's Cultural Strategy for London – 2012 and Beyond*. London: Greater London Authority.

Habermas, J. (1987) *The Theory of Communicative Action*, Vol. 2. Cambridge: Polity Press.

Haddock, M. (2003) *Report on Community Cohesion Initiatives in Oldham Primary Schools*. Oldham: Oldham Metropolitan Borough Council. Available online: http://www.oldham.gov.uk/oldham_schools_cohesion_report.pdf (last accessed 21 November 2007).

Hall, S. (1989) 'The Meaning of New Times' in Hall, S. and Jacques, M. eds. *New Times: The Changing Face of Politics in the 1990s*. London: Laurence & Wishart.

—— (1992) 'New Ethnicities' in Donald, J. and Rattansi, A., eds. *Race, Culture and Difference*. London: Sage.

—— (2001) 'Museums of Modern Art and the End of History' in Hall, S. and Maharaj, S. eds. *Modernity and Difference*. London: Institute of Visual Arts.

Hall, S. and Du Gay, P. (eds.) (1996) *Questions of Cultural Identity*. London: Sage Publications.

Hall, S. and Jacques, M. (1989) 'Introduction' in Hall S. and Jacques, M. eds. *New Times: The Changing Face of Politics in the 1990s*. London: Laurence & Wishart.

Hannigan, J.A. (1995) *Environmental Sociology. A Social Constructionist Perspective*. London/New York: Routledge.

Hare, B. (2000) 'Glasgow Belongs to Whom? Civic Identity in the Visual Arts in Scotland' in Mosley, I. ed. *Dumbing Down. Culture, Politics and the Mass Media*. Devon: Imprint Academic.

Harvey, D. (1989) *The Urban Experience*. Oxford: Blackwell.

Hay, C. (1996) *Restating Social and Political Change*. Buckingham: Open University Press.

Heartfield, J. (2002) *The 'Death of the Subject' Explained*. Sheffield: Sheffield Hallam University Press.

Hewett, I. (2003) *Music. Healing the Rift*. London/New York: Continuum.

Hewitt, R. (2005) *White Backlash and the Politics of Multiculturalism*. Cambridge: Cambridge University Press.

Hewison, R. (1995) *Culture & Consensus*. London: Methuen.

Higgins, C. (2009) 'Ed Vaizey reveals Tories' Strategy for the Arts' *The Guardian*, 17 June.

Hill, M. (2005) *The Public Policy Process*, 4th edn. Edinburgh: Pearson Education Limited.

Hoggett, P. (1997) *Contested Communities: Experiences, Struggles, Policies*. Bristol: The Policy Press.

Holden. J. (2004) *Capturing Cultural Value*. London: Demos.

——— (2006) *Cultural Value and the Crisis of Legitimacy*. London: Demos.

——— (2007) *Publicly Funded Culture and the Creative Industries*. London: Demos.

Home Office (2001) *Building Cohesive Communities: A Report of the Ministerial Group on Public Order and Community Cohesion*. London: Home Office.

Hood, C. (1991) 'A Public Management for All Seasons' *Public Administration*, 69(1), 3–19.

——— (1995) 'Contemporary Public Management: A New Global Paradigm?' *Public Policy and Administration*, 10(2), 104–117.

Hooper-Greenhill, E. (1992) *Museums and the Shaping of Knowledge*, 2nd edn. London/New York: Routledge.

Honneth, A. (2001) 'Recognition or Redistribution? Changing Perspectives on the Moral Order of Society' *Theory, Culture and Society*, 18(2), 43–55.

Hughes, R. (1993) *Culture of Complaint*. Oxford/New York: Oxford University Press.

Hunt, T. (2009) 'Enlightened Age for the Arts in Britain is Cast into Shadow' *The Observer*, 17 February.

Hussain, D. (2006) 'Bangladeshis in East London: From Secular Politics to Islam' *Open Democracy*, 7 July [internet site]. Available online: http://www.opendemocracy.net/democracy-protest/bangladeshi_3715.jsp (last accessed 29 December 2010).

Hutchison, R. (1982) *The Politics of the Arts Council*. London: Sinclair Browne.

Hylland Eriksen, T. (2001) 'Between Universalism and Relativism: A Critique of the UNESCO Concepts of Culture' in Cowan, J., Benedicte Dembour, M., and Wilson, R. eds. *Culture and Rights: Anthropological Perspectives*. Cambridge: Cambridge University Press.

Hylton, R. (2007) *The Nature of the Beast*. Bath: Institute of Contemporary Interdisciplinary Arts, University of Bath.

Imrie, R. and Raco, M. (2003) 'Community and the Changing nature of Urban Policy' in Imrie. R. and Raco, M. eds. *Urban Renaissance? New Labour, Community and Urban Policy*. Bristol: The Policy Press.

Institute of Community Cohesion (2006) *Review of Community Cohesion in Oldham*. Oldham: Oldham Metropolitan Borough Council.

James, A. (2003) 'Peace of Mind' *The Guardian*, 9 July.

James, C.L.R. (1969) 'Discovering Literature in Trinidad: the 1930s' *Journal of Commonwealth Literature*, 7: 73–80.

James, C.L.R. (1984) *At the Rendezvous of Victory. Vol 3 Selected Writings*. London: Allison and Busby

Jameson, F. (1993) 'On Cultural Studies' *Social Text*, 11(29), 17–52.

Jensen, J. (2002) *Is Art Good for Us? Beliefs about High Culture in American Life*. Lanham, Oxford: Rowman & Littlefield Publishers.

Jermyn, H. and Desaid, P. (2000) *Arts – What's in a Word? Ethnic Minorities and the Arts*. London: Arts Council of England.

Jones, S. (2007) 'Building Cultural Literacy, Museums as Spaces for Shaping the Political World of the Future'. Paper delivered at *New Collaboration, New Benefits: A Conference on Transnational Museum Collaboration*. Shanghai. Available online: http://museumandculturaldiversity.blogspot.com/2007/05/building-cultural-literacy-museums-as.html (last accessed 29 December 2010).

Jowell, T. (2004) *Government and the Value of Culture*. London: Department for Culture, Media and Sport.

Jury, L. (2006) 'Britain's Future Lies in Creative Industries, say Arts Leaders' *The Independent*, 9 June.

Kawashima, N. (1997) 'Local Authorities and Cultural Policy: Dynamics of Recent Developments' *Local Government Policy Making*, 23(5), 31–36.

—— (2004) *Planning for Equality? Decentralisation in Cultural Policy*. Warwick: Centre for Cultural Policy Studies, University of Warwick.

Keaney, E. (2006a) *Public Value and the Arts. A Literature Review*. London: Arts Council.

—— (2006b) *From Access to Participation. Cultural Policy and Civil Renewal*. London: Institute for Public Policy Research.

Keats, J. (undated) [1820] 'Ode to a Grecian Urn'. Available online: http://www.bartleby.com/101/625.html (last accessed 29 December 2010).

Keith, M. (2005) *After the Cosmopolitan. Multicultural Cities and the Future of Racism*. Oxon/New York: Routledge.

Kelly, O. (2003) 'Art' in Lewis, J. and Miller, T. eds. *Critical Cultural Policy Studies*. Oxford: Blackwell Publishing Ltd.

Khan, N. (1976) *The Arts Britain Ignores*. London: Arts Council of Great Britain.

Knopf, T.A. (2006) *Rumours, Race and Riots*. New Jersey: Transaction.

Kroeber, A.L. and Kluckhohn, C (1952) 'Culture: A Critical Review of Concepts and Definitions'. Peabody Museum of American Archaeology and Ethnology Papers, Harvard University, 47(1).

Kumar, K. (1995) *From Post-Industrial to Post-Modern Society: New Theories of the Contemporary World*. Oxford: Blackwell Publishers Ltd.

Kuper, A. (1999) *Culture: The Anthropologist's Account*. Cambridge/Massachusetts/London: Harvard University Press.

Kymlicka, W. (1995) *Multicultural Citizenship*. Oxford: Oxford University Press.

Laclau, E. and Mouffe, C. (2001) *Hegemony and Socialist Strategy: Towards a Radical Democratic Politics,* 2nd edn. London: Verso.

Laing, R.D. (1967) *The Politics of Experience*. London: Penguin.

Lammy, D. (2005) Keynote Address to Museums Association Conference. Available online: http://www.davidlammy.co.uk/da/25307 (last accessed 29 December 2010).

Landry, C. and Bianchini, F. (1995) *The Creative City*. London: Demos.

Leadbeater, C. (2000) *Living on Thin Air: The New Economy*. London: Penguin.

Lebrecht, N. (2006) 'Last Gasp for the Culture Vultures' *Evening Standard*, 8 March.

—— (2010) 'Wanted: A Keynesian Vision for the Arts' *Standpoint*, December 2010.

Lefley, J. (2006) 'Luvvie Art Celebrates "Diversity" with This Picture of a Black Man Holding Up a White Girl' *Evening Standard*, 4 May.

Levi Strauss, C. (1952) *Race et histoire*. Paris: United Nations Educational, Scientific and Cultural Organisation.

Levine, C. (2007) *Provoking Democracy. Why We Need the Arts*. Mass/Oxford/Victoria: Blackwell Publishing.

Lewis, J. (1990) *Art, Culture & Enterprise: The Politics of Art and the Cultural Industries*. London: Routledge.

Lewis, J. and Miller, T. eds. (2003) *Critical Cultural Policy Studies: A Reader*. Oxford: Blackwell Publishing Ltd.

Lloyd, D. and Thomas, P. (1998) *Culture and the State*. London: Routledge.

Local Government Association (LGA) (1993) *Creative Consequences*. London: LGA.

—— (2001a) *Realising the Potential of Cultural Services: The Case for the Arts*. London: LGA.

—— (2001b) *Tackling Poverty and Social Exclusion through Cultural Services. A Toolkit*. London: LGA.

—— (2002) *Cultural Exchange: The Contribution of Cultural Services to Modernised Local Government*. London: LGA.

—— (2004) *Cultural Services and the Shared Priorities*. London: LGA.

London Borough of Tower Hamlets (2003) *Tower Hamlets Cultural Strategy*. London: London Borough of Tower Hamlets.

—— (2005) *Creating and Sharing Prosperity in Tower Hamlets. Regeneration Strategy*. London: London Borough of Tower Hamlets.

—— (2006) *Tower Hamlets Local Area Agreement*. London: London Borough of Tower Hamlets.

—— (2007) *Tower Hamlets Community Plan*. London: London Borough of Tower Hamlets.

Looseley, D. (2001) 'Cultural Policy in France since 1959: Arm's Length, or "Up Close and Personal?"' Frederiksberg, Nordisk Kultur Institut. Available online: http://www.nordiskkulturinstitut.dk/arbejdspapirer/cultural_policy_in_france.pdf (last accessed 29 December 2010).

Lownsbrough, H. and Beunderman, J. (2007) *Equally Spaced? Public Space and Interaction between Diverse Communities. A Report for the Commission for Racial Equality*. London: Demos.

Lukes, S. (2005) *Power: A Radical View*, 2nd edn. Basingstoke: Palgrave Macmillan.

Lumley, R. ed. (1988) *The Museum Time-Machine*. London: Comedia/Routledge.

Macgregor, N. (2010) *A History of the World in 100 Objects*. London: Allen Lane.

Madden, C. (2001) 'Using Economic Impact Studies in Arts and Cultural Advocacy: A Cautionary Note *Media International Australia*, 98 (February). Available online: http://christopherdmadden.wordpress.com/2009/02/06/usingeconomic-impact-studies/ (last accessed 29 December 2010).

Madden, C. and Bloom, T. (2004) 'Creativity, Health and Arts Advocacy' *International Journal of Cultural Policy*, 10(2), 133–156.

Mahamdillie, H. (2002) 'Racism: Myths and Realities' *International Socialism Journal*, 95 (Summer).

Malik, K. (1996) *The Meaning of Race*. Basingstoke and London: Macmillan.

—— (2002a) 'Against Multiculturalism' *New Humanist*, Summer.

—— (2002b) 'The Real Value of Diversity' *Connections*, Winter.

Marx, K. (1978) 'The Grundrisse' in Tucker, R. ed. *The Marx-Engels Reader*, 2nd edn. London/New York: W.W. Norton & Company.

Maslow, A. (1971) *The Farther Reaches of Human Nature*. New York: The Viking Press.

Matarasso, F. (1997) *Use or Ornament: The Social Impact of Participation in the Arts*. Stroud: Comedia.

Mayor's Commission on African and Asian Heritage (2005) *Delivering Shared Heritage*. London: Greater London Authority.

McGuigan, J. (1996) *Culture and the Public Sphere*. London/New York: Routledge.

McMaster, B. (2008) *Supporting Excellence in the Arts: From Measurement to Judgement*. London: Arts Council England.

Meredyth, D. and Minson, J. (2000) 'Editor's Introduction: Resourcing Citizenries' in *American Behavioural Scientist*, 43(9), 1374–1394.

Merli, P. (2002) 'Evaluating the Social Impact of Participation in Arts Activities: A Critical Review of Francois Matarasso's "Use or Ornament?" ' *International Journal of Cultural Policy*, 8(1), 107–118.

Miles, M. (2005) 'Interruptions: Testing the Rhetoric of Culturally Led Urban Development' *Urban Studies*, 42(5/6), 889–911.

Minihan, J. (1977) *The Nationalization of Culture. The Development of State Subsidies to the Arts in Great Britain*. London/New York: Hamilton.

Mirza, M. ed. (2006) *Culture Vultures: Is UK Arts Policy Damaging the Arts?*. London: Policy Exchange.

Mommaas, H. (2004) 'Cultural Clusters and the Post-Industrial City. Towards the Remapping of Urban Cultural Policy' *Urban Studies*, 41(3), 507–532.

Mooney, G. (2004) 'Cultural Policy as Urban Transformation? Critical Reflections on Glasgow, European City of Culture 1990' *Local Economy*, 19(4), 327–340.

Morris, E. (2003) Speech to Cheltenham Festival of Literature. Available online: http://www.culture.gov.uk/Reference_library/Press_notices/archive_2003/ Estelle_Morris_speech_16Oct_2003.htm (last accessed 29 December 2010).

Mulgan, G. (1994) *Politics in an Antipolitical Age*. Cambridge/Oxford: Polity Press in association with Blackwell Publishers Ltd.

Mulgan, G. and Warpole, K. (1986) *Saturday Night or Sunday Morning? From Arts to Industry – New Forms of Cultural Policy*. London: Comedia.

Myerscough, J. (1988) *The Economic Importance of the Arts in the UK*. London: Policy Studies Institute.

National Advisory Committee on Creative and Cultural Education (NACCCE) (1999) *All Our Futures: Creativity, Culture and Education. Report to the Secretary of State for Education and Employment and the Secretary of State for Culture, Media and Sport*. London: NACCCE.

Nayeri, F. (2008) 'Anish Kapoor Turns Art Inside Out, Hates the Smell of Hairspray' *Bloomberg*, 29 October. Available online: http://www.bloomberg.com/apps/news?pid=newsarchive&sid=aJfgTR2ZpmCk&refer=muse (last accessed 5 February 2011).

Nolan, J. (1998) *The Therapeutic State*. New York/London: New York University Press.

O'Connor, J. (2001) *Cultural Industries and the City. Full Report of Research Activities and Results*. London: Economic and Social Research Council.

O'Neill, B. (2001) 'Why banning the BNP is bad for democracy' in *Spiked online*, 12 June [internet site]. Available online: http://spiked-online.com/Printable/00000002D121.htm (last accessed 29 December 2010).

Oakley, K. (2006) 'Include Us Out – Economic Development and Social Policy in the Creative Industries' *Cultural Trends*, 15(4), 255–273.

Oldham Metropolitan Borough Council (2002) *A Detailed Response to the Independent Review Report*. Oldham: Oldham Metropolitan Borough Council. Available online: http://www.oldham.gov.uk/finalresponse.pdf (last accessed 29 December 2010).

———— (2004a) *Oldham Borough Guide*. Oldham: Oldham Metropolitan Borough Council.

———— (2004b) *Oldham Beyond*. Oldham: Oldham Metropolitan Borough Council.

―――― (2004c) *Forward Together. Building Community Cohesion in Oldham. Impact and Outcomes.* Oldham: Oldham Metropolitan Borough Council.

―――― (2007) *About Community Cohesion.* Oldham: Oldham Metropolitan Borough Council. Available online: http://www.oldham.gov.uk/about_community_cohesion.pdf (last accessed 21 November 2007).

―――― (undated) *A Cultural Strategy for Oldham: 2003–2006.* Oldham: Oldham Metropolitan Borough Council.

Oldham Partnership (2006) *Submission by Oldham Partnership for the Local Government Chronicle Local Strategic Partnership Award 2006.* Available online: http://www.oldhampartnership.org.uk/driving_to_improve_the_local_quality_of_life.pdf (last accessed 29 December 2010).

ORC International (2003) *The Oldham Way – Listening to Oldham. Report of the Fifth Survey of the Oldham Citizens' Panel.* Manchester: ORC International.

Owusu, K. ed. (1999) *Black British Culture & Society: A Text Reader.* London: Routledge (Comedia Series).

―――― (1986) *The Struggle for Black Arts in Britain. What Can We Consider Better than Freedom.* London: Comedia.

Pahl, R. (2001) 'Market Success and Social Cohesion' *International Journal of Urban and Regional Research,* 25(4), 879–883.

Pankratz, D. and Morris, V. eds. (1990) 'Introduction' in *The Future of the Arts: Public Policy and Arts Research.* New York: Praeger Publishers.

Pearson, N. (1982) *The State and the Visual Arts.* Milton Keynes: Open University Press.

Perrons, D. and Skyers, S. (2003) 'Empowerment through Participation? Conceptual Explorations and a Case Study' *International Journal of Urban and Regional Research,* 27(2), 265–285.

Pick, J. (1991) *Vile Jelly: The Birth, Life and Lingering Death of the Arts Council.* Denton: Brynmill.

Pierson, C. (1998) *Beyond the Welfare State? The New Political Economy of Welfare,* 2nd edn. Cambridge: Polity Press in association with Blackwell Publishers Ltd.

Pierson, P. (2004) *Politics in Time. History, Institutions and Social Analysis.* Princeton: Princeton University Press.

Quilley, S. (2000) 'Manchester First: From Municipal Socialism to the Entrepreneurial City' *International Journal of Urban and Regional Research,* 24(3), 601–615.

Rich Mix (2000) 'Market Research Conducted by UBEST Services', unpublished report by Susie Fisher Group.

―――― (2001) 'Business Plan' (unpublished), 25 October.

Ritchie, D. (2001) *Oldham Independent Review: One Oldham, One Future.* London: Government Office for the North West. Available online: http://www.oldhamir.org.uk/OIR%20Report.pdf (last accessed 29 December 2010).

Robinson, G. (2000) 'An Arts Council for the Future' (original 1998) in Warnock, M. and Wallinger, M. eds. *Art for All? Their Policies and Our Culture.* London: Peer.

Rojek, C. (2003) *Stuart Hall.* Oxford: Blackwell Publishing.

Rothfield, L. (1999) 'Cultural Policy Studies?! Cultural Policy Studies?! Cultural Policy Studies?! A Guide for Perplexed Humanists'. Working Paper. Chicago: The Cultural Policy Center, University of Chicago.

Rutherford, J. (2007) *After Identity*. London: Lawrence & Wishardt.

Savaric, M. (2001) 'Political Correctness Applied: Multiculturalism in Northern Ireland' in *Contemporary Post-Colonial and Post-Imperial literature in English*. Available online: http://www.postcolonialweb.org/poldiscourse/casablanca/savaric2.html (last accessed 29 December 2010).

Schuster, M.J. (2002) 'Sub-National Cultural Policy – Where the Action is: Mapping State Cultural Policy in the US' *International Journal of Cultural Policy*, 8(2), 39–54.

Selwood, S. (2001) *The UK Cultural Sector*. London: Policy Studies Institute.

—— (2002) 'The Politics of Data Collection' *Cultural Trends*, 12(47), 13–84.

—— (2010) *Making a Difference: The Cultural Impact of Museums*. National Museums Directors Conference.

Shaw, R. (1987) *The Arts and the People*. London: J. Cape.

Shellard, D. (2004) *Economic Impact Study of UK Theatre*. London: Arts Council England.

Sinclair, A. (1995) *Arts & Cultures. The History of the 50 years of the Arts Council of Great Britain*. London: Sinclair-Stevenson.

Skot-Hansen, D. (2002) 'Danish Cultural Policy – From Monoculture Towards Cultural Diversity' *International Journal of Cultural Policy*, 8(2), 87–101.

Smith, C. (2000) Lecture to the Royal Society of Arts, 1999 in Wallinger, M. and Warnock, M. eds. *Art for All? Their Policies and Our Culture*. London: Peer.

Smith, R. (2002) 'Spend (slightly) Less on Health and More on the Arts' *British Medical Journal*, 21 (December).

Social Exclusion Unit (2001) *PAT 10 Report of the Social Exclusion Unit*. London: The Cabinet Office.

Sooke, A. (2010) 'From son of India to a Global Superstar' *Daily Telegraph*, 7 December.

Stallabrass, J. (2006) *High Art Lite. The Rise and Fall of Young British Art*, 2nd edn. London: Verso.

Stanbridge, A. (2002) 'Detour or Dead-End? Contemporary Cultural Theory and the Search for New Cultural Policy Models' *International Journal of Cultural Policy*, 8(2), 121–134.

Staricoff, R.L. (2005) *Arts in Health: A Review of the Medical Literature*. London: Arts Council England.

Steyn, J. (1990) 'The Complexities of Assimilation in the 1906 Whitechapel Art Gallery Exhibition "Jewish Art and Antiquitie" ' *Oxford Art Journal*, 13(2), 44–50.

Stonor Saunders, F. (1999) *Who Paid the Piper?: CIA and the Cultural Cold War*. London: Granta.

Strauss, A. and Corbin, J. (1998) *Basics of Qualitative Research: Techniques and Procedures for Developing Grounded Theory*, 2nd edn. Thousand Oaks, CA: Sage.

Sun (2006) 'Fury over "PC" Guy Fawkes Ban', 2 November.

Swann, Lord (1985) *Education for All: The Report of the Committee of Inquiry into the Education of Children from Ethnic Minority Groups*. London: Her Majesty's Stationery Office.

Taylor, A.J. (1994) 'Policy Chaos or Chaotic Policy? The Arts and Politics in Post-War Britain' *Talking Politics*, 7(2), 131–136.

Taylor, C. (1994) 'The Politics of Recognition' in Gutmann, A. ed. *Multiculturalism: Examining the Politics of Recognition*. Princeton: Princeton University Press.

Taylor, D. (2002) 'Education under the Skin: The Row over London Schools "Boycotting" the Queen Mum's Funeral Hides the Real Problem' *The Guardian*, 23 April.

The Asian News (2001a) 'Kids and Parents split on Curfew Move', 1 September. Available online: http://menmedia.co.uk/asiannews/news/s/480045_kids_and_parents_split_on_street_curfew_move (last accessed 29 December 2010).

—— (2001b) 'Youth Laughed after Beating Up Pensioner', 1 November. Available online: http://menmedia.co.uk/asiannews/news/s/480102_youth_laughed_after_beating_up_pensioner (last accessed 29 December 2010).

—— (2002) 'More Flags to Challenge "Racist" Kidnap", 1 March. Available online: http://menmedia.co.uk/asiannews/news/s/480559_more_flags_challenge_to_racist_kidnap (last access 29 December 2010).

—— (2004) 'Pull down Oldham's Wall of Hate – Residents', 31 May. Available online: http://menmedia.co.uk/asiannews/news/s/491234_pull_down_oldhams_wall_of_hate__residents (last accessed 29 December 2010).

—— (2004) 'Playwright Defends his "Oldham Riots Romeo" ', 2 February. Available online: http://menmedia.co.uk/asiannews/news/s/481045_playwright_defends_his_oldham_riots_romeo (last accessed 29 December 2010).

—— (2007) 'Town Hall cancels Christmas', 30 April. Available online: http:// menmedia.co.uk/asiannews/news/s/527144_town_hall_cancels_christmas (last accessed 29 December 2010).

Thistlewood, D. (1981) *A Continuing Process: The New Creativity in British Arts Education 1955–1965*. London: Institute of Contemporary Art.

Thomas, P. (2007) 'Understandings of "Community Cohesion" Held by Youth Workers' *Journal of Social Policy*, 36(3), 435–455.

Thompson, S. (2006) *The Political Theory of Recognition*. Cambridge/ Massachusetts: Polity Press.

Throsby, D. (2002) *Economics and Culture*. Cambridge: Cambridge University Press.

Travers, T. (2006) *Museums and Galleries in Britain: Economic, Social and Creative Impacts*. National Museums Directors Conference.

Turner, B. (2001) 'Outline of a General Theory of Cultural Citizenship' in Stevenson, N. ed. *Culture and Citizenship: Cosmopolitan Questions*. Maidenhead: Open University Press.

Tusa, J. (2007) *Engaged with the Arts: Writings from the Frontline*. London/ New York: I.B. Tauris.

Upchurch, A. (2004) 'John Maynard Keynes, The Bloomsbury Group, and the Origins of The Arts Council Movement' *International Journal of Cultural Policy*, 10(2), 203–217.

Wainwright, L. (2010) 'Art (School) Education and Art History' in Appignanesi, R. ed. *Beyond Cultural Diversity. The Case For Creativity*. London: Third Text.

Wallach, G. (2000) 'Introduction' in Bradford, G., Gary, M., and Wallach, G. eds. *The Politics of Culture*. New York: The New Press.

Williams, R. (1963) *Culture and Society*, 2nd edn. Harmondsworth: Penguin Books.

—— (1979) 'The Arts Council' *Political Quarterly* (Spring), 157–171.

—— (2000) 'Culture is Ordinary', Reproduced in Bradford, G., Gary, M., and Wallach, G. eds. *The Politics of Culture*. New York: The New Press.

Wolff, J. (1999) 'Cultural Studies and the Sociology of Culture' in *Invisible Culture*. Available online: http://www.rochester.edu/in_visible_culture/issue1/wolff/wolff.html (last accessed 29 December 2010).

World Commission on Culture and Development (1996) *Our Creative Diversity*. Paris: United Nations Educational, Scientific and Cultural Organisation.

Worpole, K. (1998) 'Think-tanks, Consultancies and Urban Policy in the UK' *International Journal of Urban and Regional Research*, 22(1), 147–155.

Yin, R. (2003) *Case Study Research: Design and Methods*, 3rd edn. London/California/New Delhi: Sage.

Zukin, S. (1997) *The Culture of Cities*, 2nd edn. Massachussetts/Oxford: Blackwell Publishers.

Index

Note: locaters in **bold** type indicate figures or illustrations, those in *italics* indicate tables.